A DESTINY TO MOULD

Forbes Burnham

A DESTINY TO MOULD

*Selected Discourses by the
Prime Minister of Guyana*

compiled by
C. A. Nascimento and
R. A. Burrowes

LONGMAN CARIBBEAN

LONGMAN CARIBBEAN LIMITED
TRINIDAD AND JAMAICA

LONGMAN GROUP LIMITED
LONDON

*Associated companies, branches and
representatives thoughout the world*

First published 1970

SBN 582 78008 X
Cased edition
SBN 582 78009 8
Limp edition

*Made and printed in Great Britain by
William Clowes and Sons, Limited, London and Beccles*

Contents

Preface

We have endeavoured in this book to cover a considerable period of Prime Minister Forbes Burnham's political life. The book begins in 1955, when Forbes Burnham split with Dr Cheddi Jagan, Leader of the People's Progressive Party. It covers Burnham's years in the opposition as Leader of the People's National Congress, his victory at the polls in 1964, his period as leader of a coalition government, the attainment of independence in 1966 and, finally, his leadership of the new Republic of Guyana into the 1970s.

The collection of speeches, statements and broadcasts made by Prime Minister Burnham has been made in an attempt to bring to the reader the story of the man, as radical, leader and statesman, idealist yet pragmatist and above all as champion of the small man.

The book also tells of a turbulent period in the history of this former British colony destined to become the second English-speaking republic in the western hemisphere and the first coloured republic in South America.

In his quest for the leadership of his country, his struggle for independence and his effort to gather the resources of his people and his land to build a new nation, Forbes Burnham never forgot the fight of other colonial peoples against oppression and poverty and for freedom and unity. The material we have selected also tries to capture some of his thoughts on and the influence he has exerted in this continuing struggle of the Third World.

In the final section of the book we have included the Prime Minister's speeches paying tribute to Dr Martin Luther King, President John F. Kennedy and Sir Winston Churchill because we believe that these speeches reflect Mr Burnham's equal regard and respect for great men in recent times, all of whom have affected and touched his own political life, but in vastly different ways. In particular, his speech paying tribute to Dr King, we believe, reveals the deep and continuing concern Forbes Burnham feels for the plight of the black man against the forces of bigotry and discrimination.

Rather than present the Prime Minister's speeches in simple chronological order we have arranged them so that the issues which demanded and dominated his time and consideration are isolated for easy access to the reader. Where necessary, we have prefaced each speech with a short introduction in an effort to place it in its proper context, to provide continuity and, hopefully, to assist in the telling of the story of Forbes Burnham, his philosophy, his struggle, his frustrations and successes in rising to power and in moulding a destiny for his people.

KIT NASCIMENTO
REYNOLD BURROWES

Foreword

Politics is about people and, in this context, the singular of people is person.

I have known Forbes Burnham as a person for over twenty-five years – first when I was a rather hopeless student and he was acceptedly the most intellectually gifted of the masters at Queen's College, Guyana; later when I was a so-called 'extremist-leftist-political-activist' and he a leader in our time of standing up.

In those days – the period between 1949 and 1954 – we, and I include names known and unknown, all tried together to 'storm heaven' in the face of gloomy admonitions to the effect that heaven was not in fact stormable. And even now, with him Prime Minister and me a member of the government, we still continue to have very spirited discussions as to the stormability of heaven.

Consummate politician that he is, Forbes Burnham at the conclusion of any argument in which he concedes the viewpoint of the other will usually say: 'Let me accept that you are right. But what do you suggest I should do to bring into being the end you advance?' It is at this point that the contender begins to understand that Burnham's pragmatism is political and not philosophical. What I am trying to say is that a man, like Burnham, who finds himself engaged in the heart-fracturing task of transforming an underdeveloped country, soon isolates what he knew all along – the fact of difference between theory and practice, between what is desirable and what is possible. And becomes impatient.

Forbes Burnham is, I feel, by nature and temperament an intellectual. And by intellectual I mean a person whose chief pre-occupation is the criticism or elucidation of ideas. But the economic, social and psychological pressures of a country harassed by history have made him transform himself. So that today the disposition of people and things is of the first importance to him since this, in his perception of himself in relation to the world's actuality, has become his life-work.

From the gay, witty and brilliant companion of years ago he has become the work-horse of the nation, demanding from his colleagues and himself prodigies of effort.

I am not – and no man is – equipped to say what it is that a man should do with himself.

Sacrifice is a personal decision.

MARTIN CARTER
Ministry of Information and Culture
3 December 1969

Introduction

On 26 May 1966, Linden Forbes Sampson Burnham, Prime Minister of Guyana, received from His Royal Highness the Duke of Kent, the Constitutional Instruments of the new State in the first Parliament of the first new nation on the South American continent in over a century.

On receiving the formal documents of independence the Prime Minister said:

> Your Royal Highnesses, Mr Speaker, may I, on behalf of the Parliament of independent Guyana, and the people of this new nation, express gratitude, first of all, for Your Royal Highness's undertaking the duty, we hope with pleasure, of representing Her Gracious Majesty the Queen of Guyana, on the opening of this first and significant session of the National Assembly of Guyana.
>
> Today is historic primarily because we are indulging in an exercise which is the first of its kind by the Parliament of Guyana. But there is another significance about today's date, for in the Year of Our Lord 1739 on the 26 of May, there was established a constitution by the Dutch, much more liberal than the constitution which was substituted for it in 1928, and I have a feeling that today we are redressing the events of 1928 by opening our Parliament on the same date on which a relatively liberal constitution, subsequently suspended, was established.
>
> We have come to the end of the road of colonial rule, and not without significance to our minds is the fact that Her Gracious Majesty, Queen of the United Kingdom, is Queen of Guyana. Our association with the Crown, our membership of the Commonwealth, are matters of free and untrammelled choice by the representatives of the people of Guyana.
>
> After 150-odd years of British rule, and in some cases, misrule, we are now independent. But we harbour no bitterness. Bitterness, we feel, is for children and the intellectually underdeveloped. It is

difficult, nay impossible, to change the facts of past history, and in the circumstances, though we welcome with enthusiasm our new status, we are prepared not to spend the time ahead of us abusing those who once dictated to us, but rather to seek means of cooperating with them to our mutual advantage – shall I say, self-interest.

These words marked the end of an era in Forbes Burnham's life – the struggle for his country's freedom – and projected the beginning of another – the task of building a new nation.

Prime Minister Burnham was born on 20 February 1923, in the village of Kitty, a suburb of Georgetown, the capital city of Guyana.

He is the second son of a family of five children. His father, who greatly influenced his early life, was headmaster of the Methodist Primary School in the village in which he was born. Like some 31 per cent of Guyana's population of three-quarters of a million, he is a direct descendant of one of the thousands of African slaves brought by the Dutch and British to work the sugar plantations of the South American colony.

It was in 1498 that Christopher Columbus is reported to have sailed in sight of the flat muddy shoreline of the country which is today Guyana, but he did not land.

Within the next 100 years, Spanish and English explorers foraged in the massive rivers, thick jungles, mountains and savannahs of this 'land of many waters', the translation of the Amerindian word, 'Guyana'.

Guyana covers an area of 83,000 square miles. It is situated on the north-eastern littoral of the South American continent and shares its borders with Venezuela to the west, Brazil to the south and west, and Surinam to the east.

The Dutch settlers established the first colony in the early seventeenth century in the Essequibo river.

In 1783, British privateers invaded the colony and defeated the Dutch. In 1783, the French captured it and gave it back to the Dutch. The British recaptured it in 1796 to lose it again to the Dutch in 1802 to retake it finally in 1803. In 1814, Britain paid three million pounds for the colony in the peace settlement after the Napoleonic wars and in 1831 the land formally became British Guiana.

It was in relation to this land that Sir Walter Raleigh sacrificed so many of his men in the fruitless search for the golden city of El Dorado over which he finally lost his head.

When the Dutch surrendered to the British in 1803, the 'Articles of Capitulation' stipulated that the British accept that 'the laws and usages of the colony shall remain in force and be respected'. Chief among those laws and usages was the system of government. A 'Combined Court' made up of officials appointed by the colonial power and an elected majority of financial representatives drawn from the body of sugar planters, administered the territory. The British perpetuated this system of colonial administration.

With the abolition of slavery in 1833, came an influx of indentured labour from the Portuguese island of Madeira, from China and, finally, from India. They came to replace the Africans who, now free, fled the brutal hardships of the sugar-cane fields to set up their own villages as cooperatives, planting sugar-cane and their own provisions, and for many, to gravitate towards the city.

Well before the abolition of slavery, the slaves had made their bid for freedom from the torment and cruelty to which they were constantly subjected. In February 1763, the first significant slave revolution in the hemisphere took place in what was then the Dutch colony of Berbice.[1] Historically, this was the first blow in Guyana for freedom from colonial suppression. With the Dutch in confusion, the revolution almost succeeded but failure finally came through differences over tactics among the leaders of the rebellion and the arrival in the colony of Dutch reinforcements.

The names of the revolution's leaders, Cuffy, Akra and Accabre, are written into Guyana's history books as the first of the country's martyrs in the cause of freedom and Cuffy has been chosen as a national hero of the Republic of Guyana by the government of Prime Minister Forbes Burnham. Republic day is on the anniversary of the revolution.

The sugar barons continued to control the purse strings of the colony of British Guiana and the elected financial representatives, not by any stretch of the imagination representative of the people, exercised supreme power over a population which, though nominally free after 1833, had virtually no political voice. Development of any kind – even the building of roads – was sacrificed to the interests of sugar. The Indians, indentured labourers, who remained on the estates,

1. Under Dutch rule the territory was divided into three colonies and named after the rivers which made natural boundaries: the Essequibo to the west, the Demerara to the centre, and the Berbice to the east. Today, approximately the same areas are counties retaining their original names.

were bondsmen, little better off than the slaves they replaced. The government dominated by the planters rejected the idea of developing any alternative means of employment to work on the sugar estate.

The British government refused to lend the colony money because British officials had no control over finance. By the 1920s, expenditure on health, education, public works and agriculture was virtually at a standstill. The public debt stood at a figure equal to four years' revenue and servicing it absorbed 20 per cent of the colony's annual income.

It was into this period of the colony's history that Forbes Burnham was born, destined to be the Prime Minister of an independent Guyana and destined to be the first leader of the Republic of Guyana.

In the home of the Burnhams, knowledge was the chief currency and money mattered little, for there was so little of it that it ceased to matter. Primary school teachers in those days, in spite of their importance to the community, were paid little more than subsistence wages and every day was a struggle for existence.

Burnham received all his earlier education from his father and at the age of eleven attended for a short time Central High School, and then Queen's College, the leading secondary school in the colony.

At the end of his first year at Queen's, young Burnham was told by his parents that they could no longer afford to let him continue. They need not have worried; Burnham had won an internal scholarship and went on to win two more in a brilliant scholastic career enabling him to complete his education at a level quite beyond the means of his parents to provide.

Reference to his school reports reveals a popular figure already gathering a following as a natural leader. 'He is a natural leader. . . . He is diligent and studious but not aloof. A great favourite with others in his class.'

In 1942, Burnham won the Guiana Scholarship, awarded to the top student in the colony, providing him with a university education in Britain.

The war delayed Burnham's journey to London University but he did not waste his time. He went on to complete his Bachelor's Degree externally. In the meanwhile, following in his father's footsteps, he taught for a short while at a private secondary school and then became an assistant master at Queen's College.

Burnham travelled to England in 1945 and soon after made a name for himself by winning the Best Speaker's Cup of the Laws Faculty.

He had by then decided to study law and in 1947 he received his LL.B. (Hons.) and the following year was called to the Bar at Gray's Inn.

His skill as an orator and his dedication to the struggle for independence of his own country and of all colonial peoples led him to the Presidency of the West Indies Students' Union in 1947.

A student of Marxism, he led the West Indian Students' Delegation to the World Youth Festival in Czechoslovakia, but even then Burnham's burning sense of nationalism made him suspect and eventually reject the communist creed. To him, the solution to the problems of his own people had to be found at home.

In the course of his student career in England, he also became an active member and vociferous spokesman for the original League of Coloured Peoples, and along with his fellow West Indian, African and Asian students, helped organise many of the mass demonstrations through the streets of London which helped to make the average Briton conscious of the determination of colonial people to free themselves from the exploitation by imperial powers.

During Burnham's time in London, there had been some improvement in conditions in British Guiana. Employment had slowly increased, the standard of living had risen, the dreaded disease of malaria had been eradicated and the colony's financial surplus built up.

In spite of these relative improvements, the British, though establishing a limited form of parliamentary democracy and an independent judiciary, made no effort to educate the people politically and in fact continued to deprive them of any real say in the governing of the country.

British Guiana was still a sugar plantocracy, and the intricacies of democratic government were introduced only to a chosen few, mainly white, always rich. The British were, in fact, content to rule rather than govern – until they were forced by circumstances to do otherwise.

In 1949, Forbes Burnham returned home and set up private practice in law. He returned to a Caribbean suddenly becoming politically awake and, characteristically, plunged into the ferment of political and trade union activity.

In the year of his return, Burnham joined forces with Dr Cheddi Jagan, a young Indian dentist, who had returned seven years earlier from an American education. Jagan, a zealous Marxist, had already caught the imagination of a considerable mass of the people as a fighter for their rights and as an anti-imperialist. Burnham's iconoclastic politics were, however, in contrast to Jagan's dogmatic Marxism.

Between them, they founded the People's Progressive Party, named by Burnham, and Burnham's considerable talent for organisation turned a quasi-political organisation – The Political Affairs Committee headed originally by Jagan – into a vibrant and militant political party.

Dr Jagan became leader and Mr Burnham chairman, of the first nationally organised political party in the colony.

The declared policy of the P.P.P. was simple and had tremendous appeal to the thousands of Guianese hitherto without a vote and a voice in their own affairs. The party advocated an end to colonialism, a demand for self-government and a higher standard of living for all.

By 1953, the People's Progressive Party had been forged into a strong political body ready to fight a general election under a constitution which allowed, for the first time, adult suffrage at the age of 21.

The P.P.P. had a weekly party newspaper, *Thunder*, which was widely circulated, and local party branches were established throughout the country.

Apart from a few independent Guianese politicians, most of whom were mouthpieces of the British regime, the Burnham-Jagan team was without opposition.

In the interim, Burnham had earned the respect of, and a following in, the trade union movement which at that period was growing from strength to strength. In 1952, he was elected President of the British Guiana Labour Union. As Prime Minister today he still holds the Presidency.

The P.P.P. swept the polls in the 1953 general election, winning 18 out of the 24 available seats in the House of Assembly. Dr Jagan became Premier and Forbes Burnham, Minister of Education.

The party with Jagan and Burnham at the head had united Indians and Africans, sugar workers, rice workers and city workers, and had behind it the militant young intellectuals returning from universities abroad.

The new government of Guiana swore allegiance to the British Crown in April 1953 and on 9 October 1953, six months later, the Conservative government of Winston Churchill suspended the colony's new constitution and expelled the government from office.

The British Secretary of State for the Colonies at the time, sought to justify the British decision to the House of Commons on 22 October:

> What emerges from British Guiana is a coherent picture of ministers largely dominated by communist ideas, who are ... threatening the order of the colony, threatening the livelihood of its inhabitants and undermining not only its present economic stability but also chances of building it up ... they are unfortunately all part of the deadly design to turn British Guiana into a totalitarian state dominated by communist ideas.

The British position was largely inspired by the then Governor of British Guiana, Sir Alfred Savage, who was firmly convinced that Dr Jagan was committed to the idea of turning the colony over to the Russians. The British were no less hostile to Forbes Burnham who, though a non-communist, was certainly not a witch-hunting anti-communist.

The British action came in for strong criticism in and out of Britain, as immoral and unjustifiable. A substantial percentage of the House of Commons opposed the decision, the vote in the British Parliament being carried by the slim majority of thirty-eight, as did much of the British Press. Afro-Asian Commonwealth leaders condemned it out of hand. Forbes Burnham has consistently criticised the immorality of the decision and points to it as the root cause of the subsequent division of the nationalist movement in Guiana on racial lines.

Having removed the P.P.P. from office, the British installed an 'Interim Government', an executive entirely appointed by the British government, and curtailed the movements of leading P.P.P. politicians including those of Forbes Burnham and Cheddi Jagan.

Before the restrictions, Burnham travelled to England with Jagan to protest the British decision. He knew, however, that Jagan's devotion to the communist cause transcended his commitment to his own country. As a nationalist, Burnham was already questioning in his own mind the wisdom of continuing his alliance with Jagan.

Burnham was also aware that Jagan placed heavy reliance on him as spokesman and advocate for the party's cause during their trip to London and subsequently in Europe and India. By the time they had returned to Guiana, Burnham had made up his mind to part company with Jagan unless the latter was prepared to put Guianese nationalism above posturing as an international communist.

In 1955 Burnham defeated Jagan for the party's leadership at internal party elections. Jagan walked out of the meeting, denouncing the decision, and from that point and for two years British Guiana had two People's Progressive Parties – one led by Jagan and the other by Burnham.

The split between the two leaders smashed the apparently monolithic front of the party and Jagan placed almost total reliance for his support on the nearly 50 per cent Indian population in the country. The African community placed their support firmly behind Burnham. Forbes Burnham was not happy with the situation realising that this division of the races on political grounds could quickly destroy his country. In his first public statement as leader of the new P.P.P., he warned against the danger of racial politics and strongly appealed for support on the basis of his beliefs, not his ancestry.

Burnham's hopes were not to be realised, however, and by the time the British government had decided to grant now elections under a limited constitution of self-government, Jagan was already campaigning with the Hindi slogan, 'Apan Jhaat', meaning 'Vote for your own'.

The election was held in August 1957. The votes were cast strictly along racial lines with Jagan winning 47 per cent of the total vote and 9 seats of a 14-seat legislature. Forty per cent of the registered electorate stayed away from the polls.

Shortly after the election, Burnham renamed his party The People's National Congress, and he set himself the dual task of winning political power for his party and independence for his country.

In spite of his hectic career as a politician, Burnham earned recognition as one of the country's leading barristers. His advocacy at the Bar frequently jammed the court-room with spectators, not the least amongst them his professional colleagues. In 1959, he was elected President of the British Guiana Bar Association and in 1960 he was appointed a Queen's Counsel.

Burnham's political support was mainly concentrated in the heavily populated urban areas while Jagan's was primarily rural. The electoral system of constituency voting introduced by the British therefore gave an unfair advantage to the People's Progressive Party and it was important to Burnham that the system be changed.

When the British called a constitutional conference in London in 1960 to settle a constitution for Guiana Burnham argued for an immediate change in the electoral system to one of proportional representation, that is, the country becoming a single constituency with the voter voting for the party of his choice and seats in Parliament being allocated in direct proportion to the popular vote. At the conference Dr Jagan claimed that he had a mandate for immediate independence. Burnham also demanded independence but with elections first under a system of proportional representation. Burnham was to stand by this position consistently in the years ahead before independence was finally achieved.

The British acceded to neither of the two Guianese leaders' wishes. Instead, an advanced constitution of internal self-government was given with the British retaining responsibility for foreign affairs and defence.

An electoral commission was appointed to demarcate new constitutional boundaries with 35 constituencies,[2] each returning a single candidate. Jagan said the boundaries had been 'jerrymandered' and rigged to defeat him. This accusation of rigging by Jagan has subsequently become a habitual electioneering slogan. In fact, the appointment of the boundaries proved, once again, to be in favour of the People's Progressive Party and once again the unfairness of the constituency system became apparent.

As the 1961 General Election approached, a third political party entered the scene. The new party, the United Force, was led by Peter d'Aguiar, a Portuguese businessman and generally considered the country's leading entrepreneur. In general, d'Aguiar was backed by the conservative middle and upper class community and the Amerindian population.

Isolated from the coastal areas where 90 per cent of Guyana's population is concentrated, the Amerindians were not caught up in the quest for political emancipation. They received their education largely at the hands of Catholic missionaries and were taught to believe that the Queen was their protector. In the past they had been used by the British to catch slaves who had fled the plantations into the interior and they still viewed the coloured man with suspicion and sometimes even fear. D'Aguiar, a prominent Catholic, did not find it difficult under the circumstances to win their support. The Amerindians account for approximately 4.5 per cent of Guyana's total population.

2. In 1957, the country was divided into 14 constituencies, each returning a single candidate.

The U.F. campaigned on a platform of anti-communism and free-wheeling capitalism, but diverted much of their energy from opposition to the P.P.P. to opposition to Burnham's P.N.C. This situation probably arose out of Burnham's rejection of an early attempt by d'Aguiar's party to merge with the People's National Congress.

Burnham regarded the offer of a merger with an open mind but could not accept the demand of the U.F. – a totally untried party much further ideologically right than Burnham – for significant representation at executive level.

Burnham remained convinced that this third party coming on the scene at this time would do little to reduce the P.P.P. strength but would dig into his own support, divide the opposition to the P.P.P. and put Jagan back into power through the back door. This in fact happened.

The People's Progressive Party won 20 seats with 42·6 per cent of the vote, Burnham's People's National Congress won 11 seats with 41 per cent of the vote and the United Force won 4 seats with 16·3 per cent of the vote.

Jagan now faced a situation in which the majority of the popular vote had gone against him. Once again the voting had conformed to racial patterns and a considerable amount of racial bitterness had as a result been engendered.

British Guiana had now become a microcosm of the world's most aggravating problems. Economic poverty, racial animosity, an east-west ideological conflict, class warfare and religious prejudice; all the unhappy ingredients were there.

The situation contained its irony too. The colony's Indian population, religiously committed to the Hindu and Muslim faiths, were to an appreciable extent the landed and property-owing class, yet they supported a communist-directed party; the Africans and other minority racial groupings were mainly wage earners and the unemployed but supported the liberal left and the right of centre parties. The situation was an explosive one, and it was not long before the explosion came.

Burnham was not an advocate of violent upheaval and in spite of the fact that he considered Jagan's government the result of an 'electoral miscarriage', he encouraged his supporters to accept the official result of the election, offered Dr Jagan his cooperation from the Opposition benches and pressed the demand for independence even harder. Later, however, Burnham was to remark that 'Dr Jagan appears to have interpreted this to mean that he could ignore the opposition.'

On 31 January 1962, the government introduced a Budget later to be described by the trade unions as 'a scheme to tax the poor'.

The Budget met with widespread opposition and eventually led to a general strike. Burnham observed afterwards: 'We had the spectacle of Dr Jagan springing a most unpopular Budget on the people without any advance preparation or warning that such action was contemplated. It was ill-conceived. It was bound to cause objection.'

Housewives, children, shop-girls poured into the streets of the capital and joined the strikers marching against the Budget. Forbes Burnham and Peter d'Aguiar led massive but peaceful marches around the Legislative Building while gas-masked riot police looked on. The area had been declared legally 'out of bounds' the day before, though long accepted as a traditional area for popular public protest. The following day Jagan ordered the use of tear gas on the marching strikers though no violence occurred. Suddenly the situation got out of hand and on 16 February 1962, what began as a peaceful but determined strike ended in widespread disorders and rioting, causing substantial damage to the commercial centre of the city.

The situation out of control, Jagan requested the British government to bring in British troops, the Governor having taken the precaution to have them standing by. The government was obliged to withdraw the Budget.

There was no doubt in Burnham's mind that the Budget of 1962 was the root cause of the general strike and that the disturbances which followed were the result of deliberately provocative action on Jagan's part.

Jagan asked for and got a Commonwealth Commission of Enquiry into the disturbances. The Commission comprised an English chairman, Sir Henry Wynn Parry, and an Indian and a Ghanaian judge. The enquiry was public and all the political leaders gave evidence with hundreds of others. It sat from 21 May to 28 June 1962. The enquiry produced an inconclusive report, criticising all sides but stating that: 'The disturbances ... were not the result of a deliberate plan ... (contrary to Jagan's contention) ... to overthrow by force the government of British Guiana ... the outburst ... was comparable to an act of spontaneous combustion when some highly-fermented substance is subjected to long pressures.'

The effect of the strike and the disturbances was to bring about an understanding, based on mutual self-interest, between Burnham and d'Aguiar. Jagan had weathered the storm but he now faced a much more united opposition with Burnham its *de facto* leader and which represented 57 per cent of the population. This situation formed the scenario for the 1962 Constitutional Conference called in October by the British government.

At the Conference in London, Burnham urged the British to grant independence, but pointed out that the solution to Guiana's problems must be found through the free expression of the will of its people at the polls and that this expression must be reflected in the Parliament of the nation. The only way, he said, that this could happen would be to change the electoral system to proportional representation and to hold elections prior to the advent of independence.

Britain's Secretary of State for the Colonies at the time, Mr Duncan Sandys, instead attempted to force agreement between the three political leaders attending the Conference. This proved to be a futile exercise and the conference, after weeks of argument, was adjourned.

In the meanwhile British Guiana was going down hill rapidly. Unemployment had risen to a high of twenty per cent, the economy stagnated, the *per capita* income decreased and racial tensions heightened.

Shortly after his return from the conference Burnham again made a bid to stem the tide of racial animosity. He held a mass open air meeting in Georgetown and told his audience:

> Unless and until the various races in this country cooperate on the basis of attachment to a common fatherland, this country will never, never progress. We cannot afford a division such as between India and Pakistan. We cannot afford those new zones in our country which were proposed by a certain gentleman[3]. . . . We can only go forward if we understand that we are Guianese first, Guianese second and Guianese third.

Burnham's continued efforts to bring an end to the discord amongst the races met with little cooperation from Jagan. At the beginning of 1963, throwing caution to the winds, the P.P.P. leader set about attempting a take-over of the trade union movement through legislation.

As in the case of the Budget of 1962, the P.P.P. government made no attempt to consult the trade union movement or give prior warning

3. One politician had advocated racial partition.

of their intentions before introducing the legislation in Parliament. In April, a general strike ensued and continued for three months of bitter struggle.

Jagan attempted to break the strike with the use of 'scab' labour and deliberately sent Indians to those places where the strikers were predominantly African. This further heightened racial tension and once more the government declared a state of emergency, though no violence had in fact occurred. Finally, on 8 July the strike ended when Jagan capitulated and the Bill was withdrawn. It was a victory for the trade unions and the opposition but it was won at an appalling cost to the country. The P.P.P. government announced an irrecoverable loss of $30 million (Guyana) in revenue to the country.

In October of the same year the three political parties began what now seemed to be the annual trek to London to discuss the question of independence for the country. The results of this conference were to prove disastrous for Jagan.

Burnham's position was totally consistent with, and had not changed from, his position at the Constitutional Conference held exactly one year earlier and by this time d'Aguiar's United Force had also become enthusiastic supporters for a change in the electoral system.

The 1963 Constitutional Conference might well have been a facsimile of the 1962 Conference except that Duncan Sandys persuaded the three leaders to sign a letter giving the British Secretary of State for the Colonies *carte blanche* in deciding the issues raised at the conference. When Sandys presented the letter Burnham was hesitant about signing. He felt that this was an abdication by Guiana's elected leaders of their own responsibility. Jagan on the other hand had little reservation and was the first to sign the letter with d'Aguiar following suit.

Burnham signed only when Sandys threatened to adjourn the conference and postpone indefinitely the date for independence.

The Sandys decision was:

1. New elections would be held under British supervision before the end of 1964;
2. The electoral system would be changed to that of proportional representation to elect a 53-member unicameral House of Assembly;
3. A new voters' list would be prepared under British supervision;
4. A constitutional conference to set the date for independence would be convened as soon as possible after the election.

Forbes Burnham had to all intents and purposes won the day; but it was typical of the man and his determination in quest of a cause that when he returned to his country he told his supporters that he went to London to set a date for independence and since he had returned without a date there was no cause for celebration.

At a press conference following the London meeting and after signing the arbitration letter, Jagan announced: 'I do not feel bound to accept Sandys' decision.' He refused to answer a question as to whether he would boycott the election. 'I have to first consult with my colleagues in British Guiana when I return there,' he said. He continued: 'The solution Sandys had in mind is likely to put the P.P.P. out of power.' Then in reference to the decision of the British government, he warned: 'They are only inviting trouble and I cannot be responsible for what will happen.' Mrs Jagan[3] at home issued a call to her followers at a public meeting, declaring, 'We must be prepared to die and I am prepared to die with you.'

Jagan was determined to oppose at any price the holding of elections under PR, while Burnham was equally determined to have the election held. Slogans appeared in the country districts, 'No PR – OR DEATH; KILL TO PREVENT PR.' Jagan and his Ministers virtually abandoned their offices to stump the country making inflammatory speeches. It was not long before violence, terror and intimidation aimed at total chaos and racial war began.

Burnham accused the P.P.P. of deliberately planning the violence to ferment racial fratricide and urged his supporters to stay in their homes and keep out of trouble. But the fear, suspicion and tension had gone too far. Villages along the coastal belt, once racially integrated, overnight became a succession of barricaded, partitioned ghettoes. Indians and Africans who had lived at peace together for years, innocent of the violence, were forced to uproot their homes to seek refuge in areas with their own ethnic group. Everything from military hand grenades, sub-machine guns to home-made shot guns began to appear. Arms caches later unearthed were frequently traced to Cuban sources.

In Georgetown, the minority Indian population, regardless of which party they supported, might easily have been massacred. Numerous incidents of bombed and burned homes did occur but

4. Dr Jagan's American-born wife. Married in 1943, they met while Jagan was a student in Chicago. She is a self-confirmed Marxist and was a member of America's Young Communist League.

Burnham managed to keep control of his followers in spite of the provocation. At the inland Bauxite mining town of Mackenzie, predominantly African, ugly racial incidents occurred.

Jagan callously described the situation as a 'spontaneous reaction of the people' opposed to the British 'imposition'. Withdraw the Sandys plan, Jagan declared, and the violence would cease.

Burnham declared that it was not a 'struggle for independence and national liberation against the forces of imperialism'. 'It was,' he said, 'a brutal, cowardly, self-destructive war in which Guianese were deliberately encouraged to destroy one another and the imperialists were forgotten.' It would have been easy enough for Burnham to apportion blame elsewhere, but he was not prepared to blame the British for a situation for which they were not directly responsible.

Finally, the British government intervened. Since Jagan was in power and controlled the Security Forces, the British Governor was constitutionally helpless to stop the slaughter. Stopping short of another suspension of British Guiana's constitution, Britain's Parliament amended the constitution to give the Governor powers to declare an emergency. The Governor, Sir Richard Luyt, promptly arrested and imprisoned leading members of Jagan's P.P.P. including his Deputy Premier, Brindley Benn, on charges of planning to endanger civil order and safety. Some members of the P.N.C., including Robert Jordan, now party chairman and Minister of Agriculture, were also arrested and imprisoned on the same charges.

By September 1964, the Governor, using British troops, had managed to restore a semblance of order. Registration for the elections, scheduled for 7 December, was completed and all three parties launched their election campaigns.

Over 247,000 Guianese were registered as electors and 98 per cent of them went to the polls in a general election run under the direct control of the Governor and his appointed officials.

Burnham campaigned the length and breadth of the country in an extraordinary effort to cross the enormous racial barriers which had been raised by the preceding violence of the months before. He did not spare himself and displayed an energy which his political opponents could not match and which frequently left his aides collapsing behind him. Burnham maintained a schedule which more often than not allowed him a maximum of two to three hours' sleep a day.

The campaign was the biggest ever seen in the country and surprised even the British official sent to supervise the election. Literally millions of pamphlets, posters and booklets were circulated across the country and it is doubtful if many of the population did not hear Burnham's voice at some stage of the campaign.

Burnham called his election manifesto, 'The New Road', and outlined a policy based on his philosophy of cooperative socialism within the framework of a democratic society, though it was not until later that he introduced the term cooperative socialism to define his economic and political ideology.

In contrast to Burnham's determined campaign, Jagan hardly bothered with a manifesto and concentrated his efforts with few exceptions in the Indian populated areas. It was apparent from an early stage that once again he intended to rely solely on racial support.

D'Aguiar this time had a sort of unwritten agreement with Burnham that their two parties would refrain from direct attacks on each other. He issued a comprehensive manifesto detailing an economic development programme for the country and coming much closer to the centre of the ideological continuum than before.

Two other Indian-oriented parties entered the fray, one led by Jagan's former Minister of Home Affairs, a lawyer, Balram Singh Rai. These parties campaigned on an anti-communist platform in an effort to draw the Indian vote away from Jagan but made little impression.

The election results did not differ appreciably from 1961, but this time under proportional representation there was no anomaly between the popular vote and representation in Parliament.

The People's National Congress gained 40·8 per cent of the vote, about 5 per cent more than the total African votes registered. The People's Progressive Party held 45 per cent of the vote, almost exactly the number of Indian votes registered and the United Force obtained 12·5 per cent, about 4 per cent less than the votes registered amongst the Amerindians, Chinese, Portuguese and English.

Burnham and d'Aguiar declared their decision to pool their votes and the Governor asked Burnham to form a coalition government as Premier. D'Aguiar accepted the post of Minister of Finance.

It was perhaps typical of Jagan's desperation at the time that when he discovered the constitution made no provision for his resignation as Premier of a defeated government, he refused to resign. An Order-in-Council was required to officially remove him from office.

Many of the political commentators in Guiana held out little hope for the coalition lasting. Burnham and d'Aguiar seemed to have only one thing in common – their interest in keeping Jagan out of government. Quite apart from their apparent incompatibility, Burnham and d'Aguiar were faced with the tremendous task of rehabilitation on the political and economic fronts.

The country's finances were in a mess. According to the British government, the colony was 'insolvent'. In 1962 the Jagan budget produced a $4 million (Guyana) deficit. Two strikes and 'states of emergency' in three years had left the coffers empty. Unemployment had risen to some 22 per cent and those who were employed by the government were sadly underpaid, and the racial divisions need not be further elaborated on.

Burnham, however, was determined to make the coalition government not only survive but succeed and was prepared to bend over backwards where necessary to accommodate d'Aguiar's more rigid personality. Further, d'Aguiar was anxious to prove himself as Minister of Finance. At the end of just six months in government, Forbes Burnham was able to report to the nation a remarkable recovery. His government had established peace in a country only recently torn apart by hatred and violence.

The economy was already showing signs of buoyancy. A locally floated $10 million (Guyana) debenture loan had been fully subscribed and $1·5 million (Guyana) voluntary Treasury Savings Certificates were over-subscribed to the amount of $3 million (Guyana). With this impressive effort at home, some $40 million (Guyana) in foreign aid grants, machinery, technical assistance and low interest loans had been secured.

Burnham fulfilled an election promise to raise the minimum wage of government employees from $3·04 to $4·00 (Guyana) per day and already his government was successfully rehabilitating the thousands of persons who had become displaced as a result of the racial disorders.

Burnham had won the first stage of the battle and now he set out to win the second – the attainment of independence.

In October 1965, Burnham and d'Aguiar travelled to London for what would prove to be the last Constitutional Conference. Jagan had adopted a policy of non-participation and non-cooperation and boycotted the conference.

D'Aguiar was not over-enthusiastic about the idea of independence nor did he support Burnham's expressed intention of changing Guiana's status to a republic on the attainment of independence.

The conference had some rough moments but Burnham displayed an extraordinary amount of patience and compromised on the issue of republican status by agreeing to its delay at least until after another election.

Finally the second battle was won and Forbes Burnham was able to return home and rejoice with his people, for 26 May 1966 had been confirmed as the date for independence.

Just four months before independence Her Majesty Queen Elizabeth II became the first reigning monarch to visit Guiana and as Burnham observed when welcoming Her Majesty, 'the last while our country remains a colony'.

On the Queen's arrival in Guiana, Premier Burnham offered her 'that warmth of friendship and hospitality which matches the warmth of our climate'. He told the British Monarch: 'Our country's population is as diverse as its history. . . . The descendants of the sons and daughters of Africa, India, China, Portugal and Britain, we are today Guyana's children. Guyana for us can be our only motherland.'

Burnham was not simply indulging in formal pleasantries. The message contained in his words was the message he consistently preached to his people. His was the task of picking up the pieces of a shattered nation, with a varied people for whom fear and suspicion were all-pervasive.

It was Burnham's hope and conviction that independence would bring with it a sense of internal responsibility and self-reliance, an understanding that the future of Guyana belonged only to the Guyanese and that only they could make or break it.

Before independence the official religious emphasis had been entirely Christian. Burnham took immediate steps to correct this. The Muslim and Hindu religious festivals – Phagwah, Eid-ul-Ahza, Youman Nabi, Deepavali – were elevated to the status of national holidays. He placed a new emphasis on the building of Guyana's varied cultural heritage and at formal occasions gave recognition and pride of place to local foods and dishes.

Burnham now, however, had to face increasing difficulties within his own Cabinet while grappling with the problems outside.

After independence, cracks began to appear in the Coalition Government. The United Force minority increasingly began to make demands out of all proportion to its electoral strength. D'Aguiar began to trade more and more on his holding the balance of power and increasingly used the threat of resignation and consequential collapse of the government to force his views.

Burnham, on taking office, began a comprehensive series of 'meet-the-people tours'. He realised that face to face communication was the only certain method of obtaining accurate feed-back from the people and he encouraged his Ministers to follow his example. D'Aguiar was vehemently opposed to this policy. He accused the People's National Congress of playing politics when they should have been administering the government. His approach was not realistic in the context of Guyana, and was opposed even by his own party. In Guyana, a politician who rules from his office and relies only on the mass communication media (Guyana has no television) to keep in contact with the people, rapidly finds himself out of touch.

Burnham, realising the need for rapid and tangible signs of economic progress to win confidence, favoured heavy development expenditure to get the economy going. D'Aguiar preferred to run the country's finances with conservative caution and failed to see the political consequences of too much restraint in the face of rising expectations.

Burnham was also anxious and determined to bring home highly qualified Guyanese instead of continuing the importation of expatriate skills. Where Guyanese at home could be found with suitable qualifications for senior administrative jobs, Burnham could see no reason for an expatriate to come in. This frequently brought about clashes with d'Aguiar, who often preferred to search outside for specialist skills.

Burnham's patience was frequently tried in the extreme, but he was not prepared to wreck all that he had striven so long to build while he could still find some ground for compromise with the minority party. But d'Aguiar began to publicise the differences within the coalition in an effort to justify his position should the government collapse because of these differences.

As the 1968 elections approached, d'Aguiar sought more and more to criticise in public Cabinet decisons to which he was party. By doing this he played into the hands of Jagan by feeding the opposition ammunition with which to attack the government and he encouraged new hope amongst P.P.P. supporters that the coalition government would collapse.

D'Aguiar the financier proved no match for Burnham the politician. Towards the end of 1967, he resigned as Minister of Finance while leaving his party in the coalition and appointed a 'Technocrat' Minister.[5]

Burnham knew that a public controversy could do nothing to enhance his government's position and therefore held his counsel, but he also knew that five additional seats for his party in the Assembly would make him independent of the United Force. The U.F. had only five voting members in the Assembly, having already lost one of them to the P.N.C. and another having left the country. By this time three members of the P.P.P. had crossed the floor to join Burnham's party. This left a situation in the House with the P.N.C. commanding 26 votes, the U.F. 5 and the P.P.P. reduced to 21. The U.F. then crossed the floor and joined the P.P.P. in opposition. But when Burnham's strength in Parliament was tested, another of the U.F.'s members at that point voted with the P.N.C., giving a sufficient majority.

The stage was now set for the December 1968 general election. Burnham in fact had the option of waiting until March 1969 to hold the election but decided the time was opportune to hold it in December.

The big question was, could Burnham muster a majority vote on his own or would he again be faced with the minority United Force holding the balance of power?

Burnham told the nation in unequivocal terms that he would not be prepared to enter into another coalition government with d'Aguiar and would form a government only if given a clear mandate from the electorate to do so.

D'Aguiar caused dismay among even his most stalwart supporters by holding a series of secret meetings with Jagan which Burnham discovered and made public. D'Aguiar caused further confusion in the ranks of his party by refusing to give a clear undertaking that he would not form some sort of alliance with Jagan if he thought it necessary. The U.F. pendulum had swung the full circle.

In the meantime, the Independence Constitution had introduced for the first time the overseas vote – the right of Guyanese citizens resident abroad to vote in national elections. D'Aguiar had agreed to this at the Independence Conference, but when Burnham legislated for their registration as voters d'Aguiar joined Jagan in opposing the measure and in seeking an injunction in the Supreme Court, claiming

---

5. The constitution allowed a limited number of specialist appointments to the Cabinet, but those ministers had no parliamentary vote.

that the procedure was unconstitutional. The injunction was not granted.

Once more Jagan raised a hue and cry that the election had been rigged through a fraudulent registration list. This time he found a colleague in Peter d'Aguiar. Though the P.P.P. and U.F. were able to offer isolated instances of mistaken registration, neither party could provide evidence of deliberate fraud. The election machinery allowed adequate opportunity for challenging a fraudulent election through the courts and it is significant that neither the U.F. nor the P.P.P. utilised this machinery to challenge the voting results.

It was clear why Jagan opposed the overseas vote. Most of the Guyanese living in the United Kingdom, Canada and the U.S.A. had gone there during the regime of Jagan's government to escape the violence and discord and growing unemployment. It was unlikely therefore that their votes would go to the P.P.P. and this proved to be the case.

The result of the election was an outstanding victory for Burnham. Not only were the people of Guyana tired of the turmoil and confusion of the years prior to 1964, but they were quickly recognising the value of stability and economic growth under Burnham's leadership. Burnham was able to campaign on a platform of what he and his party had achieved while the opposition could do little better than complain that the election was not fair.

The People's National Congress won 55·81 per cent of the vote with 30 seats in the National Assembly. The People's Progressive Party obtained 36·48 per cent and 19 seats and the United Force was further reduced to 7·42 per cent with 4 seats.

Prime Minister Forbes Burnham now held full responsibility of leadership and could at last build his nation with a free hand and a clear mandate from his people.

On coming to power in 1964 Burnham not only inherited the crisis of internal conflict, but found himself faced with the threat of external aggression. Guyana's powerful and wealthy western neighbour had laid claim to two thirds of Guyana's territory. Once the British granted independence, Venezuela became increasingly aggressive. Of less immediate danger but exacerbating the situation was a Surinam claim to Guyana's south-east of 7,000 square miles of territory. The resulting struggle for Guyana to maintain its territorial integrity has occupied much of the time of Burnham's government since independence.

2

As this book goes to press, Forbes Burnham prepares to lead his country into republican status – a status he had secured the right to adopt by the Independence Constitution itself. He has behind him the goodwill and support of the majority of his people and under him a vast land, relative to the size of its population, with resources yet uncovered and still to be exploited.

He has met with courage and is tackling with imagination and inventiveness almost all the problems that face the Third World and many of the problems that plague the whole world.

The task before Forbes Burnham is still a gigantic one, but those of us who have come to know him and to love him over the years look forward with eagerness to a future full of promise under his leadership.

KIT NASCIMENTO
REYNOLD BURROWES

Acknowledgements

Prime Minister Forbes Burnham very seldom writes out his speeches and as a result a great many of his speeches in this book have had to be culled from tape recordings. We are grateful to the Ministries of Information and External Affairs, the Guyana Broadcasting Service, the Prime Minister's Office, the People's National Congress and a number of individuals for making these recordings available and therefore this book possible.

We acknowledge also the kind help and assistance given by the Clerk of the Legislature, Mr Frank Narain, and Miss E. Cox of Parliament Office.

For the arduous task of preparing the original transcriptions we are indebted to Mrs Daisy Lancaster and Miss J. Ramdyhan.

Many long hours were spent and midnight lamps burned by Miss Ismay Goveia and Mrs Doreen Spooner in typing and preparing the final manuscript. We express our most grateful appreciation for their competent, cheerful and willing assistance.

C.A.N.
R.A.B.

The publishers are grateful to the following for permission to reproduce photographs:

The Associated Press Ltd., for no. 4; The Camera Press Ltd., for no. 5; The Guyana Information Services, for nos. 1, 2, 3, 6, 7, 8, 9, 10, 11, 12, 13, 14 and 15.

Part I
The political struggle

I

'Where do we go from here?' An article published
in *P.P.P. Thunder*, 16 April 1955

*Following the 1953 suspension of the People's Progressive Party
government, Forbes Burnham joined Cheddi Jagan in protesting the
decision in Britain, Europe, India, Pakistan and Egypt but on their
return to Guiana the two leaders disagreed strongly over Jagan's
determination to commit the party to the communist bloc. This
difference of opinion was tested at party elections with Burnham coming out victor.*

*Jagan then denounced the election results and the two rivals went
their separate ways both claiming leadership of the P.P.P. In an
article appearing in P.P.P. Thunder (the Burnham edition of the
P.P.P. newspaper) of 16 April 1955, Forbes Burnham defines his
political position.*

The outline of the party's approach and tactics which I am about to
discuss is the result of hours of deliberation by your General Council
and Executive Council elected in February.

It is necessary for us at this stage to restate certain aspects of our
policy and to set out clearly for discussion by members our tactics for
the ensuing period. Our party has had a strong following and support
throughout the country, but it must be admitted that though our
members and supporters recognise in general terms what we stand for
and what we are fighting for, we have never had an opportunity of
discussing in detail the tactics to be adopted and the policy to be
followed from time to time. That is what we hope to remedy today.

In doing that, it will be necessary as I proceed to refer to some

3

things the party has done in the past. These references, however, will not be made for purposes of recrimination or abuse of other people, nor yet again for purposes of vilification of those who used to be our comrades, but rather to give some idea of the mistakes of the past and to enable us to correct these mistakes and make certain changes in our approach.

At the very outset we should get fixed in our minds what the party is and what it is not. The P.P.P. from its inception (1949–50) has disclosed that it is a socialist party. In other words our party is pledged to fight for the establishment of socialism in this country, cost it what it will.

SOCIALISM

As I see it, comrades, socialism may be defined as that organisation of society where the production of goods and articles is for use rather than profit. This readily distinguishes it from the capitalist system under which we now live and where there is production for profit rather than use.

This is by no means a full definition or explanation of what socialism is. In fact another feature which follows from the one noted before and which is very relevant in our circumstances is that under socialism the control of the State is in the hands of the workers – the majority of the population. This cannot be achieved so long as Guiana remains a colony owned by Britain and controlled from Whitehall. For a colony exists in the interests, economic and strategic, of the metropolitan power, which is of course inconsistent with control of the territory by its workers or any other local group for that matter.

FIRST THE STRUGGLE FOR INDEPENDENCE

It is clear that one thing we must achieve first is national independence, because, so long as we are inhabitants of a colony, the ultimate power, political, economic and military, remains with those who rule from outside.

Socialism will mean a complete change of our present system. Even though we may make gains from time to time and there may come some improvements and reforms, we can never establish socialism in a colony, in the same way, when we want to build a house we must lay the foundation. If we want to build socialism we must lay the foundation of national independence.

With our first goal clearly in mind it is necessary to understand

4

how we can broaden our movement so as to include as many local groups as possible and thus increase the size and effectiveness of our forces against imperialism as we find it in British Guiana. At this point it is perhaps essential to reiterate what has been stated in the past, that ours is not a communist party nor is the party affiliated to any communist organisation outside or inside the country. This does not mean that this party is prepared to launch a witch-hunt against persons who call themselves communists or who are in fact communist. What it does mean is that we will not and cannot permit persons who consider an international reputation for being communists more important than the success of our struggle to thereby slow up our movement and weaken it. Such persons who seem to be geniuses at isolating themselves and the cause they espouse are liabilities unless they are prepared to discontinue their wanton conduct and put the movement above their personal fancies. We are fighting right now to get the British off our backs and will direct our energies and efforts to that end instead of having them diverted to irrelevant issues.

A BROAD POLICY OF NATIONALISM

Our party must be the leader of a broad movement which includes all Guianese who are agreed that we should no longer be a colony, all Guianese who are prepared to fight to make sacrifices for the achievement of independence by our country. These persons must also be prepared at the same time to work for the improvement of the conditions of our workers without whom we can never hope to win. This party started as a working class party and will never give up fighting for the workers, we will never and can never forsake them, the moment we do, we had better arrange for our political funeral.

But the fact that ours is a worker-based party must not prevent us from having the intelligence to learn from the history of other countries and other liberation movements. We must be able and prepared to draw our strength not only from the workers but from all sections of Guianese; workers, farmers, businessmen, intellectuals and civil servants, regardless of their race. All these, as we shall observe later, suffer materially from being colonials and have an interest in the country's independence. Their natural antipathy to colonialism must be harnessed in the struggle. Undoubtedly some of them may be inclined to favour our masters in the hope of getting the crumbs but those are not in a majority and most of them are capable of being won by patient work and intelligent explanation. This task is within the competence of every one of our members.

We have seen how we must work with all those who want a free Guiana and how we capture those who are neutral and others who through blindness and selfishness are not with us. We must not make the mistakes made in the past.

One such mistake was a tendency of the majority of our leaders to measure others in the movement, even among the leadership itself, in terms of very narrow and fixed criteria. If an individual did not agree in every minute detail with the ideological convictions of the dominant section in the executive, he became a stooge, a fraud, a coward, a sell-out, and tolerating him was a necessary evil while the contempt and disregard for him was very thinly veiled, if at all. Such a person, though otherwise devoted to the cause of liberation and fighting for the workers, could not in the circumstances display the energy and enthusiasm which he ought. Abuse, calumny, are not vehicles of persuasion or conviction. It is suicidal to the movement if differences which are at this stage immaterial and irrelevant are allowed to assume major proportions and drive from us potential allies.

In an alliance, the opinions of each ally have to be taken into account, if only for purposes of deciding on the basis of agreement.

MILITANT BUT INTELLIGENT OPPOSITION TO BRITISH RULE

In adopting this approach, it must not be felt the party will or can even afford to be less militant than it has been in the past. There still exists a dictatorship in Guiana. British troops occupy our land, a band of nominees responsible to the Governor only, make decisions which affect our destiny, we cannot meet without permission, our groups cannot function, Guianese are detained without trial. How can we hope to end all this without militant but intelligent opposition? Spineless acceptance of our present lot will win us disrespect and contempt, not success. We must fight if we want to win the right to rule ourselves.

Militancy, however, does not mean sensationalism. Undoubtedly militant acts may appear to be sensational but sensationalism for its own sake instead of carrying the movement further forward, is likely to carry it further back. Every act must be devoted to carrying us nearer our goal. Asking our members and supporters to march down the street in large numbers if they will disperse at the first sight of the police has nothing to commend it. Carrying a flag with Stalin's portrait merely because it is unorthodox and will draw the wrath of certain people is valueless. Seeking jail as an individual and not as one of many thousands who have been organised and prepared to follow you there achieves exactly nothing except some questionable personal kudos.

The people must be educated, organised and directed before you can expect them to march. Otherwise the result is frustration flowing from ignorance of the motives and purposes behind what is done. Comrades will question the honesty and expediency of flamboyant behaviour and lose confidence in a leadership which indulges in it out of sheer adventurism. Adventurism is the hall-mark of immaturity and is often indicative of loss of nerve.

Many of those who have behaved in this manner are prone to believe that they represent the norm and the only accepted or acceptable means of achieving what we all want. Others who do not accept their mode of thought are accused of being on the side of the British government. What can be said is that these same accusers are by their actions assisting the British government to whom they give an excuse for the continuation of the present rule.

RACIAL INTEGRATION ESSENTIAL

Another aspect to which we must pay careful attention is that of race. There are some of my race group (African) who express such sentiments as 'Black man must be on top' and a similar tendency on the part of Comrade Lachmansingh's[1] race group (Indian) to say 'Coolie man must be on top.' Such sentiments are inspired by enemies of our party and movements, and the British government will give anything for them to gain wide currency. This is no laughing matter. If the racialist feeling, latent, or rather patent in these sentiments is allowed to spread it will have a most ruinous effect. One of the greatest achievements of our party to date is that we were able to bring together the two major race groups. You will remember that prior to the advent of our party we had African politicians appealing to Africans, and Indian politicians appealing to Indians, and neither set appealing to Guianese. When we brought the races together our masters trembled.

If we are to continue in unity we must banish racialism. Each racial group is entitled to feel pride in its cultural traditions and

1. To be first Chairman of People's National Congress.

heritage but we must not have racial differences reflected in the politics of our country. Our masters want these differences, they encourage them, they play upon them. We must remember that Indians and Africans and all other races for that matter in this country suffer from the same oppressive system. Ours is not a fight for one race or another, it is a fight for Guiana. We know only one race, that is the Guianese race. Let us beware of the 'Divide and Rule' policy.

THE ATTITUDE TO FOREIGN CAPITAL INVESTMENT

I will, however, allude to one subject which has been very much under discussion: investment of capital. It has been often alleged that the P.P.P. is hostile to foreign capital and does not want it.

This is not a correct statement of our attitude. If foreign capital is to be invested here we welcome it but the Guianese workers must get their just deserts. Proper wages must be paid and human conditions granted. We have no desire to chase or scare foreign capital but we have no intention of allowing anyone to further grind the faces of the workers, or exploit our resources still leaving us poor. It is a matter of business. Capitalists want to invest here, we agree for them to invest here but on fair terms to our country.

2

Both Forbes Burnham and Cheddi Jagan realised that the British attitude had, since the 1953 constitutional suspension, begun to soften and that they would soon face another election. The election came in August 1957, under a constitution of limited self-government. The Guianese electorate were asked to choose between two parties under the same party name of the People's Progressive Party, one led by Burnham, the other by Jagan. Jagan won 9 of 14 Legislative Council seats, with 47 per cent of the vote, but 40 per cent of the electorate did not vote.

Burnham renamed his party the People's National Congress after the election. He very quickly established that his was a socialist party and very much a nationalist party and provided a vigorous and intelligent opposition to Jagan's government.

Burnham once more presents his party to the electorate in the first of a series of pre-election broadcasts.

The forthcoming elections are of tremendous importance. They usher in a new constitution under which elected ministers will have absolute power over, and responsibility for, all internal affairs.

We are on the threshold of a new era. From being a dependent country, an appendage of Britain, we will be free to stand on our own feet, to direct our own affairs, to take our own destiny into our hands. We shall cease being subject colonials and will have to think and act as free men who have the power and capacity to transform their

9

environment. And we must transform our environment or the achievement of independence will have been in vain.

The object of the People's National Congress will be to develop the resources of Guiana both natural and human for the good and happiness of the Guianese people, to increase the productivity of Guiana, to ensure the fair distribution of the wealth and produce of our country, to give security to all, to establish real equality of opportunity.

For us EDUCATION IS THE CORNER-STONE OF EQUALITY and one of the chief instruments for the abolition of snobbery, the removal of discrimination, the development of creative beings and the production of a race of men who will never surrender to mediocrity or dictatorship of any kind.

How can we hope to develop a modern, prosperous and happy society unless our people are well-educated and well-trained in the modern technological skills? The new education system which the People's National Congress will establish will be relevant to our experience, environment and needs, and not a continuation of the old one, large parts of which are irrelevant and meant for a subject people.

For Guiana to be a modern nation, it must have its own industries, its own factories. Many persons, in this context, dream of duplicating in Guiana the large factories to be found in countries like U.S.A., U.K. and Russia. Such a dream is both naïve and unrealistic. A careful scientific examination of our local resources has to be made first, and what industries can be easily developed on our soil ascertained. Simultaneously with this, there will have to be a survey of available human skills and a programme of training undertaken to supplement the deficiencies discovered. In some instances, it will be necessary to employ non-Guianese on contract while Guianese are being trained.

All this will be undertaken immediately, since it has been hitherto ignored; the last four years have been wasted in this respect by our present government.

To have a properly planned programme of industrial development and to avoid wastage certain institutions are necessary:

(a) An Economic Planning Unit staffed with economists, statisticians and other experts for the collection, analysis and collation of relevant data.

(b) An Industrial Development Corporation to secure the rationalisation of existing industries and the development of new ones.

(c) A Finance Corporation for the financing of various projects, and
(d) A Central Bank, coordinating banking policy and regulating local and foreign currency.

The direction and content of the programme must be the sole and undisputed responsibility of the government. On this, there can be no compromise. In this context private enterprise can and will be encouraged to make a contribution. We will not seek to confiscate or expropriate; we shall merely firmly insist on proper labour practices and the observance of the principle of Guianisation at all levels and all times.

But however ambitious and apparently realistic our plans may be, their success is dependant in the final analysis on men. Workers will have to be conditioned to appreciate the dignity of labour and the fact that work for themselves and their country truly liberates and makes them free men. This will be all the more readily understood when it is made clear that they are not working to enrich a few, but the whole community of which they are a most significant part. This cannot be done by mere preaching, but by an active and human approach and policy such as the People's National Congress offers. Not only the nation as a whole, but also the workers must be given a sense of responsibility, and direct participation in the management and policy of the industries in which they work.

We can build a country with modern industry only if there is increased productivity, only if our people learn to use modern tools in place of the neolithic ones, only if there is a stable community under a government in whom the people have absolute confidence, only if workers are part of a family of human beings whose welfare and comfort are that government's major concern. Thus we can make a success of what we have and produce the best advertisement for those who may be willing to give us assistance.

So far as outside assistance by way of technical advice, capital and capital goods is concerned, the People's National Congress will welcome it with open arms, provided it in no way trammels our freedom and our right to develop our economy as we please and there are no political strings. We will repay what we borrow. We crave no one else's goods. We will cooperate with and be grateful to all those who in one way or another will help us to develop our country but Guianese will be masters of Guiana.

One most important instrument of the People's National Congress' plan to develop Guiana now and to give social size to the little man is the cooperative. No one will be herded into the cooperative but direct government aid, financial and advisory, and encouragement will be given to establishing cooperatives not only amongst farmers, but also in marketing and the distributive trades. There will be such institutions as cooperative banks, restaurants, garages and firms. The cooperative will be for all, not for one group or race, but for all Guianese. The People's National Congress belongs to Guiana.

Our concern with industrial development must not be assumed to connote a lack of interest in agriculture, for Guianese must be able to feed themselves. Land is our second most important national asset. All lands and mineral rights, therefore, now vested in the Crown will be controlled and/or distributed for the benefit of Guianese.

The vitalising of agriculture – the getting of more output for the same or less input – is an important point in the People's National Congress' programme for development. We can, by an intelligent and determined plan, feed every mouth and have a surplus for export.

The People's National Congress will therefore place emphasis on:

1. An aggressive national campaign of mass education to animate Guianese farmers into using more modern and scientific methods to secure greater production.
2. Helping the Guianese farmer to tackle, through organised self-help and voluntary aid and government's assistance, the major problems in Guianese agriculture.
3. The provision of credit, and ensuring adequate transport and marketing facilities.
4. Land reform, making available to farmers on easy terms such land as they can beneficially use.
5. The provision of agricultural machinery on easy terms for the farmers.

The P.N.C. has always held as one of its cardinal principles, Guianisation. That is, that wherever there is a post or an office, it should be filled in the first place by a competent Guianese. If, however, such a person is not immediately available, one from outside can be employed while a Guianese is being trained to take over the post. On that we have no compromise.

The People's National Congress believes in the democratic freedoms as embodied in the Charter of Human Rights. It will establish these rights and freedoms, many which have never been in existence in Guiana before. It will protect them.

The P.N.C. believes that there should always be free elections, freedom of speech, freedom of worship and the other freedoms and, much more important, freedom from hunger and the freedom to work.

The People's National Congress, in viewing any political event of international importance or significance, will not necessarily gravitate to one block or the other but holds itself free to exercise its mind on any problem or any event as it arises.

It has been said that there is great racial tension in Guiana. It is the conviction of the P.N.C. that there is no necessity for this. We have in our country people from six continents, the Africans, the Indians, the Europeans, the Portuguese, the Chinese and the Amerindians. Each group has its contribution to make to the storehouse of Guianese culture. Each group has its contribution to make to the moulding of a free Guianese nation. The Amerindians, for instance, who have been sadly neglected, will be the particular concern of the P.N.C. They must be assimilated into our society, their rights to their land which they and their forefathers occupied must be preserved and they must be made full-fledged citizens of our country. There can be and should be no racial tension if there is justice and an absence of discrimination as between one race group and another. And that system of justice is what the P.N.C. proposes to establish. The People's National Congress is interested in the Guianese people and has no time and will have no truck with those who talk about remaining separate and distinct and maintaining their identity.

The People's National Congress is the party of Guiana and I invite you to rally under the banner of the P.N.C., the party of the new nation; to end the frustration which we have experienced so far, to join in the task of developing Guiana now, and to help in building a new society, a free society, an independent society, a society where political and social democracy will be established by the People's National Congress.

3

The 1961 election over, Forbes Burnham finds himself once again in the wilderness of opposition.

Just prior to the 1961 election, which followed from a constitutional conference in 1960, a third political party came on the scene. This was led by a wealthy Portuguese businessman, Mr Peter d'Aguiar, who essentially sought to represent conservative opinion and the maintenance of the status quo. *The United Force, as the new party was called, had the effect of splitting the votes opposed to the P.P.P. Burnham was defeated by 1·6 per cent of the popular vote while 16·3 per cent of the total went to d'Aguiar.*

It was at this election that the disparity between electoral support and representation in Parliament really became obvious. In a 35-seat legislature, Dr Jagan obtained 20 seats with only 42·6 per cent of the popular vote while Burnham and d'Aguiar, though commanding 57·3 per cent of the vote only held between them 15 seats. Two months after the election, at his party's Annual Congress, Forbes Burnham rallies his supporters and urges the necessity for an all-out campaign to have the electoral system changed.

How happy I am at the number of members and delegates attending this particular congress. In my own recollection I think this is the largest attendance we have ever had and it is a source of even greater pleasure when one remembers that this congress takes place after an election which the People's National Congress lost.

It is perhaps best for me to start from the elections, and to make a few observations and draw a few lessons from the results of the elections. You will recall that the victorious People's Progressive Party with 93,000 votes or 42·6 per cent of the votes cast, gained an over-all majority in the Legislative Assembly of 20 seats. The People's National Congress with 89,000 or 41 per cent obtained 11 seats and the United Force with 30-odd thousand or 16·3 per cent obtained four seats in the Assembly.

I desire to break down those results a little further and to point out that with 42·6 per cent of the votes the People's Progressive Party got 57·1 per cent of the seats and with 41 per cent of the votes the People's National Congress got only 31·4 per cent of the seats. The first reflection is that obviously something is wrong with our electoral system, for twice in four years has one party been over-represented and another under-represented. That is why I welcome the obvious thought on the part of some of the members of this party which was responsible for the motion passed last night that the P.N.C. should support the system of proportional representation.

Proportional representation is likely to give a much more accurate reflection in the elected house than the present first-past-the-post system, and you will remember that the P.N.C. in its campaign late in 1959 and early in '60 did recommend that elections should be on the basis of proportional representation.

Another fact which also comes out from the general election results is that by and large the voting was on the basis of race, more so in the case of the People's Progressive Party, as most of us can recognise how few Indian votes the People's National Congress did succeed in get-ting. The United Force, as I observed in the Legislative Assembly on Friday last, got the bulk of the Portuguese vote and the P.N.C. the bulk of the African vote.

In the result, the P.P.P., regardless of what its leaders may say or think, represents to its adherents and supporters as well as to their opponents an Indian racial victory at the polls on the twenty-first of August. Another fact which comes out from the elections is that especially in the last days of the campaign the People's National Con-gress particularly in Georgetown was fighting a battle, not against the People's Progressive Party, not against the United Force, but against the combination of the People's Progressive Party and the United Force.

The P.P.P. leadership has recognised that their victory has been the victory of a minority in peculiar circumstances and also that they do not enjoy the support of a majority of the people in the country of Guiana. In their usual hypocritical manner subsequent to the elections, they have been pouring forth declarations about the necessity for a single nation, but the acts of their supporters and some of their lieutenants belie their declarations. In the Legislative Assembly, what is more obvious than sincerity is the bumptiousness of the new recruits to the P.P.P. as well as those who were there before. Outside of the Legislative Assembly, the supporters of the People's Progressive Party are in the habit of making such remarks as 'we pon top' and that certain ethnic groups in this community, more especially the African ethnic group will be sent to cut cane and pull punt. On the other hand, we have the bombastic reassurance from the Minister of National Resources at Bourda Green that 'heads will roll'.

It is also significant that in the midst of his bombast he did not make the mistake of specifying the P.N.C. heads which he intends to see roll and that, comrades, is more than a coincidence: it is because we in the People's National Congress have shown such great solidarity and determination, have shown, especially on the Corentyne Coast,[1] that we can give better than we take. In the circumstances, at least there is one quality recognisable in the Minister of Natural Resources, that of discretion; he did not essay to threaten the rolling of any P.N.C. heads.

The United Force, on the other hand, virtually rejected by the majority of electors in this country, having lost 23 deposits and secured only four seats for an expenditure that has been estimated at various points from 300,000 to 600,000[2] dollars, have been unsure of themselves and show confidence only in their daily rag, the *Chronicle*.

It has been fascinating. At times they[3] have launched scurrilous attacks against the People's National Congress and the United Force. The uncertainty of their attitude is indicative of the insincerity of their purpose, and it must not be felt that the olive branch which sometimes is held out to the People's National Congress by the United Force is anything more than an admission on the latter's part that they are fearful as to what will happen in the years to come. You are all aware of the negotiations which took place between those who eventually formed the United Force and the People's National Congress. You

1. Easternmost coastline where Dr Jagan's supporters predominate.
2. U.S. $150,000 to $300,000. Approximately £60,000 to £120,000.
3. i.e. the People's Progressive Party.

remember the dictatorial and conceited attitude on their part when they felt that cooperation or unity meant domination by a numerically small but financially strong group. In the meantime, especially for the benefit of those who might have been disillusioned by our defeat, it is apposite for us to consider whether the P.N.C., as some of our detractors say, is a spent political force or a potent political weapon in the context of Guiana.

Our strength must not be assessed merely in terms of our representation in the Legislative Assembly, especially when we remember that a mere 4,000 votes is the difference between the governing party and the People's National Congress, and that too in circumstances where there was, figuratively speaking, a theft of supporters from the P.N.C. as a result of the blandishments and fancy promises on the part of the United Force.

We must also console ourselves with this thought, that hadn't it been for the terrific battle which we had to wage against the United Force in Georgetown we would have been able to concentrate more of our efforts and money on the fight in the rural areas where in fact the battle was finally lost by us and won by the People's Progressive Party.

The People's Progressive Party's minority is a fact of strength in so far as the People's National Congress is concerned, for by no stretch of imagination can the People's Progressive Party claim to speak for the country of Guyana and, in view of the fact that we control 41 per cent at the moment, it means that without us no important or significant action can be taken. When it is further remembered that the Legislative Assembly is not our only forum, we ought to take courage.

The People's National Congress controls the city, the People's National Congress controls the heart of the country, the People's National Congress, as the election results have shown, also controls all the urbanised and industrialised area of Guiana and an analysis of the sources from which we got our votes shows that of the three parties which contested, the People's National Congress had the most widely distributed support.

Most of us who live in Guiana and who know the various people in Guiana recognise that the much advertised ideology and philosophy of the People's Progressive Party does not so easily and readily mesh with the economic aspirations of the Indian community from which it draws its support. It is one thing, however, for us to recognise the weakness of our enemies; we can at the same time, ostrich-like, ignore the weaknesses within our own party, and, since I believe that you accept my promise that this is a question of war and the People's National Congress must do battle, you will no doubt agree with me that we should analyse some of the weaknesses within the P.N.C.

There are attacks on the P.N.C. from without; not a day passes nor a week without some attack by the P.P.P. They accuse us of being inconsistent on the question of federation on which I shall speak later, they accuse us of not supporting the independence movement and of being stooges of the imperialists, they accuse us of being in the pay of Bookers[4] because our chairman happens to be an employee of Bookers, while one of their candidates was also an employee of one of the big firms.

Some of the criticisms which have been made by persons who purport to be members of this party are that we should go easy with the Governor, because the Governor will be able to put in a word for us at the Colonial Office; that the leader of this party is too prone to associate with the ordinary people like the market women; that it is time that this party goes out of its way to woo the respectable middle class. Comrades, the moment those criticisms emerge, it means that those persons do not recognise the basic philosophy upon which the People's National Congress was founded and upon which the People's National Congress has flourished. It must be remembered that the People's National Congress is a working-class party, the People's National Congress is a socialist party; by that I mean that the People's National Congress draws its strength from the working people of this country, that the People's National Congress is dedicated to the establishment of a system of social justice, where the workers will get their just deserts; will get the rewards of their labours, and no longer will a few get the lion's share while the many get the jackal's pickings.

Our people, the people whom we represent specifically in the P.N.C., are people who have known what it is to bleed and to sweat and have known little about enjoying the sweets of their labour. The P.N.C. was not established to curry favour with the haves against the have-nots. The People's National Congress was established to give the have-nots an opportunity of having what has been justly theirs, but what has been denied them over the years. The seats which we won

4. A British company owning vast sugar, commercial and trading interests in Guyana.

and the votes which we collected at the last elections were won and collected respectively because of our militant, socialist, working-class policy and programme.

At this time, to attempt to change the line of the party and its philosophy would be to attempt to commit false pretences. We were returned on one basis, how can we suddenly change this basis? It may be that there entered into our ranks, in the general necessity for a broad front and unity, persons who were not convinced of the validity of our socialist policy, persons who still had operating in their minds certain social prejudices and snobberies, but I should urge them for their own self-preservation, to cast aside those prejudices and snobberies for, as I see it, the rank and file membership of the People's National Congress will have none of this shilly-shallying or selling out of our party.

It is necessary also for us in the People's National Congress to remember what must be our attitude to independence. This has been a subject that has been keenly debated and discussed by all groups and all persons in the entire community of Guiana. You will note, those of you who were present in the Legislative Assembly on Wednesday, Thursday and on Friday of last week, that the P.N.C. elected representatives, voted with the P.P.P. calling upon the British government to fix a date in 1962 when Guiana should be independent.

I know that even amongst the comrades here, there are many who have certain fears of what type of country we would have if there were to be independence with the P.P.P. in the saddle. I shall discuss those fears with you. But I may say this: it is impossible for a working-class party like the People's National Congress, it is impossible for a socialist party like the People's National Congress, to go down on record in and or out of British Guiana as being opposed to the granting of independence to Guiana, which is the God-given right of every human being that walks this land. What impression would we convey to those outside of Guiana who have been our friends, what impression would we convey to those for whom we have been fighting over the years?

The United Force from its very make-up and constitution would naturally be opposed to independence because so long as there is not independence there is the domination of the country by a foreign master, to which master, those who run the United Force have been the lackeys. So far as they are concerned, so long as the British remain here, so long as the British lord it over us, they, as the willing servants and instruments of the British, can expect to get their share out of the exploitation while we have nothing to gain from continued British rule.

And further, comrades, let us accept the reality of the situation. The British government, be it Conservative or Labour, is no longer interested in the retention of colonies as colonies. There are some who would say that this new attitude has been brought about by a change of heart on the part of our masters. I do not subscribe to that thesis. I think that this change of heart has been brought about directly by the agitation which is being carried on by colonial peoples throughout the world, more especially in recent years on the continent of Africa, where the Prime Minister of England had to admit that there was a wind of change blowing. But whether we believe that Britain's willingness to grant independence comes about from a change of heart, or from compulsion as a result of circumstances, the objective fact is that the British government does not propose to help to save you.

If we have to be saved in Guiana we have to save ourselves. And no attempt on the part of political parties or individuals in Guiana, to appeal to the British government to stay here a little longer to protect us from the ravages of Jagan, will be successful. Indeed even if we were to succeed in persuading the British to stay, so as to keep Jagan back, that makes a hero of Jagan and that increases his strength and his reputation, which he does not justly deserve, in the outside world.

What therefore is the solution, comrades? The solution is not to run but to stand up and fight.

The People's National Congress supports independence, as a matter of principle, but the People's National Congress recognises certain threats to our well-being, to our continued existence, whether we look at it politically or economically, if the People's Progressive Party's leadership were to have its own way. I was present for instance at Lancaster House and so also was comrade Kendall[5] in March of 1960, when the leader of the People's Progressive Party said that he wanted judges who were of the same political conviction as the majority party. I was present at Maracai in Venezuela in April of last year when the leader of the P.P.P. voted against a motion for free elections, freedom of speech, freedom of the Press, freedom of

5. Then a P.N.C. member of Parliament, since appointed in 1969 as Guyana's ambassador to Surinam.

worship and freedom of the radio. And when we further remember the statement of the leader of the P.P.P. at the Lancaster House Conference with respect to the judiciary, we see that there is great need for fear if the constitution of an independent Guiana were to be a constitution similar to that which exists in the United Kingdom and in several other parts of the world, a constitution which could be changed at any time by a simple majority in the legislature.

Now that we recognise these difficulties and now that we have committed ourselves, irrevocably, to independence, and for that I make no apologies, we have got to find a solution to combine the natural aspiration of our people for independence, with the natural desire of our people to continue to exist. The leadership of the People's National Congress has worked out this formula – that there should be certain rights which must be enshrined in the constitution, enshrined not only by statement but also by its being made impossible for those rights to be removed or changed in any way unless there is at least a two-thirds majority, not in the legislature, but amongst the voters of the country. And if the P.P.P. can get the support of sixty-six-and-two-thirds per cent of the electorate of this country, when it is about to pass any measure which is going to be discriminatory or any measure which is aimed at removing these democratic freedoms in which we all believe, well then I personally think that the P.P.P. is entitled to do so. For if sixty-six-and-two-thirds per cent of the voters are going to allow themselves to be present at their own demise there is nothing that the P.N.C. can do. As at present advised, however, so long as the P.N.C. continues in existence and continues to be a vital and potent force, it is absolutely impossible for the P.P.P. to get sixty-six-and-two-thirds per cent of the voters to agree with them in any legislation which will be an attack on these fundamental freedoms which must also include freedom to organise politically.

We are not impressed by Jagan's statement that he believes in these things because it is easy to say but another thing to persuade us. Neither are we impressed by the fact that some of these freedoms to which we refer have been written in the present constitution. The present constitution cannot be changed by the People's Progressive Party, it can only be changed by Her Majesty in Council and consequently, when Jagan boasts of having had these freedoms written into the present constitution he is making wisdom of necessity, because he cannot change it anyhow. But, on the other hand, when we become independent, the only way to ensure impossibility of change, is to have it written into the constitution that a sixty-six-and-two-thirds per cent majority of the popular vote must be necessary for any alteration or amendment to certain sections of our constitution.

Comrades, there are many people who have said that, in spite of such provisions in a constitution, the People's Progressive Party and its leader can, and will, attempt to dishonour those undertakings. That they will attempt to dishonour those undertakings I am willing to concede, but comrades, there is one question I desire to ask you: are we men or are we mice? Will we sit down and allow Jagan and his People's Progressive Party to rape a constitution? Remember, that if he attempts to make these changes without the referendum to the electorate, a revolutionary situation is created, and I believe we can learn a lesson from our members and supporters after the elections on the Corentyne Coast. This is why I continue to emphasise at all times and at all points that we have now entered a new phase of our struggle. It is not merely a question of struggling against the imperialist master for good or ill; he is on his way out. It will be a question of struggling against our political opponents, and always being on the *qui vive*, accepting nothing.

And comrades, in the tasks which lie ahead of us within this party, every member has an important part to play. The People's National Congress, contrary to what has been suggested in the *Sun*[6] and other publications, does not consist of a small clique which dictates; it consists of a number of people whom you have elected, a number of people who look to you for support, who look to you for assistance, who look to you on all of the important issues for advice.

If we can only realise in this party that it is possible to combine loyalty and discipline on the one hand with a democratic expression of your points of view, and a willingness to contribute to the general policy and structure of the party on the other, I think our party will be much stronger even than it is at the moment, and it is my conviction, incidentally, that the People's National Congress is stronger now than it has ever been at any time in the past.

Comrades, the task of the People's National Congress consists of the education, not only of its members, but also of the entire country of Guiana. It is my respectful submission, and I voice it without fear of contradiction, that it was the campaign of the People's National

6. The U.F. party newspaper.

Congress which started back in 1957 which was responsible for the reduction of the P.P.P. majority from 47 per cent to 42 per cent, in spite of the fact that the racial campaign on the part of the P.P.P. in 1961 was even higher and harder than it was in 1957.

If therefore, we are agreed that the People's Progressive Party is not to be retained, but contained and repelled, we must recognise that the only instrument of repulsion is a People's National Congress which continues to be socialist, which continues to be working class in its philosophy, and which continues to love the ordinary people. Thank you.

4

Speech in the Legislative Assembly in a special
motion debate on P.P.P. government's handling of
disturbances in February 1962, 1 March 1962

*Friday, 16 February 1962, proved to be a tragic day for British
Guiana and a disastrous one for the People's Progressive Party. In
January, Dr Jagan's government introduced a Budget which was de-
scribed by the Trade Union Council as 'a scheme to tax the poor'.
The upshot was a general strike ending in widespread disorder in
Georgetown and necessitating a declaration of emergency by the
British Governor and the calling in of British troops.*

*In Parliament thirteen days later Mr Burnham records his views
on Dr Jagan's handling of the general strike.*

... The government also wishes to appeal to all Guianese to work
as hard as is possible to recover the lost ground, to assure all those
who are engaged in the work of recovery that they have the fullest
support and encouragement of the government. The government
wishes to express its sincere gratitude to those members of the
Police Force, the Fire Brigade and Her Majesty's Forces who
worked to restore the public peace, and to all those who gave help
to persons who were injured or forced to evacuate their homes.

It is proposed to advise the Governor to appoint a Commission
of Enquiry to investigate the events which resulted in death, rob-
bery, arson, malicious damage to property and other offences, and
the severe economic loss which the country has suffered. The Commission will be appointed forthwith with the object of making a
full report on matters which will include the extent of the injury,

loss and damage suffered and the responsibility therefor so far as this can be ascertained upon the evidence adduced.

The findings of the Commission will be made public.

(Government statement)

REQUESTS FOR LEAVE TO MOVE THE ADJOURNMENT OF THE ASSEMBLY ON MATTERS OF URGENT PUBLIC IMPORTANCE

Government's handling of crisis

Mr Burnham (Ruimveldt): Mr Speaker, I ask leave, under Standing Order No. 11 to move the adjournment of the Assembly for the purpose of discussing a definite matter of urgent public importance, to wit, the government's incompetent handling of the crisis and of the situation which arose after 31 January 1962; the government's inability to maintain law and order, and the unnecessary use of emergency legislation.

Under Standing Order No. 11 (2), Mr Speaker, I have handed to you a notification of the matter which I ask leave to discuss on the motion for the adjournment. As Your Honour is aware, it is a matter for your ruling whether you are satisfied that the matter is definite, urgent and of public importance.

Mr Speaker: Hon. Members will recall that the Assembly gave permission to the hon. Member for Ruimveldt to move, at this stage, a motion for the adjournment of the House on a definite matter of urgent public importance. The hon. Member for Ruimveldt may now make his statement on the government's handling of the crisis situation after the 31 January 1962, including the maintenance of law and order and the use of the emergency legislation.

Appointment of a Commission of Enquiry

Mr Burnham: Mr Speaker, I am aware of the fact that since the hon. the Premier has informed this House that a Commission of Enquiry will be appointed to enquire into the incidents which occurred on Friday, 16 February, it would not be advisable in this discussion which the House has given me leave to initiate, to attempt to apportion any blame as to who was responsible for the incidents; for instance, who shot Superintendent McLeod and so on. I wish to assure you that if, perchance, I stray beyond the bonds of propriety, I will look to the Chair for the necessary guidance, assistance and, perhaps, control.

It was, I believe, on Wednesday 31 January this year that we heard the hon. Minister of Finance reading his Budget. Today I note with interest, though not with sympathy, that his tones were very much more subdued than his tones on Wednesday 31 January. But it seems to me that the crisis which arose in our dear country over the past two weeks can be, to a great extent, traced to the Budget. I do not propose to go into the details and proposals of the Budget, for my latest piece of information is that these are no more and that there is another United Kingdom specialist[1] here to advise on a new Budget.

Unbearable Budget proposals

But the fact that emerges is this: a large section of the population of this country, more especially the workers, found these proposals in the Budget unbearable and, in the case of the workers particularly, these proposals were interpreted as an attempt on the part of the government to further lower their already low standards by the imposition of heavy taxation on commodities which workers have to consume.

I remember some years ago when the Financial Secretary (as he then was) Mr Frank McDavid presented the Budget, the hon. the Premier, Dr C. Jagan, observed that the government at that time taxed items because they were in wide use and, because they were in wide use by the workers, those Budgets used to be anti-working class Budgets. There are others who would like to make us believe that the Budget which was adumbrated on the 31 January was a working-class Budget, but the objective fact is that a large section of the working class – the majority – felt that the Budget was anti-working class. There was a great deal of opposition to it – which of course is the democratic right of persons who do not agree with government's proposals.

Allegations by the government

It seems to me that the government, for no intelligible reason, took fright and then completely mishandled the situation. There was, for instance, the debate in this House on the 9 February on the question of the appointment of a select committee to draft a constitution for British Guiana. Of course, as has become normal since the opposition

1. The original budget was advised on by a British economist, Mr Nicolas Kaldor.

days of the Premier, there was a demonstration outside the legislature. He alleged that there was too much rowdyism; he says that there was an alleged assault on him and/or his car; and over the radio he alleged that threats had been made to the lives of himself and his ministers. These allegations about threats on the lives of ministers might have been based upon evidence. If they were based upon evidence, then this government ought not to have done as the Savage government did in 1953 or the British government over the same period, merely repeat the allegations. The allegations ought to have been investigated and charges laid against the persons responsible.

So far as I am aware, a plot to assassinate or kill any person is still a criminal offence punishable under Chapter 10 of the *Laws of British Guiana*.

It seems to me that the repetition of those allegations was intended to gather sympathy from some whose loyalty to, and support of, the majority party was waning. Whether that was the intention or not, and it seems to me it was, it was certainly calculated to exacerbate feelings as was the false allegation during the election campaign about violence at Mahaicony to the hon. the Premier, as he then was not.

Government provoked crisis

It is in this context that we have to view the statements and the invitation made and issued at a meeting at Windsor Forest on the Monday prior to the 9 February when the Premier told a number of his supporters in that rural area that a big demonstration was being planned against the government and that they should come down to Georgetown to defend their government. Certainly, one who is head of the government ought to realise the impact of such an invitation and the inevitable result; that there must be increased tension and further ill-will and bad feelings between one section and another section in the community. It is my feeling, or conviction, that those were deliberate acts to excite the populace. But even if my conviction proves to be wrong, certainly the conclusion is right that it did increase tension and excite the populace.

But the most alarming act by this government came on Wednesday, the 14 February. This is the government which prides itself on being working class; this is the government that has taken unto itself the description of 'vanguard of the proletariat'; this is the government whose leader over the years has been the leader of demonstrations.

I remember in 1952 the soft drinks tax demonstration, inspired and helped on by the leader of this government, when I was deputed by him to represent those who might have been arrested.

This is the government that has said, through the mouths of its leaders in the past, that in this revolutionary era the legislature is not the only forum of agitation and anti-government activity; this is the government headed by the hon. the Premier, who, in 1953, objected to the crowd's not being allowed in the Chamber; this is the same government today that on Wednesday, 14, issues a Proclamation making certain areas prohibited for the purpose of gatherings, meetings, etc.: in particular, the areas surrounding the Legislative Assembly.

The Proclamation unnecessary

To my mind, and I understand, to the mind of certain of his ministers (but since they are bound by the Official Secrets Acts, they cannot disclose whether my information is correct) that Proclamation was unnecessary and provocative. It was an attempt by a so-called working class government to intimidate the workers, to intimidate the people in this town and to prevent them from demonstrating and showing what they felt about various measures. If that Proclamation was not unnecessary, why is it there was no incident on Thursday, 15, when there was a demonstration in breach of that Proclamation?

Certainly, those who thought about that Proclamation ought to have realised how stupid they looked and ought to have recognised that they had brought the administration of law to its very nadir.

The Proclamation was not only stupid, but also wicked. It was viewed as wicked by several thousands of persons and members of the working class. It proved that this government was prepared to use force; to use the legislative machinery; to use delegated legislation to suppress any who dared to oppose it and vocally show their opposition to the measures of the government.

Request for British troops

There was, on the 11 February, a demonstration by the unions representing the employees of government – a peaceful demonstration – where there was great show of solidarity between the white collar workers and the manual workers: and then again on the 13 there was arranged a mass demonstration of all workers. Both of these demonstrations were extremely peaceful. There was absolutely no incident whatsoever, but yet my information is that prior, at least, to the demonstration of the 13, if not to the demonstration of the 11, this government had asked His Excellency the Governor to make available British troops to preserve law and order. Apart from the fact that it must represent the lowest depth to which this government can sink – and it is indeed the lowest depth when those who had cried in 1952 and 1953, 'Limey, go home' are asking the same 'limeys' to come here to preserve law and order – that request to the Governor to bring British troops here is of twofold significance. Number one, it represented an admission by this government that either it was incapable of preserving law and order in peaceful times, or it did not have confidence in the forces of law and order at that time existing in this country. And a government which has not got the confidence of those who must enforce the law is no government.

It is all right to come out after, as a rat from a hole, and to start squeaking, but those are the facts. You have the Police Force here. You have the Volunteer Force here and, in fact, in spite of the smiles from the Minister of Communications and Works –

Mr Speaker: We haven't got such a minister in the House.

Mr Burnham: You will forgive me, Mr Speaker, they change so frequently. It is to be observed that on Wednesday the 14, this government also issued a Proclamation giving certain powers to the Commanding Officer of the British Guiana Volunteer Force. So it was not *per incuriam* that they did not know of the existence of the Volunteer Force. They knew that it existed. They knew that the police existed, but yet, these people who talk about independence, who open their big mouth in an attempt to convince the world that they are the greatest nationalists, fall back on the imperialist troops.

The second point of significance in that request which was made prior, I state categorically, to the 11 and 13 of February, is that it was obviously an attempt by this government to further intimidate those who were opposed to its measures and who, up to that time, had been showing their opposition in the usual democratic fashion.

Maybe, for those of the older school, it was an unusual fashion but it is a fashion to which we have become accustomed in this country since the entry to the political field of the hon. the Premier. And then – it is not that I want to make heavy weather of this – it is difficult to erase from my mind the impression that it was not a mere coincidence that the British troops arrived on the same Friday, on the same day, that the disturbances took place.

3

Causes for the strike by the workers

During the period prior to Friday, 16, and after, there was a strike of government and other workers. It seems to me that the government showed gross incompetence and misjudged the situation at this point also. It was little short of pitiful to hear the leader of the People's Progressive Party warning workers about their being in breach of the law. Obviously, that was a very thinly veiled reference to the Ordinance which has replaced the Essential Services Ordinance of 1952, an Ordinance, the removal of the provisions of which was the main plank in the P.P.P. platform in 1953.

The question of the difference between its employees and the government is one that went back some years. Certainly, we remember the famous, not last, words that Premier uttered in November 1959, when the members of the unions affiliated to the Federation of Unions of Government Employees asked for increased wages. He said, 'Not a cent more'.

After a strike in 1959, there was an increase from $2·52 to $3·04 (Guyana), but there were several outstanding differences between those unions and the government which this government took absolutely no steps to have settled. In fact, in October 1961, there was request made to government to send to Whitley Council[2] certain differences then existing between the unions representing government employees and the government, and up to the time of the strike which started on Tuesday, 13 February, there had been no reply from the government to that request.

That is the situation; where government had obviously ignored the demands of the workers and had slyly refused to enter into discussions with the representatives of the workers by means provided by Whitley Council. Then add to that the anti-working class Budget; add to that the threat to take stern measures, as the hon., the Premier, said over the radio; add to that the unnecessary Proclamations; add to that the invitation to foreign troops to come here 'to preserve law and order' when there was no breach or no threatened breach.

Government responsible for 'the explosion'

I promised not to deal with the events of Friday, 16 February, in great detail, but it is the view of many that the situation on Friday, 16

2. A representative body for negotiation and joint consultation between management and staff.

February, was clumsily handled, and there were provocative acts for which there could have been no justification, but as to who was responsible or was not responsible I leave it to the Commission to decide.[3] But one thing is clear, that whoever might have been the individuals responsible for the several instances and events, the government by its blundering had certainly created an atmosphere in which anything was likely to happen. Indeed I remember now the words of the Premier uttered some months ago 'That there is going to be an explosion in British Guiana', and indeed the government was the body that was responsible for that explosion on Friday, 16 February.

Now, what do we have? We have a Proclamation of Part II of the Emergency Order of 1939. He who had justly complained against the declaration of Part II of the Emergency Order of 1939 in 1953 is now using the same instrument, the same legislative instrument, and the same instrument in the person of the Governor.

What is the necessity for emergency legislation at this time? To allow people's privacy to be imposed upon; to allow officers to search premises without warrant; to allow people to be detained without any proper cause being given, and to ban publications if, in the opinion of 'His Eminence the Dictator' those publications are not conducive to law and order, or 'good order', as is actually stated in the enactment?

It is true that the Emergency Order was invoked in the name of the Governor, but clearly the Emergency Order is the child of the Premier and his ministers. What more disgraceful act than that could there have been? If he had all that guts why didn't he do it before the British troops came? If he had all that gumption, if he really thought it was necessary, why didn't he, the Premier, rely upon his police and Volunteer Forces to make the Emergency Order effective and effectual? And I must say this, *en passant*, that the police have shown, from my observation, the greatest loyalty to this present government in spite of the unfortunate and ill-advised utterance by Mr Kelshall at a Press Conference.[4]

Why could not the government use the police I do not know and will never be able to understand. Why the government had to rely upon foreign armies is past understanding. Was it because the

3. The Commission concluded that the disturbance was not a result of deliberate planning by any group but rather 'spontaneous combustion'.
4. A wealthy Trinidadian and self-proclaimed Marxist employed by Japan as his personal political assistant.

government knew that it had treated policemen, who are workers, very badly, and that 'the rice farmer', to quote the Premier in a speech at Windsor Forest in 1959, 'was more entitled to assistance than employees of the government', which would include the police? Whatever might have been the reason it was certainly most disgraceful for a popularly elected government to seek, first of all, to pre-judge the police, and to use foreign troops as an instrument for browbeating and intimidating the populace.

But that is not all. Here we have another bit of clumsiness on the part of the government. The Premier gets on the radio on the night of Friday, 16 February, and talks of 'visiting the full severity of the law on those apprehended or proved guilty'. What utter nonsense, and how significant is it. Here we have clearly an attempt at intrusion into the judicial system by the Premier. (*Interruption*). Idiots will giggle and hyenas will grin, but others like the hon. the Attorney General and the Minister of Home Affairs will appreciate that no member of the executive has any right to talk about visiting upon people the full severity of the law when there are Courts of Justice and people are going to be tried for offences already known to the law. That is an indication of exactly where this government is or was tending.

Theatened censorship of the Press

Now that we have an emergency we also have a further irritation of the situation. The hon. the Premier has threatened to introduce Press censorship. That is in keeping with the Proclamation of Wednesday, 14 February. The Proclamation was intended to prevent demonstrations against the government. This threat of Press censorship is an attempt to silence those who are against the government. I see absolutely no jurisdiction for any Press censorship of any kind. I cannot possibly hold any brief for the daily newspapers. In fact I have as much reason, both as a man and as the leader of a party, to complain against the type of thing we have found in the daily newspapers over the years. In the majority of instances they are against the popular movement, and they always keep up the tradition of supporting a losing cause at every election. But a government that says it will visit the full severity of the law on people when there are Courts of Justice; a government whose leader has said he wants a judiciary of the same political persuasion as the governing party, is not a government that will stop at suppressing or censoring scurrilous articles. It is a government that will not stop until it has silenced every form of opposition. Today it is *The Daily Chronicle*[5] (perhaps I should not say whether or not it is a good thing for this country that it should continue to exist), tomorrow it may be the *Evening Post*,[6] the next day perhaps the *Guyana Graphic*,[7] and then we will find it is the P.N.C.'s *New Nation*, and then we will go on until the only publication will be the *Thunder*.[8]

That particular pronouncement by the Premier is again provocative but indicative of what he has in mind. He is the publisher, or used to be the publisher, of *Thunder*. It would not be a question of mere inaccuracies, because *Thunder* is as replete with inaccuracies as any one of the daily newspapers. It could not be a question of libel, because *Thunder* had to settle an action for libel recently with Mr Sugrim Singh. It is obviously an attempt to silence opposition completely in British Guiana. But whatever may be their intention they certainly will not be able to achieve it, or achieve it without a serious situation arising. For what the People's Progressive Party must understand is that the results of the last election did not show that they commanded a majority of popular support, and any attempt by them to suppress the rights of the majority to oppose the government by democratic means – by the Press, by demonstrations, etc. – is going to be met, shall I say, very firmly.

Whither are we drifting in the circumstances? The events of Friday, the 16 of February, were unfortunate, but if the Premier means anything by the first part of his plea on that historic night, if he means anything by that joint plea made by the three leaders of the three political parties on Saturday 17 and Sunday 18 February, the situation, at least from that stage, should have been differently handled.

You do not cool tempers by threats, especially when you yourself have admitted virtually that you are incompetent to preserve law and order without your masters' soldiers. You do not encourage people to return to serenity, sobriety and calmness by declaring a state of emergency, and by having before their eyes every day the symbol of their subjugation and the symbol of your derogation from what you promised before, and what you have always set yourself as.

5. Controlled by U.F. Leader Peter d'Aguiar.
6. Independent and locally owned.
7. Then owned by the British Mirror Group.
8. P.P.P. party newspaper.

It was the Premier who went before the United Nations Committee and said that had it not been for the armed might of Britain the people of Guiana would have declared independence. Does he expect anyone to trust him or to believe in his *bona fides* when under a panoply of foreign troops he declares a state of emergency? But let him be warned.

Let his government be warned. You can arrest me if you want; you can arrest anyone if you want, but we are not going to take it either.

You (the Premier) come back from the U.S.A. and say that you believe in the democratic freedoms, but, in the first difficulty in which you find yourself, you resort to repression – and that in the context of a pauperised country.

These poor people, who had to go on strike in order to make government give them their due, will now have to pay for the upkeep of foreign troops in this country. You say you are paying them $2·6 million (Guyana) and we will have to agree to it. I suppose you will come back here for a few more millions to pay for the upkeep of the foreign troops you have brought into this country.

Sir, is this the attitude of a working class government? It seems to me that if this government had been true to its mouthings and statements about being honest (*Interruption from the government benches*). Answer not a fool according to the multitude of his folly – as I was saying, Mr Speaker, if this government were interested in the working class, it would have, in the first place, considered favourably and sympathetically the demands of the workers.

Mr Speaker: Time!

Mr Correia (Mazaruni-Potaro): I beg to move that the hon. Member for Ruimveldt be given another 15 minutes.

Mr Carter (Werk-en-Rust): Seconded.

Question put, and agreed to.

Mr Burnham: It would not have waited for a strike before it decided to give backpay from the 1 January 1961. It would not have waited for a strike before sending to the Whitley Council those points of difference which existed between itself and its employees.

Further, it would not have panicked at the first sign of simple opposition and agitation. If this government continues in the way it has started since the beginning of February, this country is going to be ruined by increased tensions, and the majority of its population will be drawn into one camp or another where the prime concern will be how to destroy each other rather than how to build the country and repair what damage was done on Friday 16. Indeed if the present trends and traits continue, it will mean that we shall be completely burdened with a terrific debt to the British government for sending imperialist soldiers here.

Government should resign

I am opposed to the P.P.P. and that goes without saying, but after all I am a Guianese, and my heart must bleed when I see so much incompetence in such high places; and when I recognise that, as the history of the last few weeks has proved, this government's policy is tending to the ruin of this country. We will not make a great noise about the Premier's saying he will not resign. It is the right of a politician to assume the air of bravado in circumstances of difficulty and fear. That is passed now, but I must observe that the attitude of bravado did not express itself prior to the end of the strike. I would observe for myself and the P.N.C. that it must take a great deal of 'brass face' and lack of self-respect to talk about not resigning and underscoring that when he has had to withdraw the Budget on which any government stands or falls.

Mr Speaker, never have I heard of a government withdrawing the important provisions of its Budget under pressure and then saying to the foreign Press: 'I will not resign – underscore that'.

But that is not all. It was stated in the *Thunder* that the T.U.C. did not get much because what the T.U.C. got on Sunday night had already been conceded on Wednesday night. That might have been so, but the concessions were as the result of the workers' demonstration. This is not the time for bravado; this is not the time for irritating people by talking of not resigning. If you do not want to resign, the people will know that you are not decent enough to do so when your government has collapsed.

This is the time for sending back the British troops and assuming the reigns of government. Do not depend on an expatriate Governor to issue Part II of the Emergency Order. If you do not resign now or mend your ways, when you get your independence you will be presiding over a graveyard.

5

Extracts from speech at People's National Congress
Annual Congress, New Amsterdam, 14 April 1963

*With British Guiana still licking its wounds from the 1962 general
strike, the P.P.P. government in April 1963 precipitated another general strike by introducing a Labour Relations Bill on 25 March
which the British Guiana T.U.C. labelled 'a blueprint for the end of
trade union freedom in British Guiana'. The strike lasted for three
disastrous months.*

*Mr Burnham addresses his party's Annual Congress at a time
when the strike was at its height and when tension and frustration
were at bursting point. In a remarkable analysis of the situation,
Forbes Burnham succeeds in putting his finger on the pulse of the
nation at the time and succinctly sums up the cause of rising racial
tension across the land.*

Comrade Chairman, last year at our Annual Congress we met just
after the disturbances of the now infamous February 16. Though the
incidents of Friday 5 April 1963[1] were not of the order of those of
last year February they sprung basically from the same cause – frustration, unrest and protest against the political and economic situation.

It is not for me at this point to attempt to apportion blame in
terms of individuals, groups and parties who might have made their
contribution to the creation and aggravation of the circumstances.
Rather I will try to isolate and identify the conditions, facts, events,

1. Date on which the three-month general strike began.

attitudes and reactions which form the back-drop to the play which is now being acted out in Guiana.

There is the pre-eminent fact of unemployment. In 1956, according to the McGale Report[2] there were 29,600 potential workers or approximately 18 per cent of the labour force unemployed. In Georgetown the rate was 22·3 per cent or 37·5 per cent of the national figure. Unemployment was highest in the 21–40 years group which accounted for 42·6 per cent of the whole. By 1963, though there has been no detailed study similar to that of McGale's in 1956, it is accepted on all sides that both the numbers and percentage of unemployed have increased. These are estimated at over 40,000 or over 20 per cent and many observers consider this a conservative estimate. The distribution geographically and according to age, percentage-wise, is much the same as 1956. Though the disturbances of February 1962 contributed their quota of unemployment, they merely accelerated or quickened a trend which was obvious during the period 1957–61.

Large numbers of unemployed with no unemployment benefits or assistance are an upsetting element in any community. There is also in these days of welfare States a tendency for these unfortunates in the society to look to government to provide relief in one form or another and when the government cannot perform or deliver, this expectation turns to criticism and hostility. In a paternalistic colonial society this demand on, and subsequent hostility to, the government, are further accentuated to the obvious embarrassment of the government.

The situation is made more acute by the allegation and in many cases proof of political discrimination by the representatives and supporters of the government in awarding jobs.

Another complicating factor is that in Georgetown where unemployment is highest the political party forming the government is without any significant political support or strength. It therefore in the circumstances becomes the butt of further dislike and hostility.

The fact that the governing party draws the greater part of the electoral support from the Indian community while Georgetown is predominantly African does not contribute to easing an otherwise tense situation. Political discrimination and differences are accentuated and aggravated by racial considerations. For example, from the

2. A report on employment commissioned by the International Labour Organisation.

nature of things, a job for a P.P.P. supporter generally means a job for an Indian as against a non-Indian; political arrogance of a P.P.P. member means the arrogance of an Indian towards a non-Indian; anti-government sentiments and actions take on an anti-Indian flavour. And so the vicious circle runs.

The governing party professes to be socialist but by its postures, its statements, the foreign literature it distributes, it leads one to the conclusion that its aim is to make Guiana a Soviet satellite. We are entertained by such statements like that of one P.P.P. legislator (Moses Bhagwan) that 'there is too much freedom in this country' and note the government's refusal to allow radio time to any party but its own and the failure to hold a bye-election in Houston for seventeen months. These are regarded as straws in the wind and call forth more fears, uneasiness, animosities and determination to be rid of such a government.

These last fears and reactions are not peculiar to non-Indians or Africans but are shared by many Indians. The possible defection of the latter away from the P.P.P. causes that party to fall back on gimmicks and tactics to whip up Indian racial feelings for the purpose of retaining its political support with obvious deleterious results so far as the nation is concerned.

It must not be believed that these tensions which arise in the capital remain there. They spread, and people throughout the country take their sides with fatalistic resolution. It is true that the city is not Guiana but it is the seat of government and the centre of the social, cultural, literary and political activities of the nation. Its significance therefore is not to be reckoned in terms of the proportion its population bears to that of the entire country.

One of the many concepts that have been borrowed from Britain is the supremacy of the legislature. What is, however, not fully appreciated by those who have a majority in the legislature here, is that that supremacy and attendant respect are retained by an appreciation among other things of the necessity, by tolerance and sensitivity to public opinion, to take into account and give weight to what other sections of the community think and are prepared to accept.

Such an approach provides the only alternative to a military dictatorship and an elaborate secret police system if there is not to be chaos and civil war. Hauteur, arrogance, insensitivity to the realities, and a naïve belief that there is some occult magic which makes a legislative majority invincible and omniscient, are no solution.

It is in this context that the P.N.C.'s proportional representation proposal must be understood and the fact that there has been such wide support for that proposal is proof that it has given expression to a need felt by many inside and outside the P.N.C.

If a party with an overwhelming legislative majority not based on an overwhelming popular majority refuses or fails, for whatever reasons, to have regard to *the other point of view*, those who represent the other point of view lose respect for the legislature and the forum of debate and agitation shifts decisively. Such a situation is fraught with dangerous possibilities and probabilities.

Proportional representation serves two vital purposes at this stage. It removes a certain cause of tension – the feeling by a substantial section of the community that it is under-represented where it really matters. The legislature will then accurately reflect the distribution of political power and make it palpable to all sides that consensus must be the prerequisite of governing. Legislative debates will then have a meaning and the legislature can be a place where issues are settled and binding arrangements and compromises made.

There have been some who have expressed opposition to P.R. because its introduction will rob them of the chance of a legislative majority. They rationalise their fears of losing 'power' and put forward academic arguments with the greatest sophistry. But what does 'power' mean in the present context? The 'power' to rush through bills, dispense patronage at certain levels, travel at taxpayers' expense and enjoy some social kudos – nothing else. It is the 'power' to be in office coupled with the impotence of being unable to govern. Real power connotes the ability to govern effectively, to bring necessary changes to the social and economic systems, to weld the various sections of Guiana into a nation, to put the country on the road to prosperity, to be accepted by political friend and foe as the government, a government that performs and delivers.

Those who describe proportional representation as a gimmick have not been able to propose a political solution to the particular problem as outlined above. The electoral system has become the focal point of political agitation not because it is so important in itself but because on it hinges the possibility or impossibility of ensuring government by consent. It has to be resolved or our country is doomed to even greater stagnation and retrogression.

The P.N.C.'s further proposal of a referendum to resolve the deadlock is another honest attempt to have the question settled. It is noteworthy that our political opponents who reject a referendum have not been able to put forward publicly their arguments against it. They make remarks like 'you do not give sweets to children because they want them' and threaten hell and fire if a referendum were to be imposed. These statements and attitudes indicate an intellectual bankruptcy, a fear of a referendum yielding P.R. and the placing of the wishes and selfish interests of a few above the preferences and sovereignty of the people.

It is perhaps apposite to return to a consideration of the racial question to which I have made passing reference before.

No one but an ostrich will deny that there exists racial rivalry and tension and that these with notable, significant, and welcome, exceptions are coincident with political party affiliations. This is true of all three parties but I choose to note more specifically the relations between Indians and Africans; not because the other ethnic groups are unimportant but because these two are most numerous and the strains between them are most obvious.

It is a fact that at the last elections the Indians voted predominantly for the P.P.P. and the Africans likewise for the P.N.C. This does not say that the former received no African votes or the latter no Indian votes. Is this a position that we have to accept? Are the groups unaffected by differences of ideology, policy and the competence or incompetence of one party or another in government? Unless it is otherwise, there is no hope of building a Guianese consciousness and nation.

Before answering these questions we ought to go deeper. The Africans who came here as slaves, drifted away from the plantations after the abolition of slavery and in large numbers moved to the cities or set up villages. Robbed of all but the rudimentary aspects of their native culture they accepted European (English) social standards and norms, and set about being assimilated into a society dominated by the European. They seem to have placed great store on the acquiring of education and skills and though as a group they never reached the upper levels of the foreign society they were for practical purposes Europeanised.

The Indians, when the Africans had forsaken the plantations and the Chinese, and Portuguese from Madeira, had proved unsuitable agricultural workers, have from that time formed the predominant section of the plantation and therefore rural population. The very fact of their having accepted wages and conditions which the Africans for social and financial reasons rejected was a source of early friction.

The Indians found themselves in the midst of a foreign society with different values from their own. They realised that they had to be westernised to be accepted but naturally their late arrival into the environment made the necessary assimilation seem slow and all the more so since they retained much more than fragmentary traces of their native culture. In seeking entry into the society they at first placed emphasis on the accumulation of wealth, rather than educational skills and the outward trappings of the western world. Many, if not the majority, have now reversed this process and consciously or subconsciously adopted the same emphasis and goals as the other groups in the community.

The result has been that these Indians, now seeking and obtaining entry into jobs and professions in which they were hardly represented before, tend to feel that this process is slow, that they have been discriminated against in the past and the swing of the pendulum should now be in the direction of the Africans being discriminated against.

Naturally, the entry of this new group into jobs, in fact the virtual monopoly of Africans in the past, breeds resentment amongst the latter. The Indians are unsure of themselves and the Africans feel themselves threatened; with the inevitable tension. It is for the leaders of the nation to recognise the sociological problem and instead of using it for political ends to seek a solution based on cooperation and positive joint and symbolic action. A lot of idle prating about the imperialists' policy of dividing and ruling will achieve nothing.

It must be also recognised that in spite of the new values now becoming part of the Indian repertoire there is a lag between the forward group and the rest. The Indians are still predominantly a rural people and there is the usual difference in terms of experience and traditions between the rural and urban population found in all parts of the world and frequently reflected in party preferences and affiliations. This universal problem is heightened in Guiana by the visually recognisable differences between the two different racial groups whose vocational and occupational differences are coincident with ethnic distinctions.

Further, note must be taken of the cultural differences between the two racial groups. The Indian unsure of himself will find emotional and psychological compensation in emphasising the cultural legacies he has inherited from Mother India, the African will find his succour in the derogatory observation that the Indian after all is socially and culturally inferior because he has not been and may never fully be westernised – as if there is an intrinsic merit in being westernised.

These are problems that can and must be solved. Education not only in institutions of learning but through media like the radio, T.V. and joint social and community effort and activities is the most important answer as I see it.

In this the P.N.C. must take the lead if it is to justify its boast of being the most intelligent and competent party and if it is to make full use of the mental and manual skills of which it has majority control in Guiana.

6

Radio broadcast to the nation on winning the 1964
General Election, 19 December 1964

*In October 1963, Britain's Conservative government ordered that
British Guiana's electoral system be changed to proportional representation and that new elections be held under this system in 1964.*

*Burnham had been constantly pointing out from 1960 that the
electoral system of constituency voting was grossly unfair, producing
a Parliamentary strength for the P.P.P. completely disproportionate
with its voting support.*

*The general election resulted in a plurality of votes for Mr Burn-
ham's People's National Congress and Mr d'Aguiar's minority
United Force. Though d'Aguiar's vote has now been reduced to 13
per cent his party retains the balance of power. Burnham, realising
that the situation could lead to chaos now decides to form a coalition
government combining his party's seats in the Legislative Assembly
with those of the United Force.*

*The two parties command 53 per cent of the vote and 29 seats in
the 53-seat Parliament. Mr Burnham leads the new government as
Premier with Mr d'Aguiar holding the portfolio of Minister of
Finance.*

*In a radio broadcast to the nation immediately following the for-
mation of his new government, the Premier declares his government's
determination to heal the breach which has developed between the
two major race groups of his country and his resolve to bring an end
to racial violence.*

The election is now over. A hard and at times bitter campaign has come to an end. On the results, the People's National Congress, in the interests of peace and stability in Guiana, has agreed with the support of the United Force to form the government. One of the more serious tasks facing us is the attainment of independence at the earliest point in time.

One of the disturbing features of the election which we have noted is the apparent cleavage existing in our society brought about by colonialism and seven years of mismanagement and misrule. Despite the years of disaster suffered by the people of this country, a large section of the electorate was persuaded against its best interests to vote for the party formerly in power as a result of the dishonest and opportunist propaganda that unless *that* party was returned to power those people would suffer. The new government headed by me intends to show by its actions in the immediate future and indeed throughout its term of office that this is not true. The problem of racial cleavage, racial antagonism and distrust which the last government allowed to develop during its term of office is still with us, but our government recognises this as a challenge which it intends to accept and which it is determined to overcome.

My government considers that it is a matter of the greatest importance and the utmost urgency that an 'atmosphere of relaxation' be established immediately. The reduction of tension, which is already apparent, and which will become more pronounced with every passing day when it is realised that not only are we intent on being fair and just, but also that we have at our disposal the means to carry out our intention, is merely the first fruits of our attainment of office.

Enemies of this country would like to see racial division and antagonism continue among the people of this country. We will dispel the fears of the apprehensive and confound the hopes of those who seek the destruction of this country. To be specific, this government holds that all the people of this country are equally important, whether they belong to a large group or to a small group.

To us the Amerindians are important. To us the Chinese are important. To us the Portuguese are important. To us the Europeans are important. To us the mixed races are important. To us the Africans are important. To us the Indians are important. In short, all Guianese are important and valued members of our community and we cherish them and consider that as a government it is our duty and privilege to guard, protect and further the real interests of all.

It would appear that the would-be destroyers of this country have sought to convince our Indian citizens that they have cause to fear because of the removal of the former government. We can assure our Indian citizens here and now that rather than cause for fear they have much to hope for from the new government.

This government is not bent on the confiscation of property. This government will not pursue policies likely to bring the races into collision. This government will maintain law and order. This government will see that the lives and property and personal safety of all citizens are protected.

We are fully aware that attempts will be made in the future as in the past to create disturbances. All of us know those who are likely to create disturbances, and those who think that they have some benefit to be derived from chaos and violence. We have no benefit to derive from such things and we will stamp out firmly any disruption of the calm, studied and steady progress which we are determined to establish and maintain in this country for the good of all.

We wish to let our Indian citizens know therefore that they can depend upon this government as they could not upon the previous administration for justice and fairplay, peace and security, ordered progress and economic advance. And this assurance extends to all the other race groups living in this country.

Of particular interest to us also is the welfare of our Amerindian citizens who in the past have been neglected, first by the imperial power and more recently by the former government. It will be our task to explore avenues and to take steps to bring the Amerindian citizens into full participation with the rest of us Guianese so that they may share in the benefits and responsibilities of a free Guiana.

We intend to demonstrate not only to fellow Guianese but also to the world that non-European people can, in their dealings with people of varying origins, show more enlightenment and humanity and achieve greater success than in those countries and territories considered and referred to as 'developed'. And we look forward with anticipation to the gains which Guiana as a whole will enjoy from the flowering of the abilities of those of our citizens so long treated as 'children of the forest' and 'beasts of burden'.

Our government does not consider, despite the unfortunate happenings of the past seven years, that there is in this country any deep-seated antipathy between the races, but recognises that our misfortunes have stemmed from the evil machinations of those bent upon the establishment of a totalitarian dictatorship founded on hatred, violence and mutual distrust. Nevertheless the government does not consider that it is the fount of all wisdom, and in order to ensure a greater degree of harmony than has been the lot of this country during the past seven unfortunate years, is actively considering the establishment of a body drawn from all sections of our population, racial, religious, cultural, etc., to whom the government can turn for advice when matters likely to affect any section of our population arise.

We know that the world is looking at us. Some of the cynical pessimists are waiting to say 'I told you so'. We intend to confound our critics, and to prove that in the realm of human relations we can teach the world and make a name 'to point a moral and adorn a tale'.

We ask for time, patience and understanding. The damage done over the last seven years cannot be repaired in a day. We cannot and will not condone and accept the nepotism and corruption of the past seven years. Changes are necessary and changes will be made, but no one who is honest and possessed of ability need have the least apprehension. Square pegs will not remain in round holes and all thinking Guianese know that they should not so remain.

All intelligent Guianese know that the previous administration has by its actions deliberately prevented the attainment of independence by this country, so that today we are one of the few remaining colonial peoples. Indeed it is now clear that far from wanting freedom the previous government was bent upon creating those conditions calculated to delay the transfer of power from British to Guianese hands until such time as they were able, at the bidding and under the tutelage of their *foreign* totalitarian masters, to introduce the form of tyranny and slavery which is *their* conception of freedom.

We know that more than ever these people will seek the delay of independence and anyone who by word or deed contributes towards the delay of independence for even one day, is an ally of those who would enslave us.

The energy which some in our midst exercise to demonstrate to the world that the races in this land cannot live together will be matched by the energy we will expend to show that they can.

The results of the election and the formation of our government are not to be considered as a victory for one party but a triumph for the whole Guianese people. There is nothing to gloat over; nobody is 'pon top'. But all of us are I am sure sobered by the realisation of how near we came to having our country destroyed, and how arduous were our endeavours to give this country the chance to live, to breathe, to survive.

It has been reported that some established organisations have made representations to the British government about Guianese affairs. I wish to announce that in the immediate future I shall seek to hold discussions with the Maha Sabha, the Hindu organisation, the United Sad'r Islamic Anjuman, Ascria, the Chinese Association and of course with the Archbishop of the West Indies, the Roman Catholic Bishop of Georgetown, the Ethiopian Orthodox Church, the Congregational Conference, the Methodist body and other religious and cultural organisations. My purpose is to establish a consultative democracy.

And now that the majority of the Guianese electorate have declared in favour of the government in power, it is my wish that Guianese in and out of the legislature – with malice towards none and goodwill towards all – will settle down to the engaging task of binding up the nation's wounds and charting a new course of peace and prosperity for Guiana.

Thank you for listening.

7

'Report to the Nation.' Statement on the first six months of the government's term of office, 12 July 1965

Six months after taking office in December 1964, Premier Burnham stands on the open balcony of the Parliament Buildings, and reports to the nation in a public address simultaneously broadcast.

It is a remarkable report in that it describes a country completely torn apart by racial violence and hatred over a period of some four years, brought to a state of calm in six short months.

Somewhat over six months ago in a rainy night, Sunday the 13 of December 1964 on the eve of my appointment as Premier of Guiana, I stood before a large crowd of my fellow Guianese at the Parade Ground and publicly stated that my government recognised that one of its first duties was to rule in the interests of all the people of this country. I promised then to dispel the fears of the apprehensive and confound the hopes of those who sought the destruction of our country. Today I stand here with the same thoughts in my mind to give to you, my friends, my masters, a report of my stewardship, an account of what measure of success has been achieved and what obstacles have been encountered since we assumed office.

Some six months ago there were still abroad the results and fears which racial and communal violence had left in its wake. Seven long years of incompetence, ineptitude and corruption had induced an atmosphere of frustration and despair. Our country's economy had become stagnant. Our coffers were practically empty and Guiana stood poised on the brink of bankruptcy. As a nation we seemed to have lost confidence in ourselves. Many had fled from the land of their birth and many were preparing to follow. The workers were disillusioned and could see only unemployment and poverty facing them. Few investors, local or foreign, were bold enough to risk their investments. Some, indeed, had cut their losses and quit and many who remained did so against what they considered their best judgment.

I knew then that the task of rehabilitating and reconstructing our country was enormous. My colleagues on the Council of Ministers knew then the enormity of the task they would have to perform but we were moved by a deep sense of patriotism and confidence that we would be able to lift Guiana out of the morass of maladministration, mismanagement and at best, mediocrity, which were the hallmark of the previous administration. We anticipated that there was much that we would have to do to cleanse the Augean stables before a new start could be made. But none of us, as we were to discover, had previously realised how great was the extent of moral and physical decay which was our inheritance.

We knew that there were several vacancies in the professional and technical ranks of the Public Service but only after assumption of office did we realise that there was in fact a huge depletion of these ranks. Ministries like those of Forests, Lands and Mines; Health and Housing; Works and Hydraulics and Agriculture were too denuded of staff to carry out the exercises of government let alone the new responsibilities which a development programme would entail. These vacancies had arisen partly from a spate of resignations throughout the Service which was caused by the prevailing sense of frustration and insecurity, nurtured and engendered by our predecessors, and partly because the latter sought to balance the budget by refusing to fill certain vacancies.

A catalogue of vacancies and unfilled posts would take me many an hour and perhaps be a source of depression. I wish to give some idea of how near to disaster we were six months ago and how certain that disaster would have been had there not been a change of government.

Our predecessors were naïve enough to believe that the way to economise was simply not to spend. They imagined that by not making the vitally necessary appointments, to which rather larger salaries were attached, they were saving. Their myopic vision prevented them from recognising that for every technical and professional post not filled the health of so many hundreds of persons suffered and so many hundreds of artisans and unskilled labourers were left without work. It has been estimated, for instance, that one more architect at the Ministry of Works and Hydraulics would have provided regular work for at least 500 other persons in various categories within and without the Public Service.

This was a situation which could not be remedied in a short time. With the cooperation of such staff as was there the government had to introduce certain new procedures, at least temporarily, and also to call in aid the services of private technicians and technologists as well as some experts lent us by the United States AID Mission. Further, we have issued a call to technical and qualified Guianese abroad to return to help in the rebuilding of our country and we propose, shortly, to send a team abroad to recruit the necessary type of staff regardless of nationality. In addition, we propose, as from September of this year, to award not less than fifty scholarships per annum in the technical fields and these are apart from other scholarships which countries like the United States of America, Canada, West Germany and the United Kingdom, are likely to make available. In the meantime I desire to pay special tribute and to express the nation's gratitude to those officers who have most enthusiastically and with great energy been working beyond the call of duty to ensure the execution and completion of old works and new.

But the ill-judged economising to which we have referred was only one facet of the picture of disarray with which we were faced on taking office. There was another facet – inefficiency and mis-spending as the concomitants of an elaborate system of corruption and nepotism.

One hundred so-called interim teachers were appointed in the Ministry of Education. Persons, all professionally unfit, some of them morally unfit, drew monthly salaries as interim teachers and head teachers in some cases, but the majority of these persons, thank God, have, though paid, never crossed the threshold of the schools to the staff of which they were attached. Some of them worked at Freedom House,[1] others were activists and party organisers. We, as taxpayers, were called upon to subsidise from government revenue the doubtful and sometimes anti-national activities of a certain political party.

Then there were the irregularities in the Department of Social

1. Headquarters of the People's Progressive Party.

Assistance where, on the *ipso dixit* of the minister, 3,500 names were added to the lists of persons to receive social assistance as displaced persons, even without any official investigation or proof. When 11,000 families, receiving assistance, were investigated in 1965 it was found that there were only 3,000 genuine cases and of the remaining 8,000 the majority did not qualify and the others were fictitious and non-existent.

The unbusiness-like conduct of affairs was further exemplified by the fact that on land settlement schemes at the end of 1964 the arrears of rental which, in any case, did not represent an economic return on capital expenditure, stood at the astounding figure of $1,356,725·68 (Guyana) and of this, approximately one million dollars was owed by the tenants of the Black Bush Polder.

The confusion, corruption and dishonesty at the Rice Marketing Board and the revelations thereon contained in the auditors' report have already been commented on during the debate on the Rice Marketing Amendment Bill earlier this year. The Board, as you are aware, has since been reconstituted and is now carrying on its job of marketing the farmers' rice instead of providing commissions for Gimpex[2] and perquisites and feather beds for cronies.

This is but part of the chaos out of which we undertook to create a new confidence and a new nation. Many Guianese seemed to have lost their self-respect and self-reliance. Low wages and unemployment were the only future to which thousands of workers could look forward.

Within days of my government's assumption of office we gave tangible proof of our seriousness and willingness to carry out undertakings made during the election campaign by fixing the government minimum wage at four dollars per day retroactive to 1 October 1964. On my personal intervention those workers of Indian descent who had fled from Mackenzie during the disturbance were able to return as from 1 January 1965 to their jobs and their places of abode, and to this day they are singing the praises of the government and strongly criticising those who are still seeking to stir up violence and indulge in wanton acts of sabotage.

I, myself, instead of hastening abroad as others had done in the past and still others, naïve though well-meaning, would have had me do, to go a-begging, undertook to tour the country to meet the

2. Commercial enterprise run by the P.P.P.

people, to learn of their grievances, their difficulties, their hopes and their aspirations. Those visits have not been confined to areas where my party's support has been predominant but have been, in many cases, to areas traditionally hostile to the People's National Congress and the United Force, the two member-parties of the coalition government.

I have learnt a great deal from these visits. I have learnt for instance, that the majority of Guianese regardless of political affiliation or ethnic origin are sick and tired of the violence and carnage for which 1964 will go down in history. I have learnt that rice farmers want their rice sold and to get proper returns for their toil and labour. I have learnt that the simple people, the ordinary Guianese, want work and a better standard of living and are prepared to work and cooperate with the government in achieving these objectives. I have been struck by the willingness of the Guianese people, in all walks of life, to help themselves and to chart a new course to progress and these Guianese are drawn from people who supported all of the political parties that offered themselves to the electorate in December last.

Fellow Guianese: your faith, trust and your willingness to help yourselves and country have paid great dividends. We have received road building equipment to the value of five million dollars from the United States and will receive 2·25 million dollars in similar equipment from Canada, putting us in a position to satisfy our country's need in this respect for many a year and helping us to carry out our programme of at least 300 miles of first class all-weather highways within the next five years.

Construction of the road from Atkinson to Mackenzie, a dream of many a past administration, will begin within a few months. Government buildings, starting with this one on the verandah of which I stand, are being rehabilitated after several years of neglect and decay. Our hospitals particularly those in Georgetown and Suddie will be re-equipped pending a final decision with respect to the building of a new hospital. Six new all-age schools will be built this year to accommodate 5,000 children. Nearly two million dollars-worth of food will be made available for distribution to school children, needy families and self-helpers, and a private investment fund of 3·4 million dollars (Guyana) will shortly be made available for the promotion of local industries as soon as the necessary arrangements can be made for the servicing of the fund.

May I pause here to express the gratitude of the government and the people of Guiana, to those countries, those nations like the United States of America, Canada and the United Kingdom, and those agencies like the United Nations, for all the very kind and generous assistance which they have given us. We appreciate this type of assistance, assistance to help us to rehabilitate and reconstruct our country, assistance which does not entail meddling in our local political affairs by any of our benefactors.

These are some of the results of your efforts. These are some of the consequences which have flowed from your display of faith and confidence.

Within a few short months my government has been able to convert what has been a rapid downward progression into an equally rapid upward progression. From being a country which was a living example of disruption, discord and disunity, ours has become one at which many of our neighbours gaze with undisguised envy. The ship of state which had run aground has been salvaged and with a new captain and crew aboard and no room for passengers, is making its way with certainty towards the port of economic recovery and prosperity.

One of the greatest tasks which faced and still faces our government is the necessity to reduce and ultimately eradicate unemployment. You no doubt remember that the MacGale Report of 1957 disclosed that approximately 18 per cent of our work force was unemployed in 1956. This percentage by December 1964 had risen to well over 20 per cent representing more than 40,000 persons. This is a staggering figure to contemplate but we must do more than contemplate. We must do more than utter loud noises and attempt to apportion blame. We must settle down to the difficult but challenging task of dealing constructively and effectively with this problem and this is what we have attempted to do.

The labour exchanges in the three districts have been strengthened and new procedures adopted to make them more efficient. For the first six months of this year the labour exchanges have been able to place in employment more Guianese than they did in the two years 1963 and 1964. Up to the 30 of June 1965, jobs were found for approximately 6,000 unemployed and this figure does not take into account appreciable numbers who have been placed in employment outside of the agency of the exchanges.

But we do strike our chests at putting 6,000-odd people in jobs out of over 40,000, when there are thousands more who will be entering into the employment market within another two weeks. Ours has been some achievement, but there are still thousands who are experiencing the humiliating and dehumanising frustration of being without work. Able-bodied men, women and young people are amongst us with their strength, their talents, their skills and their knowledge going to waste.

No government that claims, as we do, to represent the working-class can ignore the situation. No government which claims the right to lead its people to independence can turn the Nelson eye to this problem.

But even while we embark upon crash programmes we recognise that in the final analysis, significant projects and undertakings must be attempted, not merely on the basis of there being several thousands unemployed, but also after there has been a proper discovery and inventory of our human resources, skills and special aptitudes. That is why an extensive Man-power Survey has been undertaken with the kind assistance and under the competent supervision of a United Nations Specialist, Mr Oliver Francis of Jamaica. This survey which began in January has progressed satisfactorily according to schedule and, by 31 July, we should have available a preliminary report on certain aspects.

Meanwhile the Minister of Labour is working on a scheme for the training of young men and women in the age-group 18–25, a scheme which will teach to those participating, skills as mechanics, electricians, printers, bookbinders, drillers and technicians in many fields.

The government's emphasis is on providing training that is relevant rather than academic and irrelevant.

New spirit and hope have been given to the University of Guiana to ensure that it will no longer be a second-class institution for indoctrination in irrelevant ideologies.

The youth, too, have received new inspiration and with government's encouragement 42 new youth clubs have been organised and an Area Youth Committee established. A successful congress was held in April as well as several seminars and games clinics. The youth are now involved in schemes being drawn up by the Ministry of Youth for the execution of a number of community projects including the clearing of lands and the building of roads.

There have been indications of valuable metals like copper, a report on which is expected shortly. If, as is believed, our mineralogical potential is great and economically exploitable we can rest assured that it will be fully developed in the basic interests of the people of Guiana. It is this government's policy that the minerals within the bowels of our earth belong to the Guianese for whose benefit they must be won. We will not, like the dog in the manger, refuse to encourage or give licences to foreigners, but we shall ensure at all times that the country and its citizens are not robbed.

In a country like ours, not only must agriculture supply the means for substantial employment but also it must be an important medium for contributing to our capital accumulation and growth. Looking at examples and lessons from other nations we are convinced that agriculture can be made viable and play its proper role provided the proper discipline, supervision, education and assistance can be assured. It is a fallacy to believe that this country's economy, at this stage, can move on the basis of perpetual large-scale subsidisation of agriculture. There will have to be large capital expenditure but, unlike our predecessors, we are determined to ensure that there are the proper returns for this expenditure.

It will be recalled that before the Ministry of Economic Affairs was created, Development and Planning came within my portfolio, and I found then to my horror and dismay that there was no planning secretariat or planning unit worthy of the name. There were three officers acting when there should have been a complement of nine, and yet, you will find this difficult to believe, those whom we succeeded in office were blithely talking about drafting and executing a development programme.

I have no doubt that now for the first time Guiana will have a sensible development programme, expertly prepared and expertly serviced. If there were no other achievements to point to, I would have been satisfied with this alone for it marks an intelligent and serious approach to the task of developing our country's resources and setting Guiana on the road to economic progress. In this context, on behalf of the government and people of Guiana, I deem it my duty to express the deepest appreciation and gratitude to the civil servants, the international agencies, the foreign governments and all who will have contributed to this *magnum opus*.

A rehabilitation committee widely representative of various social and religious organisations and under the chairmanship of a distinguished Guyanese, Sir Stanley Gomes, has been set up to advise government, after proper investigation, on what steps and action may be taken to rehabilitate and bring assistance to those persons, those Guianese, who have in any way suffered as a result of the disturbances which plagued our country from 1962 to 1964.

There have been allegations about imbalances and, in response, my government has invited the International Commission of Jurists to mount a commission to enquire into the balance of the races in the security and public services and government agencies and undertakings including land settlement schemes and other areas of governmental responsibility. This invitation has been accepted and within a few weeks a three-man commission will begin its investigations. It is difficult, if not impossible, to find a more detached and reputable body than the International Commission of Jurists to undertake an enquiry of this kind. The International Commission of Jurists is a non-governmental, non-political international organisation which has consultative status with the United Nations Economic and Social Council.

In inviting the International Commission of Jurists to carry out this exercise we were fulfilling our pledge to the people of this country made in my speech on the 13 of December 1964, to remove sources of racial tension and mistrust within our society and to restore to it a climate of racial tolerance and harmony. I deeply regret the irresponsibility of the opposition (whose seats again today are vacant), in declaring its intention to boycott the team of jurists, but we shall not be deterred from carrying out our functions as a government and to hold the balance fairly between all the peoples of this country, exposing in their stark nakedness those who seek every opportunity to divide.

Within three months of the formation of this government we were the hosts, thanks to the generosity of the government of Barbados, to the Third Conference of Caribbean Commonwealth Countries. There were no loud noises issuing from this conference, but the conference itself was a success. Not only did it indicate that Guiana was capable of playing its proper role in the region, but out of it came positive decisions calculated to make regional cooperation and unity a fact. In the spirit of this conference, within the last week, the governments of Guiana and Barbados have agreed to set up a free trade area as between these two countries and to work towards the eventual establishment of an economic community and a customs union. This agreement is aimed at furthering the economic interests of the region. It is not intended to be exclusive nor is it directed against anyone.

In fact the two subscribers to the agreement are prepared to welcome new members to the club. It is time that we in the Caribbean seek every means of rationalising our respective economies, making them complementary instead of competitive and lay the basis for giving a better and richer way of life to the peoples whom our respective governments claim to represent. I have good reason to believe that very shortly there will be an announcement of further accessions to the community which Barbados and Guiana have decided to establish.

The Commonwealth team which came here to observe the conduct of the elections has written that the results of the elections mirrored the political preferences of the nation. The British government undertook in October 1963 to call a conference after the elections and to fix a date for independence at that conference. Since we have been in office we have displayed our competence to deal with the problems that we have met. The Commonwealth Prime Ministers' Conference issued a communiqué in which all the prime ministers, except one, welcome the British government's intention to call an early conference and fix the date for independence.

We are grateful to the British government for the assistance they have given us by way of loans, grants and technical personnel, but we are tired of being a second-class people. We are tired of tutelage. When one looks at the other nations which have won their independence in recent years one sees all the criteria and more which qualify us for independence, if indeed a people have to 'qualify' to enjoy their God-given right to rule themselves and run their own affairs. We will not be distracted or side-tracked; we will not be drawn into pointless and academic arguments about real and imagined grievances and differences. Britain cannot solve these. Britain cannot remedy these. She has never in the past attempted to do so prior to the granting of independence. If differences there are in our community then we Guyanese must settle them and not our erstwhile tutors who, however well meaning, can never fully understand or appreciate our conditions, our way of life and our attitudes. Guianese must solve their problems and no one else.

The majority of the electorate and the population, including a significant section of the opposition, want independence and we will no longer be thwarted by little selfish men or those who believe that God gave them the burden of settling the destinies of other peoples and other nations, and we shall have independence no matter how great the sacrifice.

And after we will have achieved independence we shall set it as our task to work in community with our West Indian brothers for the complete removal of the last vestiges of imperialism from the Caribbean, for the building of a brave, new and just society, for the projection of the Caribbean personality on the international scene and in the councils of the world. We shall be no man's satellite; we shall be no man's slave.

It is my conviction that Guiana as part of the Caribbean has a contribution to make to the world, a tale to tell – the tale of how a small nation can act independently without making itself a participant in the cold war – a tale of how a small nation can evolve a way of life of its own – a tale of how a small nation can, with the energies of its people and the assistance of real friends, banish poverty, plan its economy and maintain democracy. This contribution we cannot make, this tale we cannot tell, unless we achieve full independence.

8

Speech at a mass open air meeting on winning the
1968 General Election, Independence Square,
Georgetown, 22 December 1968

*The first election held since Guyana's attainment of independence
is won outright by Prime Minister Burnham's People's National Congress. Burnham's supporters are jubilant and they gather in their
thousands to listen to their Prime Minister.*

*Forbes Burnham knows, however, that the struggle to build his
nation has just begun and that the people must be prepared for this
struggle – he strikes a serious note. The Prime Minister's speech re-
flects his determination to cross the racial barrier still to be broken
down, to rule in the interest of all Guyana and to introduce as quickly
as possible his economic and political philosophy of cooperative
socialism.*

Comrades and friends, tonight as I stand before you I am deeply
grateful for the way in which you by your votes have responded to
the call of the P.N.C. for a clear majority in the election just past.

The success which the efforts of the P.N.C. and you have achieved
is a victory for the Guyanese people and for Guyana. I thank you both
for your support and for the calm and restrained manner in which you
conducted yourselves during the trying period when all manner of
abuse and provocation was directed at you. You have shown the
world that the Guyanese electorate is a mature and sophisticated one.
Your behaviour has surprised our detractors and has disappointed
those who came to scoff.

In victory we have not been jubilant. We have not sought to gloat over the defeat of our opponents and this alone has both surprised and embarrassed those who in the past were accustomed to victory parades.

Seven days have passed since you went to the polls to indicate your will that the People's National Congress should continue to administer the affairs of our country. The vote which has returned my party to office is in my opinion a vindication of the last four years of P.N.C. administration – the policy of national conciliation which we have pursued; a policy dedicated to the consolidation of peace and harmony in our country.

The result of the poll has shown that, contrary to the expectations of the bigots and the short-sighted, we have crossed racial frontiers in a significant manner. We have breached the P.P.P. stronghold in the Corentyne and elsewhere. This is of importance to us as a party but it is of even more importance to the Guyanese nation. It is the most significant development of the election. For now we know and the P.P.P. knows and the world knows that Guyanese, regardless of their ethnic origin are not the property of any one political party; that the majority of Guyanese are interested in the welfare of the nation as a whole rather than in the narrow interest of a part of the nation.

The support which we have received from all races and classes in Guyana compels recognition that, whatever label was put on us before, we are now recognised as the truly nationalist party which we have always claimed to be, and can speak for, and are responsible to, all the people of Guyana.

We hold as sacred the trust which Guyanese have placed in us and are both proud and humble in contemplation of the awesome responsibility which is placed upon our shoulders. We shall not fail the Guyanese people.

Those who have supported us will not be forgotten, but even those who have opposed can rest assured that in no way will their legitimate interests be neglected, for we are committed to the proposition that Guyanese as Guyanese are entitled to our concern and assistance and that the national good must transcend party or sectional interest.

We hope that by our efforts the next election will find us with more support than we have at present.

Now that the tumult is over, it is time to turn our attention to the many and varied tasks that lie before us. It is to be hoped that those who, unmindful of the harm which can be done to the image of

Guyana, have sought to sully the government for election purposes will now desist. But whatever the attitude taken by our opponents, we will not be deflected from the tasks which face us and which would have faced any other government that found itself in office.

We do not deny the right of the opposition to oppose but as a government we will not permit the disruption of our national life in any manner. We are equipped materially and psychologically to deal firmly, impartially and swiftly with all who by any means or in any guise may be so ill-advised as to seek to spoil our record of peace and tranquillity to gratify their puerile ambitions.

I speak to you tonight in two capacities – as party leader and as Prime Minister.

As leader of the P.N.C., I view the leader of the P.P.P. as one with whom I am in political conflict. As Prime Minister, I recognise him as leader of the opposition and a necessary part in the functioning of the democratic machinery of government. A responsibility devolves upon him as it does upon me to make the democratic processes of our young country work and whatever stand he or his party may care to take, I and my party shall not abandon our responsibility.

Let us now turn our eyes to the future for there is much to be done. First of all we must rid ourselves of all vestiges of colonialism. The process of decolonisation now barely begun must be accelerated. There must be decolonisation both of institutions and of minds. We must open the interior and truly possess our country. We must settle once and for all the Amerindian land question. We must put behind us the paradox of indigenous people without land. We must overhaul our legal system. We must lay a solid foundation for a new society functioning in freedom.

I cannot emphasise enough our intention to create a new society completely orientated towards the people as a whole and based on the principle that man is the most precious of all resources. To this end we will accelerate the process of decolonisation already begun. And when I use the word decolonisation I include in that concept the veritable creation of a new man. I include also a complete break with past attitudes of subordination and differentiation.

The problem of racial cleavage has been considerably lessened since the P.N.C. took over the administration in 1964, and the results of the election confirm this. Nonetheless, we do realise that much work remains to be done in the area of race relations. The realisation of a national identity requires a resolution of this problem. The absolute necessity for national unity arises not only from the need for a national consensus. In the face of threats from abroad, we need national unity if we are to maintain our independence and to implement the schemes for the rapid development of the economy.

I want to tell you tonight that the forging of national unity and the decolonisation of our minds are as important as our economic problems. They are important because they are related to the ideological position we take as we prepare to go forward. The identification of our ideological position is important because it is this identification which will determine our future in the psychological as against the statistical sense.

Comrades and friends, the question in issue before us all is: What do we want for ourselves? Do we want to remain a mere residue of a colonial past? Do we want to continue accusing ourselves and allowing others to accuse us of being a divided people or members of an anthropological aggregate within which there is no social cohesion? Do we want to continue aping the ways of our former masters? I am fully aware of course that the means of communication in this twentieth century have had a tremendous influence on our ways of thinking, and that it is only too easy for us to forget our origins and fall into the cultural trap of our times, the trap which has made cardboard Europeans of so many of us.

Guyana, like other developing countries must needs be preoccupied with economic problems. But there is a physical limit to what Guyana or other countries with similar social and economic handicaps can do. And I would be failing to do my duty if I did not make it clear to everyone that whatever the future holds for us is already in our own hands. I have said before that in my view the economic development of Guyana lies in the diversification of agriculture – with a concomitant emergence of industrial processes – and the exploitation of our mineral resources.

The hydro-power project at Tiboku will liberate vast areas of our hinterland for forest exploitation as well as provide employment for our people during the various stages and steps of construction.

The diversification of our agriculture will make it possible for us to develop new industries from its by-products. But no matter what plans we make or what dreams we dream, I want you to keep remembering that the great lesson of the years behind us is that we ourselves will have to provide the workers, the technicians, the scientists, and the guts, to accomplish that which we want to accomplish.

We are a people in our own right, with brains and talent of our own, with a knowledge of our own people and our own history, with an understanding of our own problems and our own resources, with an appreciation of the kind of world in which we live. We must apply our own brain power to our environment, develop our own philosophy and our own ideology. This, I think, is the best way of serving our people and the true alternative to strutting and fretting upon a petty stage seeking the acclamations of a cynical audience.

And let me remind you, comrades and friends, that the working class holds a special place in modern society. In Guyana we must recognise this in deed as well as in concept and word. In the public sector of the economy, that is to say in ministries and corporations, a new policy of workers' participation in planning and decision-making will be introduced next year. Employees who work in an enterprise, at whatever level, must necessarily acquire knowledge of certain aspects of life of the enterprise. There must be a machinery for self-expression that is compatible with a well disciplined work-force. Apart from this, it is our conviction that people called to a vocation of labour by hand or brain must in this age realise their full social, economic and spiritual emancipation. The public sector sees no reason to hesitate in leading the way on terms to be worked out with the Trade Union Council and other interested parties.

Comrades and friends, in thinking about the future of Guyana we have at all times to apply our minds also to the people of Guyana. The young people particularly and those who, as a result of our past social structure, have always felt that there was no use in our system for them, must take pride of place. In this regard, your new government will take action to bring into being a series of reforms ultimately resulting in a revolution of our social life.

Of the various areas that suggest themselves, the concept of co-operative development comes first to my mind. Chief in any programme of cooperative advance must be a high priority allocation to the training of young people and other people who would form the spearhead of this new movement to transform our society. The objective I have in mind is to build a corps of cooperators who will make for themselves a new, a real life, in selected areas of the near or far interior, and who will be fully equipped for this role.

A central cooperative credit society established by my government in 1966 will next year blossom forth into the foundation of a cooperative bank and by 1970 become our first indigenous bank. It will be the apex of the cooperative credit system, mobilising cooperative savings and channelling credit to cooperative societies engaged in economic activity.

Also high in the priority list is our pre-occupation with the welfare of the farmer and the consumer. There is a close relation between both of these so far as the cost and standard of living is concerned. We must make Guyana a country in which farmers enjoy secure marketing facilities, favourable prices that are guaranteed and subject to increase in scarce periods. At the same time, we must ensure that a regime of cheap food in Guyana is established. We have already started to make this possible by a programme of increased buying of farmers' produce and we intend to set up a great number of retail outlets in the rural and urban areas. We know, of course, that we cannot control all of our consumer prices, but we do promise that a great deal of attention will be directed to the whole issue.

A new land policy must be evolved. One of our pre-occupations is that there must come to an end the non-beneficial holding of land and the rapacious adventures of speculators. We intend to make sure that all persons who work land have land to work. Limitations must be placed upon the extent of land a person or persons may hold in order to prevent the emergence of a class of 'Latifundistas'. As I am on this question, I should say here and now that we are very disturbed at the high rents people are paying for houses. The nature of the present legislation and the question of supply and demand are the chief factors at work here.

We feel also that the whole area of taxation should be scrutinised and overhauled. The philosophy behind a taxation policy should be not simply or merely to raise revenue but to liberate energies and to channel them into creative endeavours. As for the tax-dodgers, the present government has already started a clean-up. I can assure you that the future will find us devoting more care and attention to see that people who should pay taxes are made to pay them.

9

Elected with an overall majority and a full mandate from the people, Prime Minister Burnham now moves his country rapidly towards republican status. At the Constitutional Conference of 1965, Mr Burnham made clear his intention to make Guyana a constitutional republic as soon as possible after independence was attained. This was resisted by the minority United Force, at that time still a part of Burnham's coalition government. A compromise was reached whereby the independence constitution would provide for Guyana to change from a monarchy to a republic through a simple majority vote in the National Assembly but that such a motion could not be introduced until 1969.

In the 1968 election campaign the Prime Minister declared that his party would invoke this provision if elected, as soon as possible after the election, and the result of the election gave him the mandate he wanted.

The motion to declare Guyana a republic was opposed only by the United Force and was carried by 46 votes to 2.

Mr Speaker, sir, on the morning of Friday, 19 November 1965, in London, to be precise at Lancaster House, a report was signed. That report was of the British Guiana Independence Conference of 1965, the last of three, the two others having proved abortive. The report was signed, sir, by the representatives of the People's National Congress and the former leader of the United Force... At paragraph 13 of the report, one finds the following sentence:

There will be provision for the Parliament of the new State, if it so wishes, after 1 January 1969, to bring into operation scheduled amendments establishing a republic on the Parliamentary system.

Subsequent to the report, the Guyana constitution was promulgated and one finds that in article 73 paragraph (5) provision is made for the National Assembly, upon a motion introduced by the Prime Minister and supported by the votes of a majority of all the elected members of the National Assembly, to pass a resolution declaring Guyana a republic as from a given date subsequent to the passage of the resolution. There were two provisos, however, to paragraph (5) of article 73 of the constitution. The first one was that the motion seeking to have the House agree to the declaration of a republic should lie in the House for a period of not less than three months, and the second proviso was to the effect that notice of the motion should not be given in the House prior to the 1 January 1969.

As one of those present at the conference, Your Honour, my recollection is that both of those provisos had specific significance. The one with respect to the three-month period was put into the constitution to ensure that the public of Guyana would have a reasonably long time to discuss the pros and cons of Guyana's becoming a republic as against a monarchy. The other proviso which relates to the motion not being tabled before the 1 January 1969, was intended to give the electors of Guyana an opportunity at the election, either directly or inferentially, to express their preference for the monarchical or the republican system. Notice of this motion, Mr Speaker, was given on the 20 March of this year and today, over five months after, I seek to have the House agree to the motion.

In paragraph (5) of article 73 of the constitution, reference is made to the amendments to the constitution concomitant on the passage of the motion which is now before the House. Those amendments are set out in detail in the second schedule to the constitution of Guyana and since it is not my intention to make of this discussion a legalistic argument or a foray into the field of legalism, I would content myself with alluding to the main amendments which will flow if this motion were to be passed. 'If', I said, Mr Speaker. But I would recall or note that under paragraph (5) of article 73, all that is required is a simple majority of elected members of this Parliament.

Mr Speaker, if this motion is passed and the day proposed in the motion sees the fulfilment of our intention, there will cease to be a Governor-General in Guyana and in his place a titular head of State, there will be substituted a President. The President, who will have to be a Guyanese citizen, not disqualified from being a member of this Assembly, and of the age of 40 or over, will be elected by the Parliament by secret ballot.

Looking at it as a matter of mere words and lifeless form, one would come to the conclusion that all that would have been done was to substitute a President for a Governor-General, except of course that whereas the Governor-General is appointed by Her Majesty the Queen on the advice of the Prime Minister, the President will be elected by the National Assembly by secret ballot.

The powers of the President as proposed in Schedule II of the constitution will be no less, as I understand it, than the powers of the Governor-General. But when one departs from the mere form, I would submit, sir, that there will be a difference between Guyana, a monarchy, and Guyana a republic.

In the first place, though we accept the fact that Her Gracious Majesty Queen Elizabeth II is Queen of Guyana merely titularly and exercises no executive powers within her Dominion of Guyana, though we accept the fact that Her Majesty's representative the Governor-General performs his duties in the name of Her Majesty the Queen but again on the advice, which has to be taken, of the elected ministers of the government, one must confess that looking at the history of Guyana, looking at our own former connection with and relationship to the United Kingdom, a natural fulfilment of our history should be the cutting of even formal ties with the Queen or the Royal House of Great Britain. Now that we have matured, the element of bitterness has lessened, if not disappeared, but I would submit, that in the context of Guyana there is an indescribable incongruity about having the Queen of Great Britain, the Queen of Guyana.

Moving to the status of a republic represents, to my mind, a further step in the direction of self-reliance and self-confidence. It is to be noted that there have been other constitutions promulgated within the Caribbean and outside of the Caribbean before and subsequent to the Guyana constitution. It is to be further noted that in most of those constitutions the monarchy has been retained. And in moving this motion, I desire to make a special point. We, in Guyana have decided that the monarchy should go. But we do not criticise anyone

more knowledgeable of his own circumstances and environment outside of Guyana who wants to retain for his particular country the
monarchical system, because every politician, every leader of a
country, must be deemed to be more conversant with his own circumstances and attendant facts than outsiders.

As we look around the walls of this Assembly, we see brilliant examples of photographic and painting art, but with one exception the
physiognomies there set out do not seem to be familiar in the context
of Guyana. In fact, one particular picture reminds us of that part of
our history when Guyana and several parts of the Caribbean were
merely settled for the pillage and the loot with which another country
could have been enriched. I say this merely to attempt a broad historical narrative, not in any bitterness, because those days are past.
Naturally, when we become a republic we will not dispose of these
pictures. What we will do will be to put these into a special place in
our museum, reminding us of the past to which we must not and
cannot return.

It is the contention of the party in government that the establishment of the Republic of Guyana should coincide with the celebration and/or anniversary of an event of peculiar Guyanese significance.
When we were younger we remember being told about Henry V
attacking at Agincourt and saying something about England and St
George. That was part of our education. Our own history was
neglected, if not vilified. In fact, some of those who instructed us
made a point, sometimes subtly, sometimes clumsily, of establishing
to us that we had no history.

A country without its own history, without its own heroes, without its own legends, I contend, would find it difficult to survive.
There will be nothing to look to, nothing to admire, nothing to write
or sing about. Looking over our historical landscape we came upon
what is undeniably a most significant event, the slave rebellion, as it
is called by some, the slave revolution, as it was called by others,
which started on the 23 February 1763, at Magdalenenberg in
Berbice.

I may observe, *en passant*, that Berbice has given us not only our
leader of the opposition, but also our national hero.

Cuffy led that revolt. The revolt was different from many an uprising which had taken place in Guyana. There had been previous uprisings but those were, so to speak, flashes in the pan. Those were,
so to speak, merely spasmodic reactions to cruelty. In the case of the

Berbice revolt, we found that for the first time the slaves, under a leader, decided not only that they should end their slavery but also that they should run the country and though, in their tradition of reasonableness, they suggested that perhaps a partition of Guyana between the whites and blacks was desirable, through their leader Cuffy they made it particularly clear that there was no intention, desire or willingness, on their part, to return to the system of slavery. What they saw as the future of the country was the existence of two separate and independent nations. No one will disagree that the revolution in Berbice, which started on 23 February 1763, differed from previous uprisings and was the forerunner of the much better known one led by Toussaint l'Overture some 30 years after, in what is now the Republic of Haiti.

It was decided to propose that Cuffy become our national hero and that the 207th anniversary of the revolution which he led should coincide with the date on which Guyana becomes a republic. We do not envy the British their St George. We will not beatify Cuffy, but at least we can respect him, respect the statesmanship and insight which he showed when he led the revolution.

Cuffy's efforts, may I note by the way, were all the more impressive in the context of the existing social structure of the time, when one remembers that he was a house slave as distinct from a plantation slave. He would have belonged to the group that would have been treated less badly. He would have belonged to the group that got the few crumbs and paltry favours, and the fact that at that time he was the leader showed that his spirit was such that he could not be bought with the crumbs and the favours.

One may remark on the dignity and the presence of Atta and Accabre,[1] but had there not been a Cuffy there might not have been an Accabre. I think the majority of members of this Assembly share the recognition of the sterling worth of men like Cuffy and Accabre. I cannot speak for the minority but if, as we expect, this motion were to be passed, if, as we expect, the 23 February will be Republic Day, it is more, I contend, than merely changing St George for Cuffy. If we are to give any substance and content to the concept of independence and mature nationhood what better opportunity is there than the 23 February 1970 for giving the new content which we, the majority, concede is necessary.

1. Other leaders of the slave revolution.

The party to which I belong is a socialist party. The party to which I belong believes that the instrument which can, and ought to, in the context of Guyana, be used for bringing in socialism is the cooperative. *Bona fide* cooperatives are our ideal. To this end, at the practical level, the Cooperative Department has been reorganised, but at the philosophical level, a campaign within and without the party has been carried out and is being carried out as part of a process of re-education and re-orientation of the people pointing out (*a*) the advantages of the cooperative as an institution in ordinary, practical, day to day terms; and also (*b*) its importance and significance in bringing about a change in the social and economic relationships in this country.

It is noteworthy perhaps that this position was taken by this party, way back in the early 'sixties, and equally noteworthy is a resolution adopted by E.C.O.S.O.C.[2] in June of this year urging, if I may put it this way, a proliferation of cooperatives in the underdeveloped and undeveloped world. It is not for me to expand greatly on this subject, that will be done by my most competent colleague, the hon. Minister of Education, Mrs Patterson.

So *pari passu* with the establishment of the Republic it is proposed that a serious and earnest effort be made to establish firmly and irrevocably the cooperative as the means of making *the small man a real man* and changing, in a revolutionary fashion, the social and economic relationships to which we have been heir as part of our monarchical legacy.

The government of Guyana has indicated to the Secretary-General of the Commonwealth its intention of having Guyana a republic and, at the same time, having Guyana remain a member of the Commonwealth. May I, without attempting to cause any offence one way or another, put my government's position with respect to the Commonwealth very simply. On economic grounds, our continued membership of the Commonwealth is justified. There are some who would explain their membership in terms of philosophy, but this sometimes seems empty when one looks at the different and differing constitutional and parliamentary systems to be found in the Commonwealth. Most of those who speak on this subject will admit that, economically, it is advantageous to be a member of the Commonwealth. It may be that some day membership of the Commonwealth will have some new

2. Economic and Social Council, an organ of the United Nations.

dimension attached to it, maybe, but as I see it – and speaking for myself and, I believe, the majority of my colleagues – the economic justification is predominant. And I may remark that there is no difficulty in our remaining a member of the Commonwealth.

It has been suggested in some quarters that the republican system as envisaged in Guyana removes the protection of Her Majesty the Queen from her loyal subjects in her dominion of Guyana. That is a good reason for ending the monarchy in Guyana because, psychologically, there are so many unemancipated minds who still believe that protection can come from without an independent country. It is in their interest and the interest of the progress of the country that the monarchy be removed so that there can be no illusions and it can be recognised that power and protection are to be found here in Guyana.

There is one other question to which, in deference to my learned and hon. Friend who will speak after me, I should allude. Traditionally, our final Court of Appeal has been Her Majesty in Council or the Judicial Committee of the Privy Council. Lest there be any illusions, lest there be any suggestions that the cards were not put on the table, and today is the day for putting the cards on the table, let me first observe that there is an inherent inconsistency behind Guyana becoming a republic and Guyana still having Her Majesty's Privy Council, the Judicial Committee or what have you, as the final Court of Appeal.

To continue to have the Judicial Committee of the Privy Council as the final Court of Appeal is to admit our inferiority which our erstwhile masters have attempted to instil in us, it is to admit that we are incapable of finding within the boundaries of our country such legal talent and such sense of justice as would lead us to leave the final arbitrament of matters legal to our fellow Guyanese.

Far be it from me, Mr Speaker, to suggest that the Judicial Committee of the Privy Council does not consist of eminent lawyers. Far be it from me to attempt to suggest that it might not be the fount of justice, but far be it from me, a nationalist, to tolerate this inconsistency, this incongruity so far as I have any power to bring it to an end. Those who have ears to hear, let them hear.

Whatever may be our differences, there cannot be differences between the majority in this House as to the suitability, desirability, of having a British court decide for us in Guyana. Whatever may be our differences, I would hope and expect that the same overwhelming majority which will pass this resolution will pass any proposed amendment to the constitution brought to let the right of appeal inhere in the Court of Appeal of Guyana.

My learned and hon. Friend (Mr D. Jagan[3]), for whom I have the highest regard in all fields, has suggested *sotto voce* that we can have a West Indian Court of Appeal. We can discuss. Our minds are open, but on one question I believe, we have closed minds, that is, continuing to have the Judicial Committee of the Privy Council as the final Court of Appeal.

Mr Speaker, I would submit that this is not a motion which should engender any sharp differences of opinion. There may be differences of opinion as to tactics and details, not substance, not important things, because both of the larger parties are pledged and have been pledged for years to republicanism.

I recall that at the 1962 conference which was the first of the abortive conferences, the only difference of opinion between the other large party and the P.N.C. was that of timing. The other large party, an integral part of our parliamentary institution, argued for the republic being the first stage, in other words, moving to the republican stage immediately after independence. The party which I led and lead, argued for a phasing in the context of what we considered the realities of Guyana; therefore, I cannot see any difference of substance.

I agree that there will be differences so far as the details are concerned. I do not think that there can be any argument about the date because I recall that last year the hon. Leader of the Opposition, Dr Jagan, said that the 23 of February should be a holiday every year. We are not only concurring with that but we are going further and making it a national holiday of the highest significance. There can be no disagreement on the choice of hero for it was the leader of the opposition who in 1963 thought officially to celebrate the events of 1763.

There can be no difference of opinion between thinking Guyanese because as Vere Daly, historian, remarked, regardless of ethnic origin, ours has been a history of a community of suffering. Let us therefore, conscious of our community of suffering, undertake a community of cooperation to make the cooperative republic of Guyana an institution which can change vitally our social and economic relations and ensure any real progress and socialism.

3. Brother of the leader of the opposition, Dr Cheddi Jagan.

Mr Speaker, on the question of Guyana's becoming a republic on Monday 23 February 1970, there seems to be virtual unanimity. I say 'virtual unanimity' for I am thinking of the country as a whole, rather than merely the National Assembly where a small group of three opposes the change.

Red herrings have been dragged across the trail, but there is no one with a modicum of intelligence and desire for truthfulness who will deny that the P.N.C. and the P.P.P., whatever the permutations and combinations, speak for almost 90 per cent of the population of Guyana. In view of the fact that neither party has other than stated quite clearly its support of a republic, it is safe to say that the overwhelming majority of the people in Guyana accept the change.

The other section of the opposition, apart from the P.P.P., has put forward some ingenious but unconvincing arguments against the main subject matter of the motion. All I can do at this stage is to quote a short passage from *A Short History of the Guyanese People* by Vere T. Daly at page 125:

> Cuffy had trouble with the faithful slaves. Faithful slaves were really those who were beginning to assimilate the culture of the Europeans and felt that they would lose their status in a revolutionised society.

We hear that we must have national unity before we have a republic. Those devotees of the American system do not realise that according to their own prescription, the United States of America should have had a few hundred years as a monarchy before it became a republic. The community of the U.S.A. consists of a number of minorities yet no one in the U.S.A. thought, 'Let us wait until we become one people either by inter-marriage or miscegenation.' To say this is to abuse the intelligence of this House and insult its members.

What are the advantages? I have said there are advantages. That has been admitted on both sides. What is the content of the republic is the question on which there has been some debate, debate worthy of answer. I have been told that what we need to make a success of the republic is to adopt scientific socialism. It all depends on which is your dictionary and which is your Bible. Everyone who claims to be a socialist claims that his particular brand of socialism is true socialism.

In these days it has become popular in one political party to say that the scriptures are the tablets, as handed down by Marx, amended by Lenin, brought up to date by Stalin, with some erasures by Khrushchev, and further elucidated by Brezhnev – these tablets represent true scientific socialism. There will be others who will tell you that the only true socialism is the socialism of Mr Harold Wilson, though some will say that Mr Harold Wilson's socialism was right when he was the President of the Board of Trade and not when he became Prime Minister. And so we can go on with a long set of arguments.

We do not claim omniscience. We know we are moving towards our goal. We know we shall have to experiment with one institution or another. We know that we can learn from the experience of others but we can never achieve by copying absolutely from any part of the world outside Guyana, like certain dogmatists. The dogmatist is an ignoramus and he is usually a dogmatist because he is afraid of his own capacity to think, therefore he accepts dogma and shuts out everything. He parades as reason what other people have written down in the catechism, which he, like the intellectual infant he is, learns by rote.

Because of the history of our people, we have decided that we will use the instrument of the cooperative. There again we do not approach it dogmatically. We do not join with those who say no good things come from the West nor do we join with those who say no good things come from the East. We recognise that in the western world, the cooperative is an appendage to the given capitalist system. We recognise that in the East the cooperative is an appendage to a given system of state monopoly. We are not prepared to sell ourselves short. We feel that we are capable of using the cooperative as the main institution in our economic progress and in our attempt, desire and irreversible goal to make the small man a real man. We want to see what we can learn and what we can adopt. We have no illusions. One thing we are confident of is that whether it be Nixon or Brezhnev, none of them can lay down the law for Guyana.

Part II
Towards independence

10

Extracts from speech to a mass open air meeting on
the collapse of the 1962 Constitutional Conference,
Parade Ground, Georgetown, 18 November 1962

*The October 1962 Constitutional Conference presided over by
Britain's Conservative Secretary of State for the Colonies, Mr Duncan
Sandys, was held against the background of violent disturbances which
occurred in February of that year resulting in 5 dead, 200 wounded and
millions of dollars of property damaged in Georgetown by rioting.*

*The government of Dr Cheddi Jagan was maintained in office by
British troops and emergency powers. Mr Burnham's party together
with the small United Force controlled 57 per cent of the popular
vote, but Dr Jagan still demanded immediate independence for British
Guiana under his rule. Mr Burnham also demanded immediate independence but with the proviso that elections be held prior to independence and that the electoral system be changed from constituency
voting to proportional representation.*

*Mr Sandys told the three leaders, when agreement could not be
reached between them, to return home and resolve their differences
before his government would consider granting independence. This
did not prove to be a very realistic decision and led to further division
and difficulty.*

*Mr Burnham on his return home reports to the people on the failure
of the conference and urges his supporters on to even greater efforts
to attain independence.*

Six weeks ago, on this same platform at this point, I drew for you a
picture of what we had hoped for, a picture of Guiana marching for-

ward in freedom, Guiana moving forward with a constitution which was acceptable to the majority of the citizens, a Guiana on the road to establishing once and for all, freedom, equality and opportunity for all. But it was not to be, and our fondest hopes have been dashed to the ground.

The failure of the conference is the failure of Guiana, the failure to achieve independence must be a source of disappointment to any right-thinking Guianese. It does not matter that the foulest and most cynical intentions of our political opponents have been defeated. The fact is that Guiana has suffered a setback, the fact is that we are still colonials, the fact is that Trinidad and Jamaica are independent and Guiana is dependent.

As I said six weeks ago, independence is not only an emotionally satisfying status, it is also the vehicle by means of which the people through their elected representatives can fashion their own destiny, can change the economic system which under a colony is orientated outwards to serve the interests of those outside.

Independence is the means whereby we can change that emphasis, revamp our economy and make full use of the energies of our people in setting up a system where there are no rich men in their castles, no Lazaruses at their gates whose sores the dogs of poverty lick. The failure of the conference means that our struggle has got to be heightened, the failure of the conference means that we shall have at least for a short while the incompetent and obscurantist People's Progressive Party on our backs.

We must not believe that we have won. We must understand that we now have to do some rethinking, we must understand that we now have to bring all our forces together for the final thrust towards independence and the removal of all obstacles in our way, whether it be the People's Progressive Party or what have you.

The conference began on Tuesday the 23 October 1962, as you are all aware, with the opening speeches. There was of course, the speech of the Secretary of State for the Colonies, Mr Duncan Sandys, there was the speech of the hon. the Premier, there was the speech of Mr Peter d'Aguiar, and there were the brief remarks of the leader of the People's National Congress.

The leader of the People's National Congress intimated from the very beginning that a constitution to his mind and to the mind of his party was not a scissors and paper exercise, was not a document geared for one party or another but should be a document which embodied in written form the political realities of the particular territory and at the same time be acceptable to the majority of people.

Constitutions I suppose are implemented or run by politicians but in the final analysis, constitutions are not for politicians and political leaders and political parties, constitutions are for people, that is why we insisted that any constitution that was to come out of the conference should be such that would be acceptable to the majority of the people. Compromises we were prepared to make, compromises we did make, but certain principles could not be compromised on. Such a principle is that of proportional representation.

What was very interesting from the first day of the conference was the difference in approach of the three parties as exemplified by their three leaders. The People's Progressive Party said that it wanted no new-fangled ideas and systems, but it wanted British precedents and traditions. Most damnable equivocation, Shakespeare would have said. How can a nationalist leader be satisfied merely to copy British precedents, British traditions, which may have absolutely no relevancy in the circumstances, atmosphere and environment of his own country? He who had with justification in the past so roundly abused the British system was hoping while he mouthed such phrases as 'transfer of residual power' that the British would confirm him in office regardless of the wishes of the majority of the people.

I do not want to be hypercritical. They say: 'of the dead, speak no ill'; I would say: 'of the weak, speak no ill'.

But basically what came out from that very early stage was this: the leader of the People's Progressive Party is a congenital colonial. He wanted Britain to pull his chestnuts out of the fire. He wanted Britain to say 'You young man, since you have flattered us by asking us to continue our system, we shall do so and we are very happy.' The greatest form of flattery is that which comes with copying.

The leader of the United Force also spoke but it was obvious that there too, was a colonial mentality, because he was telling Britain that she had no right to give up her responsibility to the people of British Guiana. He wanted Britain to save Guiana from a communist dictatorship. Comrades, free men do not need a liberator. Men who have that spirit of freedom will free themselves, and let us understand; Britain or anyone else or any other country cannot free us from a communist dictatorship, or any other type of dictatorship. The fault and the remedy are with us in Guiana.

The People's National Congress told them immediately 'Thank

you very much for all that you have done for us, real and alleged, but we have to settle our differences and we have to fashion a constitution, a state which will be acceptable to us and which will embody our aspirations and our ideals.' It is a contradiction of freedom, it is a contradiction of independence to ask, whether you be Jagan or d'Aguiar, him who is about to cease to be your master to help you to fashion something. It is the best argument against independence.

Our approach to this conference was not based on who would win the next election, or who would lose the next election. We wanted a constitution which would have given the majority of people in this country a feeling that they were secure, a feeling that whether or not they as individuals were supporters or members of the governing party, their basic rights would not be trampled upon, their aspirations and attitudes would not be ignored and that they could live with a certain feeling and sense of security, in their native country. For, mark you, unless there is that feeling of security, that acceptance of the government of the day, there is bound to be instability, which instability cannot be removed by the recruitment of a political army. If there is instability, it will mean that the prerequisite for economic progress will be lacking.

A country cannot really progress economically if it is socially and politically unstable, because instability premises the absence of agreement; it premises an unwillingness on the part of the populace to accept any measures passed by one government or another, as for instance, we have witnessed in the case of the Exchange Control Ordinance.[1] This measure has been virtually ineffective because the majority of the people have not been persuaded that where the government is going is right or what the government is doing is right.

The conference, however, if I may depart from my philosophising, proceeded. The question of whether or not we should have a Governor-General or President came up. The People's National Congress very early and readily agreed with the People's Progressive Party that we should have a republic from the beginning. Other questions arose, such as how the Public Service Commission was to be appointed and the People's National Congress adopted to a large extent the proposals put forward by the Civil Service Association which included giving representation to the two staff associations representing government employees. Then the People's National Congress urged the case for

1. Introduced by P.P.P. government in an attempt to check transfers of capital abroad.

proportional representation. It is to be noted that since 1959, the People's National Congress has been agitating for proportional representation and that in spite of the vain claims of some who have only recently understood what proportional representation is. As we pointed out before we left, proportional representation was not a political gambit or cheap gimmick for putting out the P.P.P. and putting in the P.N.C.; it was a solution which we had arrived at after careful thought. It would ensure that every political party got the number of seats to which it was entitled. It would ensure that cooperation between the political parties would then be compulsory, would then be obligatory rather than optional. It would mean that the general masses of the country would recognise that no political party could dominate the country or any other political parties, or threaten with any hope of success 'to roll heads'. It was our solution coming from the other side.

At one time a rosy carrot was dangled and the United Force Leader bit at it when it was proposed that if we did not have proportional representation there could be an upper house. He was prepared at one stage to accept an upper house as an alternative to proportional representation. I do not think that we should make heavy weather of the fact that bargaining around the table and skill in matters political are things that come with experience, many years of experience. But the People's National Congress said quite clearly that we were not interested in an upper house. An upper house is a brake on the will of the elected house if it is effective, and if it is constituted in the same proportions as the lower elected house, then it is a rubber stamp like the present Senate and a waste of tax payers' money and a place to which you send your political cronies.

In any emergent territory like Guiana we cannot afford the terrific brake which an effective upper house will have on progressive and modernistic legislative measure. If there are brakes to be built in, let those be built into the one elected house; and that is what proportional representation is. The brakes inherent in giving the various political parties their proper representation operate by compelling the government, if it wants to remain in office, to understand to appreciate and come to terms with other serious points of view.

The leader of the People's Progressive Party was enamoured of it (an upper house) because he saw in it a way out which his British friends were offering him, a comfortable exit from his troubles.

Now it was apparent by the time we reached the second Thursday of the conference when the major question of proportional representation was being discussed that the conference was likely to founder on this rock. But the People's National Congress did not go to the conference for the conference to fail, and the People's National Congress was anxious to find a way out consistent with its attachment to principle and the preservation of its dignity.

The Secretary of State called the three leaders separately, I also spoke to the two other leaders separately. Then I said on the Friday when the Governor was attempting to get the three leaders together, that we would be prepared to offer a revision or reconsideration of proportional representation at the end of four years and so that the conference could come to a successful conclusion I would not ask that proportional representation be entrenched. We wanted to come to a successful conclusion of the conference.

The leader of the People's Progressive Party said he did not want that; he said that the people were not going to agree to change back from proportional representation once it had been accepted. Of course that had a certain significance to me. What it meant to me was that the leader of the People's Progressive Party was prepared to allow the people to have a say, so far and no further, and had been caught up by his messianic complex. He knew better for the people than the people themselves what the people wanted and what was best for the people.

Then finally the People's National Congress through its spokesman proposed that this question, which was the main one at the conference, should be submitted to a referendum. The main question at the conference was what should be the electoral system. Should it be first past the post or should it be proportional representation? I said, therefore, that we all as democrats should be agreeable to the voters of Guiana deciding what electoral system they would live under.

Now, what could be fairer than that? It is the thesis of democrats, even self-styled democrats, that the final arbiter is the people, the final power and the real sovereignty rest with the people. If political leaders honest or dishonest cannot agree, if it is difficult for sides to be taken at the conference, to be given up, let the people decide. To my mind that is the epitome of democracy but alas the wolf shed his sheep's clothing and said that he was not prepared to have a referendum.

You are intelligent people. Most of you can draw your conclusions as to the motives which led them to reject this eminently democratic solution to the difficulty unto which they had moved. We thought that the proposal would have resolved the *impasse*. I need not remind you, need I, that it was the same People's Progressive Party that had suggested that the referendum be held on the question of British Guiana's accession to the West Indies Federation?

Well, the conference broke. There were some who were glad, and there were some people like myself who were sad. What saddened me most were the pleas of the Premier to the British government to come down on his side. He said that the difficulty should be resolved on the basis of precedents and tradition and that the British government should not be interested in the internal power struggle. He was asking Britain in effect to impose his solution against the wishes of the majority.

Guiana has peculiar problems. Guiana has a history, a tradition different from those of the British. Guiana has a different climate from that of Britain, political and natural. It must be the height of insincerity for any nationalist leader in the context of Guiana to believe that the British can proffer a solution along British lines. There are lots of things that we can learn from the British, but there are lots of things that we can learn about the British which we cannot accept for ourselves. That is independence. Independence is not a mere word, independence is not expecting your boss, your master, to pull your chestnuts out of the fire. Independence means finding your own solution among yourselves.

It is not for me to apportion blame. I shall not substitute myself for history. Let history judge who was responsible for the failure of the conference. This is what I want to say. It seems to me, I may be wrong, but I have never been so sure in my life of anything, that he who seeks to support an electoral system which robs some political parties of the number of seats to which their popular votes entitle them has a tremendous onus placed upon him to justify such an electoral system. In other words, you have placed upon you the onus of justifying electoral theft. In the context of Guiana, with our deep political and ideological differences and I hope merely superficial racial tensions, a system which is and which has been proved to be unfair cannot be advocated or defended by anyone who wants to see harmony, who wants to see peace in this country.

Many people have been talking about independence, without recognising what it really means. It is a new thing, it is no question of carrying on the old order and substituting new masters into exactly the same seats occupied by the old.

We have put forward proportional representation as a vehicle for solving the basic problem in this country because unless and until there is a political consensus, unless and until there is a cooperation or understanding or acceptance at the political level, nothing else is likely to be successful. Nothing else. We have not heard a counter proposal to proportional representation. We do not claim infallibility. We do not say that there is no other solution. But we have heard no other solution proposed and therefore we rest on our solution – proportional representation.

Now what do you people in this country of Guiana think about it? You must show the way you think clearly and strongly. If, of course, the majority of people prefer first-past-the-post, the People's National Congress is prepared to accept such a verdict. But if, of course, the majority of people prefer and want proportional representation, the will of the majority must be heard and carried by every possible means.

There still remains the necessity for our party to be militant and fearless. While I was away, I understand, that there were certain 'militant exercises' to which we were not a party. The People's National Congress, as always, will be a party of peace. But the People's National Congress reserves to itself the right to defend itself.

We are aware that violence will be no solution. We are aware that civil war will harm the country. We are aware that civil strife will probably destroy us all. We shall never encourage violence. We shall never, never do anything to start civil war. But in the final analysis, it is better to die on your feet, than live on your knees.

But comrades, let us seriously attempt to look into the future. We have come here tonight not to abuse anyone. We have come here tonight not to blame anyone particularly. We do not blame the British. We do not blame the Americans. We do not blame Jagan. We only say that a minority thwarted the wishes of a majority. We merely ask if the People's Progressive Party wanted independence as badly as it claims, why could it not agree to proportional representation which would make the cooperation which it has said is necessary and obligatory? You draw your own conclusions.

We still have to achieve independence. We still have to ensure that we get into the ranks of the People's National Congress everyone in this country who seriously and really wants independence and who seriously and really believes in freedom. The People's National Congress has no place in its ranks for those who do not want independence.

We are threatened in this country at the moment with a breakdown of the machinery of government. We are threatened in this country at the moment with an economic and financial situation which Jagan has admitted is a thousand times worse than the political situation. This is no time to be squabbling, this is a time to be thinking and thinking intelligently. This is no time to behave like the fool and seek to advertise the fact that you want the Soviet Union and Eastern Europe to come and take over your economy.

The position is that small nations like our own have got to accept certain geographical facts. Secondly, we have got, after we have come out from under British tutelage, to be sure that we do not become a Russian colony or a colony of any other country or any other bloc. We know in the People's National Congress that if there is to be economic progress, assistance from outside at a certain stage will be necessary. The People's National Congress has always said that it is prepared to accept economic assistance from any source provided that it is advantageous to Guiana. There are some who would like to tie our economy irrevocably to the Soviet Union. There are others who would like to tie our economy unequivocally to that of the United States of America. The People's National Congress will not be interested in tying the economy of this country to any large metropolitan country. It will consider each and every question on its merits.

The People's National Congress believes in certain democratic principles which it shares with the West. The People's National Congress wants to lead an independent Guiana, independently. What has got to be understood is that friendship does not connote the willingness to be dictated to. Be sure, we do not want another colonial master. Be sure, we want to proceed along a path chosen by us and in the best interests of our country. And one of the things I think that distinguishes the People's National Congress from the other political parties in Guiana is this: that the other political parties behave as if the only way towards economic progress is via largesse from outside. In other words, the factories that are to come from Russia or the billions that are to come from America are the total answer to our problem.

Jagan said in London that all that was involved was a struggle for power. Now we politicians want power; the politician who tells you he does not want power is either a fool or a rascal. But the important thing, comrades, is, what are you going to do with the power which you want? Is it power to threaten to roll people's heads? Is it power to discriminate against people so far as employment is concerned? Is it power to be able to hand out the plums to your friends and your political cronies? Or is it power to weld the people together into one mass, rubbing off the rough bits and removing the tensions by inspiring them with a loyalty to Guiana, by translating for them as the P.N.C. proposes to do, the significance of being a socialist party? Is it power to build an economy which is aimed at and geared to serving the people, which is more productive than in the past and which distributes its products to all the people and not a few?

This country will never get on its feet if you try to toady to America. This country will never get on its feet, if you want to make it a satellite of Russia. This country, we contend, can never get on its feet unless the People's National Congress' philosophy prevails.

We further believe that unless and until the various races in this country cooperate on the basis of attachment to a common fatherland, this country will never, never, progress. We cannot afford a division such as between India and Pakistan, we cannot afford those new zones in our country which were proposed by a certain gentleman.

We will not go forward in this country, you know, if 'aphan Jhaat'[2] continues to have its attraction. We will not go forward in this country if 'voting for your mattie black man'[3] continues to be the philosophy of a section of this community. We can only go forward if we understand that we are Guianese first, Guianese second, and Guianese third.

2. Hindu phrase meaning roughly 'vote for your own race'.
3. Guyanese phrase with similar meaning.

11

Statement before the United Nations Special
Committee of 24 on the situation with regard to the
implementation of the declaration on the granting
of independence to colonial countries and peoples,
United Nations, New York, 8 March 1963

*Mr Burnham made his appearance before the United Nations Com-
mittee of 24 essentially for the purpose of setting his party's record
straight in regard to its position on independence for Guiana and also
to state his party's case for a change of the electoral system to proportional representation.*

*The question and answer period is particularly interesting in that
it reveals Mr Burnham's great ability to marshal facts and figures while
'thinking on his feet'.*

HEARING OF PETITIONER CONCERNING BRITISH GUIANA

The Chairman (interpretation from French): The first item on our
agenda is the hearing of a petitioner, from the territory of British
Guiana, whose request was approved by the Special Committee at its
124th meeting on 8 March 1963.

I would invite Mr L. F. Burnham to be seated at the petitioners'
table.

At the invitation of the Chairman, Mr L. F. Burnham, leader,
People's National Congress, took a place at the petitioners' table.

The Chairman (interpretation from French): I now call on Mr Burnham to make his statement.

Mr Burnham (Leader, People's National Congress): May I thank
you, Mr Chairman, and your committee for having so kindly and

graciously consented to hear me as a petitioner today, out of turn, so
to speak.

The question on which I have sought leave to be heard is that of
the independence of my country, British Guiana.

The constitution in existence now and under which elections were
held on 21 August 1961 instituted full internal self-government. At
those elections the People's Progressive Party, led by the Premier,
Dr Jagan, secured 42·6 per cent of the popular vote and twenty seats;
the People's National Congress, led by me, 41 per cent of the votes
and eleven seats; and the United Force, led by Mr Peter d'Aguiar,
16·3 per cent of the votes and four seats.

On 1 November 1961 the Premier introduced a motion in the
Legislative Assembly calling upon Britain to grant independence to
British Guiana during 1962. This motion was supported by the
People's National Congress and was carried on 3 November by 31
votes to 4.

The People's National Congress has always advocated and agitated
for independence of our country and, in fact, was the first political
party during the election campaign of 1961 to suggest a date – 31 May
1962.

Speaking on the motion of November 1961 as the spokesman for
my party, I made it pellucidly clear that independence was not an
issue between the two major parties. The question on which there
would have to be serious discussion and which would have to be
settled was the constitution under which an independent Guyana
would come into being.

The People's National Congress put forward as its thesis that such
a constitution must be one for the people and not for a particular
political party or a number of political parties; it must be acceptable
to the majority of the people, guaranteeing for them the protection
of certain basic rights and ensuring them freedom from all but un-
reasonable fear.

To this end my party proposed an electoral system of proportional
representation which would reflect in the legislature less inaccurately
than the first-past-the-post-system, the electoral support enjoyed by
the various political parties, and the enshrinement and entrenchment
in the constitution of certain basic human rights.

The People's National Congress welcomed the decision of the
United Kingdom government of 14 January 1962 to hold a constitutional conference in London in May of the same year to discuss

the date and arrangements to be made for the achievement of independence of Guyana.

When, on 4 May 1962 and 30 June 1962, the proposed conference was unilaterally postponed by the United Kingdom government because of the alleged necessity to have available the report of the Commission of Enquiry into the disturbances of 16 February 1962, the People's National Congress publicly criticised and opposed the postponement. In fact, I stated that such a postponement was unjustified and unjustifiable. The conference was eventually fixed for 23 October 1962.

Prior thereto, the People's National Congress, through me, proposed to the Premier, the leader of the People's Progressive Party, that we jointly decide to hold the conference in British Guiana, where we should resolve our differences. That proposal was rejected by the Premier, who was supported in this instance by the Governor of the colony. By that time it was clear that the main difference between the People's Progressive Party and the People's National Congress referred to the electoral system. One People's Progressive Party spokesman, the Parliamentary Secretary to the Minister of Natural Resources, publicly declared that his party, rather than accepting proportional representation, would abandon its demand for immediate independence and continue to rule under the present constitution until 1965.

At the conference in London, the United Force supported the People's National Congress in the latter's proposal that proportional representation should be the electoral system. This meant that the elected representatives of 57·3 per cent of the electorate favoured one system, as against that favoured by the representatives of 42·6 per cent of the electorate.

The People's National Congress was very anxious that the deadlock should be resolved and that independence should not be delayed. Believing as we do that the people are the ultimate sovereign and that the constitution should be acceptable to the majority, the People's National Congress proposed that if the political leaders could not reach agreement on this matter, a referendum should be held for the voters to decide between the first-past-the-post system and proportional representation. This was rejected by the Premier and his delegation, and no logical or intelligible reason was given for that rejection.

The United Kingdom government used that as an excuse not to fix a date for independence, and the position now is that there is a dead-lock, or stalemate.

The economic and fiscal problems of British Guiana are many and grave, but these are hardly likely to be resolved unless the political one – the choice of an electoral system – is resolved. In this matter the United Kingdom government continues to drag its feet.

Independence, we feel, is the inalienable right of the people of Guiana. It would mean the final recognition of their human dignity, an end of the long period of foreign rule and domination and an opportunity for them to replace the old, oppressive and dehumanis-ing colonial system by one where there would be real freedom for all and political democracy combined with social democracy. This is the people's just entitlement.

The only thing that keeps the Guyanese from the achievement of that goal is the unwillingness or refusal of the British and British Guiana governments to let the sovereign people speak.

The Chairman (interpretation from French): Do any representatives wish to put questions to the petitioner?

Mr Gebre-Egzy (Ethiopia): If I understood the petitioner correctly, he said that his party had eleven seats in the Assembly and the Prime Minister's party – that is, the government now in power – had twenty seats, and that, when the Parliament had been elected, his party had received 41 per cent of the votes and the Prime Minister's party, 42 per cent. What is the cause of this disproportion in terms of the number of seats?

Mr Burnham: The electoral system in vogue at the moment in British Guiana is what is called the single-member-constituency system or first-past-the-post. Under that system there is a number of con-stituencies and the candidate with greatest number of votes in each constituency is returned as representative for that constituency. In the circumstances it is easy to see that a party in one constituency may win the seat by a very narrow margin and another party in another constituency may win that seat by a wide margin. It is pos-sible, therefore, as so frequently happens under this system, for a party to get a greater proportion of the seats than the proportion of popular votes which it gets. This difficulty or this disparity is endemic in the system of first-past-the-post. The actual votes polled were 93,000 votes to the People's Progressive Party and 89,000 votes to the People's National Congress. Under proportional representation the seat distribution would have been fifteen to the People's Progressive Party and fourteen to the People's National Congress.

Mr Gebre-Egzy (Ethiopia): I should like to ask, as I did the other time last year of the Prime Minister of British Guiana, a question about the last disturbance which took place in British Guiana. In that disturbance some people said that the police and the civil service people did not discharge their duties properly. Or if it was not said openly, there was some insinuation that they did not do their duty properly. Since you are a member of the opposition, I am sure that you will be able to tell us what the situation was from your point of view.

Mr Burnham: In refutation of the suggestion that the police did not carry out their duties loyally and effectively, I would cite the then Minister of Home Affairs, a member of Dr Jagan's government, Mr Rai, who actually congratulated the police on the way they carried out their duties. I also refer you to the report of the Commission of Enquiry into the disturbances which took place during February. That report particularly stated that the police carried out their duties well and loyally and that there was no question of any disloyalty. So far as the civil servants were concerned, it was not a question of their disloyalty to the government but of their going on strike as a result of an industrial dispute which they had pending with the government for over two years prior to February 1962.

May I mention that the members of the Commission of Enquiry, whose report refutes the suggestion of disloyalty on the part of the police, were Sir Wynn Parry of Great Britain, Sir Edward Asafu-Adjaye of Ghana and Mr Khosla of India.

Mr Blake (United States): I should like to ask the petitioner for perhaps two points of clarification here. In most democratic countries in the world it is not found particularly necessary to have a system as complicated as the one of proportional representation. I wonder if there is any particular or special justification why that should be done in British Guiana and whether this is likely to delay independence.

I should like to ask the petitioner for some clarification on the question of racial organisation among the parties. We have heard in this committee before that this was the case. Does the petitioner feel that that is a system that will work for the welfare of the people of British Guiana?

Mr Burnham: The proposal for proportional representation which the People's National Congress advocates is not a complicated system.

The proposal is to have the entire country as one constituency and the voters being permitted to vote for the party of their choice, and then the parties being allocated seats in direct proportion to the number of popular votes polled. We do not accept the suggestion either that in the majority of democratic countries this system of proportional representation, or some variation of it, is not to be found. It exists in Tasmania, it exists in the Scandinavian countries, it exists in a number of the Latin American countries also. In our case, we have found it necessary to propose this system of proportional representation.

I did not want to raise this because it struck me as being primarily a domestic matter because we are convinced that if the opportunity were given to one party, the party in office at the moment, it would get an overwhelming majority of seats on a minority of votes. There is reason to believe that it would seek to establish an authoritarian regime through the legislative process. But with proportional representation, in the foreseeable future that is an impossibility and an overall majority of seats would express an overall majority support throughout the country.

The representative of the United States asked about racial loyalties so far as the political parties are concerned. It is true that in the 1961 elections the greater part of the voting was along racial lines. The majority of Indians voted for the People's Progressive Party, the majority of Africans voted for the People's National Congress and the majority of Portuguese and mixed peoples voted for the United Force.

It is our opinion in the People's National Congress that that is most undesirable, and that voters should be led to support a party on the basis of programme and capacity rather than on the ethnic origin of the respective leaders. It is further our opinion that if proportional representation, such as we propose, were to be instituted in Guiana, that would assist in the lessening of racial voting or, as we put it, in hurdling the racial obstacle because no party under proportional representation can possibly in the foreseeable future get an overall majority of seats if it merely appealed to race. If, however, any party under proportional representation really desired and worked for an overall majority of seats, it would have to cross the ethnic barrier and lessen this racial voting. That is our opinion.

Mr Sonn (Cambodia) (interpretation from French): I should like to put a few questions to the petitioner. The clarifications that I seek will permit me to form my opinion which I shall express later in due course.

The first question I wish to put is the following. I should like to ask Mr Burnham whether it is true that the last elections were engaged within the framework of obtaining independence, and is it true that you had said during the electoral campaign that the party which will have won the elections would lead the country to independence.

Mr Burnham: It is true that all political parties contesting the last elections did so on the assumption that the next stage was independence for our country and when the various parties spoke of the party winning being the party to lead the country to independence, that was with the tacit understanding of the particular party obtaining a majority of the votes. Incidentally, the leader of the People's Progressive Party, recognising this fact at one of his final meetings before the close of the campaign, particularly asked for an 80 per cent support because he realised that unless a majority of popular votes supported his party he would hardly be able to speak definitely for the people of the country.

There is this practical difficulty that both the People's Progressive Party and the People's National Congress favour a larger House. It is impossible to have a large House unless there are new elections.

Mr Sonn (Cambodia) (interpretation from French): The second question deals with the following point. I should like to know whether there was any discussion during the electoral campaign for any possible change of the electoral system – whether this had at all been discussed during the electoral campaign?

Mr Burnham: The People's National Congress since 1959 had been suggesting a change of the electoral system from one of first-past-the-post to one of proportional representation, and the People's National Congress never changed its stand on this matter but merely at the 1960 conference accepted a compromise solution which we subsequently found did not work in the peculiar circumstances of British Guiana.

Mr Sonn (Cambodia) (interpretation from French): A few moments ago I listened most attentively to Mr Burnham's statement. I understand that he is anxious to achieve independence for the people of British Guiana. Am I correct in saying this? And I should like to ask Mr Burnham to tell me why he has been unwilling to accept the offer to be the Vice-President of the government with four ministers, and lastly, that of forming a coalition government which would have hastened the achievement of independence for the people of British Guiana?

Mr Burnham: It is without foundation to suggest that I have ever been officially offered four ministries in the present government. That is absolutely untrue. It was in December last that the Prime Minister sent me a letter inviting me to enter into coalition discussions. Those discussions have started. But whether they continue or not, the People's National Congress is insisting on a fair electoral system, or that the people of Guiana be allowed to decide which electoral system should be in vogue when independence comes into being. May I further state that if the Prime Minister is indeed sincere in his talk about coalition, proportional representation in the circumstances of our country, since neither party will get an over-all majority, makes coalition obligatory or compulsory rather than optional.

Mr Sonn (Cambodia) (interpretation from French): I have gone through my questions and I wish to thank Mr Burnham for the answers which he has been kind enough to supply. I should like to point out that my requests for information were designed to help me find a solution to the problem. We in our delegation wish independence to be granted as soon as possible to the people of British Guiana.

Mr Collier (Sierra Leone): I should like to know from Mr Burnham whether the racial situation, which has been freely admitted to exist in British Guiana, is not likely to be emphasised by this matter of proportional representation?

Mr Burnham: In the opinion of the People's National Congress proportional representation will not further emphasise the racial differences and racial voting. As I have had occasion at another time to say, to imagine an increase of racial voting is to imagine that any quantity can be more than 100 per cent of itself. Rather, as I said in answer to the representative of the United States on the question of proportional representation, the necessity to cross the ethnic barriers for the purpose of getting an over-all majority will make the parties sincerely attempt to do away with racial voting and to attract voters from other ethnic groups than those from which they now draw their respective support.

Mr Collier (Sierra Leone): I should like to know from Mr Burnham what positive suggestions he has to offer as to how best to get out of this stalemate in the country where a situation has existed where the government party insists on one course of action and the opposition are insisting on another course of action. I should like him to tell us what he suggests would be the best way out.

Mr Burnham: The proposal which the People's National Congress makes is the same as that which it made at the London Conference in November last, that is, that the voters of the country be consulted on this single issue which is the only important issue separating the two major parties – in fact, separating the three parties. It is our conviction that the people are sovereign. The People's Progressive Party alleges that the majority of the people favour first-past-the-post. The People's National Congress alleges that the majority of the voters favour the system of proportional representation. And the only means we can suggest of breaking this deadlock is that the people, on whose behalf both parties claim to speak in a majority, be consulted, and we ask that they the people give their verdict on this matter which alone separates us from the desired state of independence.

Mr Collier (Sierra Leone): I should like to know from Mr Burnham what sort of suggestion has come from the British government on this, because they have had experience in the Commonwealth where independence has been given to many countries, where the system is different from what Mr Burnham is advocating. It has been the system of first-past-the-post in most of the Commonwealth countries if not in all of them. I should like to know whether they have had any reactions from the British government on this particular point.

Mr Burnham: It is true that the majority of the countries within the British Commonwealth do have the system of first-past-the-post, but it is also true that there are two countries that I can remember at the moment in the British Commonwealth, Malta and Tasmania, which have a system of proportional representation.

May I say further that, in tackling the peculiar problems of our territory, though some assistance can be got from the experience of other territories, we have to apply our minds to our territory, to our difficulties and to our troubles and to seek a solution within that context. The United Kingdom government has expressed this point of view in *White Paper 1970* of 1962. On page 4, in paragraph 11, it is stated that since the governing party has a majority of seats and

95

the opposition a majority of votes, and the two sides have not been able to come to any agreement on this question of the electoral system, it would not express an opinion or seek to do anything at this moment. That has been the British reaction so far. Our contention has been that it should be the duty of the government of British Guiana and the British government to seek a means of ascertaining the wishes of the peoples on this sole question which divides the two major parties.

Mr Traore (Mali) (interpretation from French): On the basis of the statement he has made, I should like to ask the petitioner why, as he has indicated to us, his party in 1961 joined the People's Progressive Party in order to vote for a resolution calling for the setting of a date for independence.

Mr Burnham: All of our members in the legislature supported the resolution for the simple reason that we are wedded to independence in principle, and, therefore, there was no issue as to whether or not independence should be granted within the shortest possible time. But, as I noted in my statement, during the course of my remarks in the legislature on this motion, I pointed out to the government that we were with them on the question of independence but that we, the parties in British Guiana, would have to get down to drafting a constitution which would be acceptable to the majority of the people. Our differences are not on the question of independence; our differences are on the question of the constitution, and, in fact, on one particular question in the constitution, because we are as anxious as anyone else to cease being colonial subjects.

Mr Traore (Mali) (interpretation from French): I should like to put the following question to the petitioner. Would the referendum he requests be a prior condition to the granting of independence to British Guiana?

Mr Burnham: Yes, that is so, because once a constitution for independence is granted, that will be the end of the matter. In any case, we have to have a constitution for moving into independence. The present constitution under which the country operates is not a constitution for independence, and in any case it will not be the constitution for an independent Guiana. It is merely that we, in our suggestions for the drafting of the constitution for independence, are asking that the electoral system in that constitution be proportional representation. Since there is a deadlock, prior to writing the electoral system into the constitution, there should be a referendum so that we can know what will be the electoral system to be written into the constitution.

Mr Traore (Mali) (interpretation from French): I should like to ask the petitioner what he expects from our committee at the present time with regard to the accession of British Guiana to independence, in accordance with General Assembly resolution 1514 (XV).

Mr Burnham: It is our conviction that if an opinion were expressed by this committee on the desirability, if not the necessity, of consulting the wishes of the people of British Guiana, that opinion would carry great persuasion both so far as the British government is concerned and the British Guiana government because this question is indefinably bound up with the question of independence.

The Chairman (interpretation from French): I wish to thank Mr Burnham for the information which he has been good enough to supply to the committee. The committee will weigh this information when it deals with the examination of the situation in British Guiana.

Extracts from speech at People's National Congress
Special Congress before holding of Third Constitutional Conference, Georgetown, 29 September
1963

*Whenever a matter of major importance to his party's future was
about to occur or had occurred, Mr Burnham kept his party fully informed through the medium of the Party Congress. The Special
Congress called on 29 September 1963 was for this purpose.*

*The British government had scheduled yet another constitutional
conference, exactly one year after the abortive 1962 Constitutional
Conference and there was wide speculation in Guiana that this time
a date for independence would be settled. Mr Burnham and his colleagues were about to depart for the conference when he spoke to
the Congress.*

*The three-month-long general strike precipitated earlier in the year
by Dr Jagan's attempt to force through a Labour Relations Bill had
cost the nation some $30 million in lost revenue and had resulted in
the second state of emergency in less than a year-and-a-half under the
P.P.P. government. The strike and its aftermath prompted Mr Duncan
Sandys, Britain's Secretary of State for the Colonies, to visit Guiana
and urge a coalition government be formed between the three political
parties, at least until the 1963 October Constitutional Conference.*

*In his speech Mr Burnham deals at length with the strike and the
futility of the Sandys proposal.*

Comrade Chairman, comrades. We have not met as a party or as a
congress since the general strike which ended on Sunday the eighth

of July. And perhaps it is good for us to recapitulate briefly and consider what lessons may be learned and what role the People's National Congress played in that event which took place between April and July.

We are all aware of the fact that the particular incident which sparked the strike was an attempt on the part of the government to pass the Labour Relations Bill, ostensibly to give workers the opportunity of choosing by ballot, trade unions which they desire to represent them, but in point and in fact the real and cynical reason behind this Bill was obtaining control over the trade union movement. The absence of control, the absence of significant support in the trade union movement on the part of the People's Progressive Party, has always been a source of embarrassment and the People's Progressive Party thought that by the passage of this Bill it would be able to remove that embarrassment and increase its support.

The strike was a magnificent effort on the part, not only of the trade union movement, but on the part of the entire community of Guiana. It is to be remembered that when the strike was over, when the agreement was signed between the T.U.C. and the government, the T.U.C. had actually got more concessions from the government than it had sought prior to the strike. That alone represented a victory for the Trade Union Council and for the workers particularly.

It has been said that the strike was started, supported and encouraged by the People's National Congress and the other opposition party.[1] In my view the P.N.C. did not have to start or encourage any strike. The strike represented in the main the reaction of the rank-and-file of the trade union movement to an attempt to establish a dictatorship in this country by a government which is in fact representative only of a minority. So far as the leadership of the T.U.C. itself was concerned it should not be felt that they were anxious to start the strike. As a trade unionist myself and a member of the General Council of the T.U.C. I can say that most definitely the leaders on many occasions were inclined to be cautious, but it was the rank-and-file that pushed them, and here we saw one of the first examples in this country of the vitality and determination of the working-class group, of the rank-and-file of an organisation.

The strike as you know lasted many weeks and there was a great deal of privation and suffering, and may I pay a compliment to those

---

1. The United Force.

who bore those sufferings, including tear gas, and the purple liquid which was sprayed on people. May I congratulate them upon the fine job which they did. One thing, comrades, comes clearly out of that: that if a people are determined to stand up against dictatorship, if they are prepared to stand up against an attempt to rob them of their freedom in any field, it is very unlikely that the would-be dictator can succeed.

We are aware that the working-class movement in this country was largely supported by other sections of the community. Other sections of the community as I see it supported the struggle for two reasons.

First, many of them were convinced beyond the shadow of a doubt that the struggle of the workers was the struggle of the entire community and what was being attempted against the workers at the trade union level, would soon be attempted against other sections of the community and the nation at other levels.

The second reason for the support which other sections of the community gave to the strike and the struggle, was that many of them were opposed to the People's Progressive Party government and found useful allies in the working-class movement. It must, however, be remembered that in a war and in a fight one takes assistance from anyone who offers that assistance, but when one is carrying on a fight one must keep perspectives clear and never permit the ally to control one's strategy or tactics.

It has been suggested by the People's Progressive Party that the whole struggle and strike were dictated by a reactionary movement in the country and outside of the country. Blame has been placed on the American government. Blame has been placed on the American trade union movement. But, speaking as one who was on the inside, it is my clear view and contention that, though assistance was received from the American trade union movement, though assistance was received from many sections and quarters not normally friendly to the workers, number one, the workers kept full control of the struggle, and number two, no one from outside was capable of directing, or competent to direct, the struggle.

One advantage which flowed from the strike was a clearer recognition than that which existed before on the part of the People's Progressive Party that a majority of seats in the legislature did not confer on them the right to rule regardless of the feelings, reactions and points of views of other sections of the community.

Subsequent to the strike, as we are all aware, Mr Duncan Sandys, the Secretary of State for the Colonies, came to this country in an attempt to find as he saw it, a solution to our political ills. He came here and after spending a few days left. One of the first remarks which he made on his arrival in the United Kingdom was that the problems of Guiana had to be solved by the Guianese people.

We in the People's National Congress do not necessarily take any pride in the fact that our point of view on any particular matter coincides with the point of view of the British government, but we cannot help noting that on this occasion the British government was in fact taking the cue from the People's National Congress. For it was since 1961 and again in 1962 and in 1963 that the People's National Congress leadership had said clearly and unequivocally that if the problems of this country were to be solved, they have to be solved by the people in the country itself.

You will no doubt recall that sometime in December 1962 the Premier had written to the leadership of the People's National Congress proposing a coalition and that talks had started tentatively but had been broken off because agreement could not be reached as to how they should proceed and what should be the form of representation during these talks at these conferences.

On Mr Sandys's visit another proposal was made for coalition by Mr Sandys. At first the proposal was that the three political parties should get together in a national government, in an attempt to ease the present tensions, in an attempt to introduce an atmosphere of calm and serenity, which would ensure to the settling of our problems in going forward to the Independence Conference in October resulting in independence shortly thereafter.

The proposal for a national government of all three of the parties did not find favour with the People's Progressive Party, subsequent to the demand on the part of the United Force, that they, the United Force, should have two ministries, one of which should be Finance and another of which should contain the subject 'Amerindian Affairs'. It seemed, however, that the People's Progressive Party leadership represented by the Premier was more inclined to discuss and consider a coalition between the People's Progressive Party and the People's National Congress.

The original proposal that such a coalition if it came to fruition should be specifically for reducing tension and tiding the time over until independence, was not particularly acceptable to the People's Progressive Party. The P.P.P. leader suggested that in conformity with an earlier discussion between himself and me we should rather get down to discussing whether or not there could be a common agreed programme, on the basis of which a coalition could be formed, a coalition which he hoped would be more lasting than one until independence.

You will also remember that the People's National Congress leadership agreed to start those coalition talks and consequently on Thursday the eighteenth of July of this year a team from the People's National Congress met a team from the People's Progressive Party and fixed an agenda for discussion. We insisted, however, that substantive talks should not begin until the emergency was removed.[2]

The argument of the People's National Congress is clear and reasonable. The emergency, which we held in the first place was unjustifiably introduced, was being kept on to facilitate the government, as admitted by Dr Jagan, in its disposal of Russian gasolene, Russian kerosene and Russian flour imported by the P.P.P. trading arm Gimpex. Furthermore, the continued emergency in other respects was directed primarily against Georgetown which is the stronghold of the People's National Congress. Only in Georgetown in the whole of the country of Guiana was it against the law to hold a public meeting or stage a procession save and except a funeral procession. Only in the county of Demerara was it an offence punishable by life imprisonment to commit breaking and entering and larceny. This is to be understood in the context of a request made by Mr Brindley Benn[3] when he went to London during the strike, to the British government to pacify Georgetown.

Obviously the emergency was being used for two purposes:

1. The pacification of Georgetown so to speak, and
2. The putting of profits into the pockets of the People's Progressive Party.

For every schoolboy knows that the Guiana Import Export Corporation, commonly known as Gimpex, which imported the Russian goods, is the trading arm of the People's Progressive Party and donates a substantial share of its profits to the said People's Progressive Party. We considered it therefore no evidence of sincerity or *bona fides* that the emergency should have been kept on while the talks were going on.

2. Declared by the P.P.P. government as a result of the general strike.
3. Deputy Premier in the People's Progressive Party government.

You no doubt will remember that eventually on Wednesday the fourth of September the emergency was lifted. The emergency was lifted just a few days before Dr Jagan and myself were due to go to the United Nations in answer to an invitation from the Sub-Committee of Five of the Committee on Colonialism of 24 of the United Nations.

It was clear, as the People's National Congress has stated in public, that the removal of the emergency at that stage was an attempt to beguile, an attempt to fool those who were not aware of the facts of British Guiana. It was an attempt to give the impression outside of Guiana that the People's Progressive Party was not as ruthless a machine as we in British Guiana ourselves know.

In any case we had originally proposed that we would continue the talks immediately after the emergency was over; I held a preliminary meeting with Dr Jagan on Thursday the fifth of September. That meeting itself did not bring out anything in particular, except that it disclosed to me two things which we must particularly note in our deliberations:

1. The absolute financial bankruptcy of this country under the People's Progressive Party government and its inability to find money even for projects which could be financed from abroad, and
2. the fact that the People's Progressive Party is now in fear, in absolute fear, of the People's National Congress.

As you are aware, on Saturday the seventh of September, I left this country to meet the 'Good Offices Sub-Committee of Five' of the Committee of 24 of the United Nations. I arrived in the United States of America on Sunday the eighth, and from Monday the ninth until I left New York on Monday the twenty-third, I was engaged in a series of discussions, conversations and talks – some of which included Dr Jagan, others of which did not include him. The moving figures in these discussions in so far as the informal ones were concerned were the Ambassador of Mali, Mr Sori Couribaly, and the Ambassador of Sierra Leone, Mr Collier.

It is my intention to relate to you in as great detail as possible exactly what took place, because not only is it my duty to report to the highest colleagues of our party, but also I think that our members should be fully informed as to exactly what transpired, to be in a position to form an opinion and to combat rumours, lies, misrepresentations and distortions which are sure to be promulgated by the other side in this matter.

Very early in the discussions the proposal was made that there should be a coalition between the People's Progressive Party and the People's National Congress. You will remember that we had accepted that as a possibility back in July when Mr Sandys was here. You will remember also in July we made it very clear that if there was to be any coalition it had to be on the basis of an equal distribution of ministries between the two parties, an equal distribution of seats between the two parties in the Senate[4] and an equal distribution of nominations to the various advisory and executive boards which operate in the country and under the aegis of the government.

The position which I took in July, having a mandate from my party, I took again in New York, during the course of these discussions. My proposal was, if the coalition was to be agreed on, the People's National Congress would agree to it on the following terms:

1. Absolute equality as set out and discussed prior to these discussions.
2. Elections before independence.
3. The preservation of democratic rights and human liberties in our country.

Dr Jagan wanted to be assured of a coalition which would last until after independence. My proposal, on the other hand, was if there should be a coalition, let there be a coalition to provide the atmosphere in which further discussions could take place with a view to having electoral reform and settling the other differences between the two political parties, and, if we were able to resolve all of them successfully, after the elections which would take place prior to independence, then it could be considered whether there should be any further coalition between the two parties.

In any case, I contended that whether the coalition was to be, as Dr Jagan wanted it, from now until after independence for an indefinite period, or, merely until independence was assured, the things which the P.N.C. demanded had to be satisfied. There was, for instance, the question of the distribution of power and the allocation of ministries within any coalition.

4. Upper House with power to delay some Bills but not financial legislation. Its members were all appointed with a government majority guaranteed.

It took me three meetings, and at the first of these meetings I stated my position with respect to the question of the distribution of power and allocation of ministries. It took me three meetings before Dr Jagan condescended to give his point of view on how the portfolios should be distributed. I pointed out that whichever coalition one is going to have, there had to be settled the question of allocation of ministries and I was particularly interested in hearing what his point of view and what was his party's stand.

Eventually, we came up to the proposal that the ministries should be distributed on the basis of six for the People's Progressive Party and five for the People's National Congress. Of course, I did not find it possible to accept such a proposal considering the mandate which I had from my party and the views I have heard expressed by strong active members and activists of the People's National Congress. I also had proposed that Dr Jagan could maintain, or retain rather, the Premiership, but the People's National Congress must have the Ministry of Home Affairs. There was a great deal of argument on this question by Dr Jagan. For he contended that the People's National Congress already controlled the police force, and, if to the actual control which he said existed there were to be added the legal control, then he and his party would be in jeopardy and to quote him accurately and precisely, 'their heads would be in danger'.

Dr Jagan actually suggested that if the portfolio of Home Affairs were to be given in a coalition to the People's National Congress there was a likelihood that a *coup* would take place and that the People's Progressive Party would be thrown out or overthrown and the People's National Congress would take over the government.

On the question of the distribution of seats in the Senate, Dr Jagan had no clear idea.

On the question of the distribution of nominations on various advisory and executive boards, he was quite clear that he, speaking for the People's Progressive Party, wanted a majority as against the People's National Congress. It seemed to me then, and it seems to me now, that if a party is in office and has failed absolutely, and that party turns to another party and says come over to Macedonia to save us and to help us, the party making the request is not entitled to any edge in representation, or distribution of portfolios or power.

The fact of the matter as I saw it then, and I see it is now, that the People's National Congress, so far as its popular support is concerned, is growing in strength while the support of the People's

Progressive Party is decreasing in strength. And apart from the question of popular support there is the question of the significance of the support of the People's National Congress. We say this not to make a boast, we say this not necessarily with any feeling of pride, we say this not to throw our weight around or to cause displeasure to those on the other side, but the historical fact in the country of Guiana is that the majority of mental and manual skills are within the ranks of the People's National Congress.

We came to a virtual deadlock and at one stage it was suggested by one of the intermediaries, that perhaps the distribution of portfolios, six to the People's Progressive Party and five to the People's National Congress, could be agreed on and conceded provided the People's Progressive Party was prepared to accept an equal distribution of nominees on the advisory and executive boards and commissions. I did not accept that, but promised that I would report it back to my party for its point of view. But in my case, the People's Progressive Party did not accept it either, because it wanted a majority not only in the Cabinet but a majority as well on all boards and commissions that were to be appointed by the government.

It must probably be clear therefore to anyone who seriously considers the situation that what the People's Progressive Party wanted was a coalition intended, not as an instrument of cooperation, not as a forum in which two sides could sit in equality and fairness, but as a gathering together of superiors and subordinates, we being the subordinates, and the People's Progressive Party the superiors.

One argument which was put forward by the hon. Premier was that if there were equality of distribution of portfolios, that would lead to deadlock and to prevent deadlock he wanted the extra vote to resolve that deadlock. The suggestion displays the typically naïve logic of the hon. the Premier Dr Jagan.

There was nothing to be gained by having an extra vote, or an extra ministry if there was to be cooperation. If there were equality, when there was disagreement some attempt would be made at tolerance, give and take, and compromise. If one side has a majority, knowing the People's Progressive Party leader as I do, he would undoubtedly have used his extra vote which would have caused the breaking up of the coalition and the last state no doubt would have been worse than the first.

The talks came to a virtual halt but there was an intercession by Mr Kojo Botsio the Foreign Minister of Ghana, who at that time had just arrived in New York to lead his country's delegation to the General Assembly. Dr Jagan and myself had lunch with him along with the Ambassador from Sierra Leone and the Ambassador from Mali. The discussions between us were carried on again in the evening of the same day on which we had lunch and no solution was arrived at. Dr Jagan stuck to his point of requiring one extra vote, at least, in everything and I stuck to my point of requiring equality. More than that I could not give, less than that I could not take.

In addition to those informal discussions the U.N. full Sub-Committee of Five met Dr Jagan and me separately at first, together on another occasion and then separately on two other occasions.

I am not aware at first hand what Dr Jagan communicated to the Sub-Committee of Five when he met them alone, except that the Sub-Committee told me that he had expressed a willingness to enter into a coalition and an anxiety to have the problems of Guiana solved; a willingness to cooperate with the People's National Congress, and a hostility towards the imposition of any solution by the British government.

On my first official appearance before the Sub-Committee of Five I expressed exactly the same sentiments. But when we appeared together, Dr Jagan informed the committee in my presence that he had made several vain attempts to have a coalition established between the People's Progressive Party and the People's National Congress and that one of these alleged attempts was in London during the October Independence Conference in 1962. I can say categorically that no such offer was received by me or by the delegation as a whole when we were in the United Kingdom last year attending the Independence Conference.

In fact I clearly remember, that on Thursday the first of November 1962, Dr Jagan and I alone, in the conference room, had a long discussion which lasted about an hour-and-a-half. During the course of that discussion he made no such proposal to me. Nor again did he make any such proposal on Friday the second of November, when he, the Governor, Mr d'Aguiar and I, spent about five hours in an attempt to save the conference from breaking down.

I found it necessary to point out to the Sub-Committee in the presence of Dr Jagan, that the People's National Congress was prepared to come to an arrangement for cooperation but not domination. That clearly the People's National Congress was not satisfied that when Dr Jagan spoke about his attachment to democracy that he meant exactly the same sort of thing we meant. Because, for a period of slightly over eighteen months, more than eleven months have found us in this country under a state of emergency. It is therefore empty for Dr Jagan to say that he believes in certain things being entrenched in writing in the constitution, certain human rights and civil liberties, when, we who have lived in Guiana have seen those human rights and civil liberties suspended twice in two years and suspended for a period of eleven months in a period of eighteen.

It was clear by that time, that there was going to be no rapprochement between the two political leaders on this question of a coalition arrangement. Naturally the People's Progressive Party will say that it is because of the sternness of the People's National Congress – the suggestion in fact was that we were influenced by the United States of America. But so far as the People's National Congress is concerned, so far as its leadership is concerned, you know, all of you know, that we have said quite clearly that we are prepared to come to terms, provided they are honourable terms. And you too yourselves know, comrades, how much difficulty I have had in persuading many of you that I should have talks with the leadership of the People's Progressive Party. In those circumstances no one can suggest that the leader of the People's National Congress is not anxious and willing to discuss peace, cooperation and understanding.

I also told the Sub-Committee that the People's National Congress was prepared to submit its case for proportional representation to the people through a national referendum, and I questioned the sincerity of the democratic sentiments uttered by Dr Jagan who was unwilling to consult the electorate which he claimed to represent.

I mentioned to you before that part of the informal discussions which were carried on was one with the Foreign Minister of Ghana which started at lunch on Thursday the nineteenth and was resumed in the evening just before dinner on the same day. During the course of those discussions Dr Jagan made a categorical statement, that regardless of the electoral system the People's Progressive Party would capture more votes and therefore, would win; to which I countered with the question, why then are you afraid of a referendum? The answer to that, comrades, was a stutter and a stammer.

Mr Burnham then described at length a P.P.P. proposal to send a Commonwealth Commisison to Guiana to draft a constitution and why this too was rejected.

You may ask, therefore, after all this what has been achieved by the visit abroad. As far as I can see nothing much has been achieved. We are where we started, we either solve the problem at home or not at all. There is no solution to the problems of Guiana outside Guiana. Outside Guiana we can get assistance, outside Guiana we can get advice, outside Guiana we can get good wishes, but neither advice, assistance, nor good wishes can solve the basic problems of Guiana.

As I had to tell the Sub-Committee, none of them could be keener than I was to see Guiana accede to independence, because they themselves were citizens of free and independent nations while I continued to be a colonial without a State really and without a nation. But the problem is not merely an early accession of Guiana to independence, the problem is an accession of Guiana to independence at the earliest possible time in circumstances and under conditions and with a constitution which would leave the majority of people in this country satisfied, willing to live side by side with each other, to mould a nation and to bring economic and social progress to that nation.

13

Statement at the opening session of the 1965 Constitutional Conference at Lancaster House, London, 2 November 1965

The political picture in Guiana had by this time undergone considerable change. At the 1963 Constitutional Conference, the three political leaders signed a document giving the British government full powers to arbitrate on the issues in dispute in regard to the granting of independence for Guiana. Duncan Sandys then announced a decision incorporating a change in the electoral system from constituency voting to proportional representation and ordering a general election which was held in December 1964.

Mr Burnham's party, in coalition with the small United Force, defeated the People's Progressive Party at the election. The coalition government won a 54 per cent popular vote with a 98 per cent poll.

Under Mr Burnham's premiership, the year had passed peacefully and racial tension had reduced considerably.

The People's Progressive Party refused to attend the conference called by the British government in November 1965 to discuss a date for independence but Forbes Burnham paid little attention to the P.P.P.'s absence. As he rose to his feet to address the conference he was in no mood for any further delay of independence for his country.

The conference concluded by setting a date for British Guiana to become the independent nation of Guyana on 26 May 1966.

This is the third independence conference I have attended in four years. The previous ones in 1962 and 1963 proved abortive in that a date for the independence of my country was not fixed. The 1963

Conference, however, did represent some achievement in that the fair electoral system of proportional representation under which each vote has the same weight and significance was decided on. Her Majesty's government of the day did give an undertaking that after the first elections under that system, a subsequent conference would be called primarily to fix a day for independence. That commitment has been accepted by the present British government and it follows that all that remains to be done is to get through the settling of certain details and the agreement of the date when Guiana shall cease to be a colonial territory and become a free and independent nation in the world.

My delegation and I have not come here to enter into arguments and disputations as to whether or not my country is entitled to independence. This was settled a long time ago. *We have come here now to write* finis *to one phase of Guiana's history.*

General elections were held in December 1964 and of these a Commonwealth Commission wrote:

> It is our conclusion that this election reflected the political conviction of the Guianese electorate. The election was keenly contested and the extraordinarily high percentage of votes cast bears testimony to the effectiveness of the administrative arrangements which ensured that the electors were not intimidated into keeping away from the polls.

On 14 December a new government, in which my party was the senior partner, assumed office. Since then the violence and tension, for which the previous two or three years had been noted in our country, came to an end. There has been a return of confidence and the people of Guiana have shown their faith in Guiana by contributing over twelve million dollars towards their country's development.

In answer to allegations of discrimination and racial imbalance in the security and public services, the government invited the International Commission of Jurists to set up a mission for the purpose of examining the balance between the races in the security forces, civil service, government agencies and undertakings (including land settlement schemes) and other areas of governmental responsibilities; considering whether existing procedures relating to the selection, appointment, promotion, dismissal and conditions of service of personnel were such as to encourage or lead to racial discrimination, in the areas concerned; and making such recommendations as were considered necessary to correct any such procedures with a view to the elimination of imbalance based on racial discrimination having regard to the need to maintain the efficiency of the services concerned and of the public interest.

That mission has investigated and reported. Its recommendations have been welcomed by my government. One of these stressed the desirability of, or rather the necessity for, early independence. Another emphasises the need for substantial capital assistance in executing the type of economic programme upon which the country must embark, in order to bring a higher standard of living to its people and 'shed the fears and suspicions that lie behind racial discrimination and violence'.

I hope that my government's willingness to accept these recommendations which are within its power to execute will be matched by an equal willingness on the part of the British government to honour the recommendations which are within its competence.

The present government of Guiana has sought at all times to involve in important decisions all sections of the community, and even though the opposition has not been remarkable for its willingness to respond to consultation, we have offered them every opportunity of making their views known.

More than symbolic of our conviction that the parliamentary opposition has a significant role to play, embodied in the draft constitution which the two parties in the government have brought with them, is a provision for the appointment of a leader of the opposition, consultation with whom on all important appointments will be obligatory. We also want to see in the constitution coming out of this conference, the institution of the office of Ombudsman, the holder of which will have statutory authority to investigate complaints of discrimination and irregular use of State-power, and to take the necessary action in terms of the spirit of the constitution and the public interest.

The draft constitution contains several provisions aimed at ensuring the independence of the judiciary, and the enshrinement of human rights, but it is not so much what is written in the constitution as the spirit in which it is worked that counts. And as we cut the political chains which have bound us to Britain in the past, we take with us the legacy of the democratic concept while we embark upon the building of our new nation – a nation in which we hope to abolish poverty and unemployment, and for the first time ensure the little man full participation in all the affairs of the country and a recognition of his innate human dignity.

As an independent Guyana moves to take her place amongst the nations of the world it will do so as an integral part of the Caribbean and, as I said in 1961: 'a pawn of neither East nor West'.

I must express regret at the absence of the parliamentary opposition, but their absence or presence will in no wise influence the insistence of my delegation and me that the date for independence be fixed for late February 1966.

Part III
A nation to build

14

After eight long years in the opposition Mr Burnham becomes Premier of British Guiana at the head of a coalition government. Eighteen days after his election victory he wishes the nation a 'Happy Christmas'.

The people of British Guiana have suffered through eight years of tension, economic stagnation and racial turmoil and now they listen to their radios anticipating a reprieve.

Mr Burnham tells the nation: 'We have a nation to build, we have a destiny to mould.' He makes as the central theme of his broadcast the need for national unity in the wake of national division coupled with the need and the will to build instead of tear down.

Fellow Guianese:

Even though I shall speak to you again before, or on the break of, 1965 you will forgive me if I attempt to look back on 1964 even before it is ended, in perspective.

The year did not begin happily. There were wars and rumours of wars. And who were the combatants on both sides? – Guianese. With every passing day things seemed to grow worse. The tensions increased, violence stalked the land. Brother raised hand against brother and there were the cries of the widows and the tears of the orphans.

But there came 7 December and elections under a fair democratic electoral system. The people spoke and spoke clearly and unequivocally. A new government came into office and then Christmas.

117

I wish as head of the new government to congratulate and thank the majority of Guianese for the peace and calm which has reigned over the last few weeks. Our country is rapidly on its way to normalcy. People are breathing and moving more freely.

I have received many kind wishes and earnest pledges of the fullest cooperation from every section of the community and every racial groups that dwells herein. I am heartened as I embark upon this great task of restoring peace and harmony in our land and building and re-building Guiana. In the very near future I intend to draw heavily on this fund of goodwill which I am sure will continue even after Christmas, indeed for all time.

In view of the lessened tension in our land and the season, I have held consultations with His Excellency the Governor on the question of those persons who have been detained under the Emergency Order. Taking into account the security situation which is always of the utmost importance, His Excellency accepted my advice to revoke the detention orders in nine cases. The persons affected are now, I hope, safely in the arms of their families and relatives, re-united and having a real Christmas. May I send them my especial greetings and feeling that they will forget the past and like so many others work for the advancement of Guiana. May I at the same time announce that the other detainees' cases are being actively studied and that it is my fervent and real hope that soon they too will be able to rejoin their families.

Christmas is the time of goodwill to all men. What more appropriate time can there be for us to forget the hurt, the animosity, the frustrations and the bitterness of the past? Let us, each one of us, hold out the hand of friendship to neighbours, friends and those from whom we have been estranged. Let us recapture the spirit of the message brought to this world by the 'Babe of Bethlehem'.

We have a nation to build, we have a destiny to mould.

Today, there are some who will have and enjoy many a good thing. But alas! there are so many for whom today will be another meal-less day which only charity may lighten somewhat.

But is it charity we want? Is not justice our quest? As we contemplate, let us pledge ourselves to work together to free Guiana from that monster of poverty and its twin, chronic unemployment. Your government headed by me will spare no pains to rid our beloved country of these twin monsters. I hope, rather, I know, that you are with me in this commitment.

Today many true Guianese must also feel the embarrassment of spending Christmas as colonials. To those who share my feelings, I say, let us not despair. The remedy is in our hand. Nothing can stand in our way if we take the peace and goodwill of this season into 1965, if we emphasise our common heritage and goals rather than our superficial differences.

When I say Happy Christmas dear countrymen, I mean that not only you enjoy the season in peace and happiness but that you should renew your pledge to free our country from poverty, want, hate and fear and foreign rule. Shall we not work towards our country being free, independent and well-knit by Christmas 1965?

Happy Christmas and may God bless you all brother Guianese – my friends, my people.

15

'Change our Society: Revolutionise our Economy.'
Extracts from speech to the Institute of Decolonisation, Congress Place, Georgetown, 16 July 1965

Guyana is now on the verge of independence and Forbes Burnham foresees the problems ahead. Rather than assume the all too familiar role of demagogue, Mr Burnham talks with his people instead of at them. He takes on the role of teacher in order to point the way to a responsible future.

By tracing the colonial history of his people he succeeds in identifying attitudes of mind which need changing and patterns of behaviour which must be abandoned in the struggle to build a new nation.

Many people believe that independence is a good thing because a particular party or parties which they support are going to be responsible for the administration and running of the country.

Many people believe that independence is a good thing because we shall no longer have to sing 'God Save our Gracious Queen', which has little or no meaning to the truly nationalist Guyanese.

Many people believe that independence is a good thing because they are going to get the fat jobs which used to be enjoyed by the sons and daughters, the representatives and wards of the colonial rulers.

Independence, I grant you, is very satisfying emotionally; it gives us the opportunity to say that we belong to an independent country which issues its own passport, and gives us an opportunity to stand up in the Councils of the world at one level or another and say, 'I come from country X Y Z'. But that is not an end in itself. Independence to my mind is a means towards an end. The end which I see must be *the changing of our society and the revolutionising of our economy.*

The political and constitutional implications of independence are known to us all. We shall have full initiative in and control over matters like defence and foreign affairs. We shall be able to make trade pacts and treaties. We shall be able to have our own army. We shall be able to have our army trained the way we want.

The fact that the constitution will be a constitution entirely under our control which cannot be suspended by the imperial government is one of those implications which we all know and find easy to understand and recognise. But deeper than all those reasons is the potential for economic advancement which comes from independence. Independence will give us an opportunity to re-organise our community; to re-organise our society.

Some nations have won their independence and some nations have been granted their independence. The leaders of those nations, without exception, I would say, are very interested in their countries being independent and are very interested in their countries taking their proper places in the world at the United Nations and various other international councils but since these leaders in many cases have not gone any deeper than the mere accession to independence, with the best wills in the world they have not really succeeded in making their countries truly independent.

You will find for instance that countries, nominally independent, model their economies on one foreign nation or another. Some countries, nominally independent, permit their own economies to be taken over by large foreign corporations or monopolies or to be controlled by the agencies of foreign nations. And yet these leaders in whose countries these things may be happening conscientiously and seriously believe in independence. The tragedy is that they have failed to recognise that the mere achievement of independence and the nominal and theoretical running of one's affairs are not the end.

What is necessary is a decolonisation of behaviour and attitude. Colonies we know have existed for the profit of the colonial powers. Colonies are the places from which raw materials are got at prices fixed by the mother country and at the same time are the automatic and exclusive markets for the manufactured goods of the colony-owning power.

Brainwashing and carefully directed systems of education have been a much more effective means of preserving the loyalty of a colony's inhabitants than the use of naked force and the most successful colonial power in the world, Britain, learnt that lesson very early. Otherwise how could a little island with a comparatively small population have held down millions of people throughout a quarter of the globe until the second world war? If we in Guiana are therefore not to suffer the difficulties which others have suffered and are to avoid the traps into which others have fallen we have got to go back into the history of our own society and understand the historical forces which influence our behavioural patterns today.

We have come from a slave society. The slaves were brought in from Africa at first, and later people were brought from Madeira, China and India. Slavery by any other name is no less brutal. There was little difference between the lot of the slaves and indentured labourers except for the fact that the indentured labourers were not as brutally treated as the slaves and were at one time paid the 'grand' sum of eight cents per week.

A hall-mark of the slave society was its brutality. Otherwise sensitive and sophisticated persons could find nothing wrong with the cries of slaves who were being horse-whipped brutally just outside their windows and sometimes in their very homes; sometimes by themselves, sometimes under their instructions. This past brutality of the slave society continues on today, but at an economic level.

Part of the efficacy of the system was the obeisance which the black slaves had to pay to their white masters. One chronicle reports that many of the slave owners, the Dutch in particular, enforced a ritual every morning in which the slaves, before going to the fields, went to the owners' homes and paid obeisance in a sort of chant and in the evening when their work was over, they went back to the homes of the slave owners and there again in a chant sang the praises of, and paid obeisance to, their owners. This was very much a part of education; it was a bending of the mind; it was, we would say today, a carefully planned system of brainwashing.

You will find the slave society out of which we have all come was based on the precedence given to the white master, and the results today are readily recognisable. One result is that today you find that many young men and women who are not prepared to go and do manual work are looking for white collar jobs formerly held by whites and near whites, and which in some cases are not as well paid as the manual job and in many other cases are not available. This inherited revulsion from physical or manual labour is, to some extent, responsible for the shortage of good, skilled, well-trained manual workers in our community, even today.

Subsequently, our education, when later we were granted the facility and privilege of education, was totally Europeanised. Look at us all today, many of us are still dressed like Europeans. Listen to the sort of things which we talk about, the ideals which we hold up, are almost always European.

This presents us with a difficult but necessary choice. We are going to have to choose between what we consider relevant and good for our nation and what we consider merely a legacy without any relevance; a legacy from our colonial and slave past.

To this day there remains also the dichotomy in people's minds between black and not so black; less black or less white and not so white. I relate these facts of history with absolutely no bitterness but in an attempt to let us see our society as it is.

More recently, and until very recently in the civil service, there were only two men who made decisions – the Chief Secretary and the Colonial Treasurer. They call him Financial Secretary. Consequently you find the whole civil service is groomed, not to make decisions, but to make recommendations. Every civil servant learns to summarise the minutes just before the minute he was writing or all the minutes before the minute he was writing and to set out all the facts as he saw them or found them for decision to be made by the Chief Secretary or the Financial Secretary. And then there stood in the background His Excellency the Governor. He was the final arbiter in the colonial territory, and if you were not satisfied with his decision then there was His Majesty or Her Majesty to make the final decision through her Principal Secretary of State for the Colonies.

Our society was therefore structured to centralise responsibility and to leave responsibility with the boss; and you still find it abroad today. You find it in political parties. You find it in clubs. You find it in all sorts of organisations. 'I cannot make this decision unless the boss makes it,' and that is because, to keep the slaves in their place – to keep the colonials in their place – it was necessary to rob them of all the initiative in order that they recognise their 'innate inferiority'. That is an attitude of which we shall have to rid ourselves. Another attitude which we find is that things foreign are always better.

We can go on like this and recognise attitude after attitude traceable back to our colonial and slave past. All too often we seek to rationalise these attitudes, but when we recognise that these are merely rationalisations of attitudes which have been bequeathed to us, attitudes which have come out of the fact that we have been slaves, physical at one time, and mental, economic and intellectual at another time, it should be easier then for us to decide to have an end to them and strike into new fields. And no one is going to do it for us. This has to be an exercise of self-liberation.

If we are to end the slavery of colonialism in our minds, the slavery of colonialism in our economy, the slavery of colonialism in our society, we have got to liberate ourselves and that has to be a joint operation as between the government and the people.

You notice that one of the first things the government has been emphasising is self-help – that people must help themselves. The first thing the government did was, not to go around the world begging for alms or grants and loans, but to seek to have the people subscribe to their own development. You may or may not agree with the mechanics of that exercise, but certainly you can recognise that behind that exercise was an attempt by a government to emphasise to the people: 'You don't look up to the boss outside, the first thing you do is to try to help yourselves and rely upon your own devices.'

The second token of government's attitude and point of view in this matter is the great emphasis which the government has been placing on the cooperatives; the cooperatives which give every Guianese the opportunity of coming together with so many more other Guianese in a grand effort for building something of economic significance and importance.

When people want jobs what do they usually say in colonies and ex-colonies? They say: 'We want big investors'; they say: 'There is no other way to give the people jobs but to get the big businessmen to come in and invest.' Little do they realise that such a means to imagined prosperity is also the surest route to economic serfdom. If a new country relies solely on foreign investors it leaves no initiative to the government in dealing with the said investors.

Now comrades, what I have been trying to say (I confess probably laboriously, I confess possibly cumbersomely, I confess sometimes rather vaguely) is this, that if we achieve independence we have got to look not only to hauling down one old flag and the putting up of another flag, not only to the changing of 'God Save the Queen' to an anthem which has meaning, not only to having a coat of arms which has relevance; not only to having formal control of our economic affairs and our international affairs.

1   The Prime Minister with President Kenneth Kaunda of Zambia, who
paid a State Visit to Guyana in 1966 at his special invitation.

2   On the occasion of Guyana's becoming a member of the United Nations in 1966, the Prime Minister poses for a picture with the U.N. Secretary-General, U Thant (on his left) outside the U.N. Building in New York – at which the Guyana flag flies for the first time.

3 The Prime Minister greets the Ambassador of Nigeria, Chief S. O. Adebo, on the occasion of Guyana's admission to the United Nations.

4 The Prime Minister being greeted by the British Prime Minister,
Mr Harold Wilson, at No. 10 Downing Street.

5. The Commonwealth Prime Ministers' Conference, 1960. (H. M. the Queen is in the centre)

6 The Prime Minister with the former Prime Minister of Canada, Mr Lester Pearson, at the Conference of Commonwealth Caribbean heads of government in Ottawa in 1966.

8 A conference of Amerindian leaders was called by the head of government for the first time in Guyana's history in 1969. Here the Prime Minister addresses 169 chieftains in the Parliament Chamber.

9 India's Prime Minister, Mrs Indira Gandhi, is presented with a photographic album by the Prime Minister. It depicts her tour of rural areas in Guyana during her State visit in 1968.

10 Campaigning at the General Election in 1968, the Prime Minister stands on a street corner surrounded by his comrades and supporters.

11 At a rural exhibition, the Prime Minister displays interest in a locally-made ornamented candlestick holder. He is wearing a 'Shirt Jac', designed to replace the jacket and tie as formal wear in the National Assembly and on other formal occasions in Guyana.

12　The Prime Minister at work in his office.

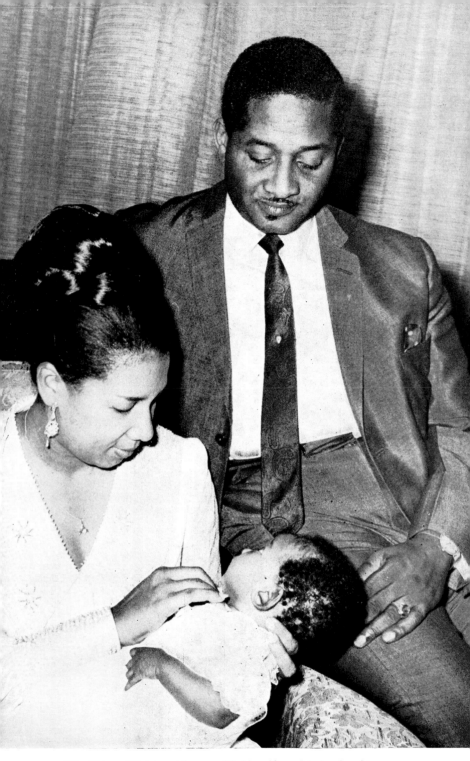

13 The Prime Minister at home with his wife and baby daughter.

14 The Prime Minister shares a joke with (left to right) Jamaica's Prime Minister, Mr Hugh Shearer, Guyana's Minister of State and Attorney General, S. S. Ramphal, and the Prime Minister's P.R.O., Frank Pilgrim.

15 On taking office the Prime Minister covered Guyana from end to end in a series of 'Meet the People' tours. Here, in a country village, he listens while one of the community leaders describes some of the village's problems.

We must see to it that we achieve more than these – namely, the decolonised attitudes of our leaders and of our people. Otherwise, we shall be nothing more than appendages to some big metropolitan country, otherwise we will be as independent as Guatemala is, we will be as independent as East Germany is, we shall be as independent as a number of small countries. Some of them not so small are formally independent, but in fact take orders from outside.

16

'The Spectre of Unemployment: The Search for Skills.' Speech to the opening of Manpower Seminar, Georgetown, 22 June 1966

On coming to power at the end of 1964, Burnham inherited a legacy of maladministration and the grim reality of 20 per cent of his country's work-force unemployed. Guyana, now independent, has to find a solution to this problem.

The Prime Minister takes a unique approach among the world's newer nations by ordering an in-depth survey of the country's manpower and available skills and obtains the assistance of the United Nations to carry it out. In spite of the initial cost – the main opposition argument against the survey – the exercise proves immensely beneficial in helping the government's economic planners to utilise the talents of the country's limited human resources.

The Prime Minister attaches sufficient importance to the occasion of his speech to assemble his entire Cabinet.

The Man-Power Survey Project was one of the first large-scale exercises approved by the Cabinet soon after this government assumed office. In fact, the decision was made by the Cabinet before it formally met, at a place in Cove and John,[1] on Boxing Day. It was on Boxing Day of 1964, the Cabinet, before it had a formal meeting, went into retirement, so to speak, and decided that there should be a thorough man-power survey and today, in spite of the uninformed criticisms which were forthcoming when the project was launched, we are now

1. Village on the East Coast of the County of Demerara about 10 miles from the capital, Georgetown.

able to see the tangible results and the value to be derived from our investment in these investigations.

The administration of any government in the modern world is very complicated. This is an age of sophistication, not naïvety and puerility. Trade between countries no longer takes the form of simple barter agreements, but is influenced by international price formulae and rather involved and complicated agreements such as the General Agreement on Tariffs and Trade, commonly known as GATT.

Activity, for instance, in the field of diplomacy has also reached higher levels, and it is now necessary for emerging countries to have their representatives trained before they can be considered fit to present properly and effectively, the cases of their countries in other parts of the world and in international councils such as the United Nations.

Again, the development of communication facilities including radio, television, telephone and the aeroplane, have contributed to a wider recognition of the disparities which exist between the levels of living of peoples in developing countries on the one hand, and developed countries on the other. One of the prime objectives of many international organisations and governments of nearly all nations, including that of Guyana, is eradication or lessening of these disparities, by making concentrated efforts to improve the living conditions of people in the less developed societies.

The present government, on assuming office, recognised that a substantial contribution could be made to the maintenance of this country's stability if there were greater opportunities for all, but it was also frighteningly obvious that these greater opportunities could not be created unless there were sound planning and cooperation coming, in the case of the latter, from all sections of the society and community. But, sound planning cannot be done on the basis of guestimates and hunches, neither can a plan be properly formulated merely on the foundation of past experiences. Patrick Henry could say he knew only one way of which to judge of the future and that was by drawing on the experience of the past. That is good for history; that is good for politics; but not good enough for economic planning.

An essential ingredient of proper planning is a complete and exhaustive analysis of various aspects of our present position and in recognition of this fact, a team of international consultants, working in conjunction with local experts and officers and headed by Sir

Arthur Lewis,[2] was invited to draft a development programme suited to the needs of this country. You are all no doubt aware of the release and publication of the programme during the past few months, and some of you might have listened to the debate on this programme in the legislature before it was passed.

The success of this programme, however, will depend not only, as some neophytes believe, on the amount of local and foreign loans and investments, but more definitely and to a greater extent on the capabilities of Guyana's people to provide the initiative, the drive and the skilled man-power, without which there can be no effective execution of the programme. It was, therefore, inevitable that whilst we were making an assessment of our development needs in financial terms, we should also be paying proper and adequate attention to preparing an inventory of human resources available within the country. On some occasions, development programmes have been known to fall short of their original objectives, not only on account of lack of finance or balance of payment problems, but also on account of shortage of persons with the required skills to execute those programmes, and therefore, I regard it as very opportune that we should have at this time, a comprehensive assessment of the human resources available in this country.

The volumes which have now been presented, are much more important than previous surveys we have had and go far beyond compare in profundity and depth with those like the McGale Report[3] of 1956–7.

During the seminar sessions, you will no doubt be given detailed information on our present situation. Certain obvious shortages will be revealed. One of the most alarming was that, in spite of the emphasis on agriculture, there was a paucity, if not absence, of training courses provided for agriculturalists and agricultural specialists up to 1964. I wish to assure you that this government will do everything in its power to prepare the country for its future responsibilities, by helping as many as possible to improve their skills. And, I am to assume that from the presence here this morning of representatives of private industry, that government's anxiety and willingness

2. Renowned West Indian economist; professor in economics at Princeton University, U.S.A., Vice Chancellor of the University of the West Indies up to 1963, and presently Chancellor of the University of Guyana.
3. An unemployment Report carried out by a British Labour Ministry expert under I.L.O. auspices.

to give leadership in this field, will be matched by the enthusiastic support of the private sector.

Turning to the reports being published, it is interesting to note that in addition to information on employment, unemployment and under-employment usually contained in publications summarising the results of labour force surveys, like the McGale Report for instance, other matters of especial significance for Guyana have been dealt with quantitatively for the first time in the history of our country. These include the extent and pace of Guyanisation in private establishments (not as rapid as some publicists would have us believe), the numbers of professionally qualified persons of various types in the community, the factors surrounding the resignation of many university-trained persons from the public service, more especially from the medical service, and the effect which past training policies or absence of policies and total absence of vocational guidance programmes have had in contributing to present shortages in certain fields and continuingly low standards.

The fact that professionally qualified persons in Guyana were found to number about 1,000 may, at first blush, appear encouraging, but closer examination of the statistics reveal areas in which there are significant shortages. These include certain branches of engineering and physical sciences, particularly those relating to mining and mineral exploration, graduate teachers for the expansion of our secondary education programme, doctors, dentists, public administrators, management specialists and sociologists.

Of course, there is an international shortage of persons with certain types of skills and expertise, but I am hopeful that Guyana's development programme will not be retarded in any way because of a shortage of skilled man-power. To recognise, identify and isolate the problem is to take the first step towards its solution. This hope is not without foundation, since it was observed during the survey that fifty per cent of the unemployed persons had attended school for between seven and eight-point-five years, so that there is a good basis for training of the unskilled.

One of the advantages which we do have in this country is the high literacy of our population which is the *sine qua non* for the absorption of skills which we can turn to great advantage. I personally, on behalf of my government, hope that your deliberations will result in mutual benefit to all the participants.

I see here permanent secretaries and principal assistant secretaries and would-be diplomats and other persons involved in the development programme. I see here members of the executive level in private enterprise. I see here senior officers in age and in status from the Georgetown Town Council and I am hopeful, nay confident, that all of you participating here today in this seminar will benefit immensely and will be able to pass on some of the benefits to your colleagues in the various services and business houses from which you come.

I am hopeful that as a result of this seminar, those of you who had given up the habit of reading, will now resume that habit. I am hopeful that you will recognise the importance of analyses and reports such as we have here in these volumes. I feel confident that your very presence here this morning proves that you have a deep and consuming desire to contribute to the progress of Guyana.

It is my humble, but great pleasure to declare this seminar open.

17

'The Purpose of Efficiency.' Speech to representatives of the commercial community and employer/
employee organisations, Chamber of Parliament,
Georgetown, 15 September 1967

*The paternalistic attitude of colonial powers has, in almost every case,
left newly independent nations devoid of efficient management skills,
and consequently an inefficient work force. Prime Minister Burnham
sets out early in his administration to deal with this problem by bring-
it out into the open. He initiates a year-long National Efficiency
Campaign.*

I think that all of us here are Guyanese and, if I may qualify my
definition of Guyanese, you are Guyanese because you are working
here and devoting your energies to the development of Guyana. Some
of you are the more fortunate to have been born here. All of you are
engaged in exercises here, out of which you draw an income. I am sure
that none of you would have reached the position you have reached
unless you had given an indication that you regard your task seriously,
and feel that it must be done efficiently and effectively both in the
context of the organisation which you happen to work for and in the
context of the nation of Guyana.

Here in Guyana we have reached the stage of political independence, and one of the things which that status connotes is the capacity
of self-criticism and introspection. If we indulge in self-criticism and
introspection we soon come to the conclusion that political independence is not the be-all and end-all. Inevitably we learn that the success
of the nation depends on the capacity and ability of the government

and those controlling certain sectors of the community and economy, to bring a better life to the country and to the masses.

The success of the nation is dependent upon our being able to produce more. I am sure that you will accept the fact that greater productivity can to a large extent be procured by means of greater efficiency. I expect that some of us will point to the fact that many people are lazy; many people do not carry out their jobs with enthusiasm; many people, at all levels and in various places, do not work the number of hours for which they are paid.

Though observations like these can be made, I am sure that at our level of sophistication we can agree that efficiency is not merely a matter of working harder and putting in more hours per day, per week, per month of the year, but also a question of adopting techniques, methods and procedures which make for quicker accomplishment of the jobs which we undertake or are paid to undertake.

On Wednesday the senior public servants and chairmen and executive officers of public corporations held a discussion here with me and the rest of the Cabinet. Today the private sector has been invited.

There are some who claim that, from what they observe, the private sector is always more efficient than the public sector. There are others who put forward this argument on the basis of an ideological orientation – to wit that the running of all business must always be left to private enterprise. I am not here this morning to indulge in any argument about this sector or that sector. It is a fact of life in Guyana, and accepted at all levels, that these two sectors exist.

Even if we assume, whatever the reason, that the private sector is more efficient, *ipso facto*, than the public sector, you gentlemen, who are here this morning, must certainly agree with me that even if the private sector for the purpose of the present argument is more efficient, there is still a great deal of inefficiency. Every day, for instance, we see, in both the public service and private sector, sloppy service to the public. In both cases, what is worrying is that many of the persons who are guilty of sloppiness and discourtesy to the general public have a keen sense in distinguishing those persons to whom they feel they should show courtesy.

I am sure most of the large organisations in this country have efficiency experts, work study experts, and in many cases, as a result, have improved their procedures. But the improvement of procedures is not the only answer. It is also a question of inculcating, into the minds of those who are responsible for the day-to-day running of the business enterprises, a new attitude, a new approach and dedication to do better than they have done before.

Systems are on paper. These systems, however, have to be worked by people. People are not automatons and consequently it is an attitude of mind adjusted towards efficiency which we want to develop in the people, both in the private and public sector.

You will note that this morning the invitations were issued, not to the employer nor the employee but to the employers and employees through their respective representational associations or groups. It is my conviction that unless both sections can be imbued with the same ideas, goals and objectives, we are wasting our time.

We want in this country to make a reality of the claim that industry consists of two parts and neither part can make a success of industry alone. The workers are most important. The managers are most important.

Recently when I had the good fortune to be present at a seminar on management I took the opportunity to emphasise the need for management recognising that workers are human beings. That was a management seminar. Now we have management and workers here today, I wish to emphasise that workers must also understand that managers are human beings.

In so far as the managers are concerned it must not merely be a question of seeking profits at all costs and in all circumstances. So far as the workers are concerned it must not merely be a question of seeking better wages, better conditions and fringe benefits at all costs and in all circumstances.

In both cases there must be an additional and most important dimension – that of regarding the good of the country and the economy of the nation, considering what contribution can be made towards advancing the economy and furthering the interests of the country.

It was observed on Wednesday, when the public servants and senior public servants met, that trade unions must understand that they have an important role to play in the building of the country, and though they must always seek to further the interests of their members, though they must always seek to get the best possible scales of remuneration and the best possible fringe benefits, they must also at all times regard what is good for the economy and what contribution they can make to improve the economy.

Being a trade unionist myself perhaps I know more about trade unions than about management, but may I say this, that it is the duty of responsible trade unions to see to it that laxness amongst their members disappears. Trade unionists must stand up to management when there is discrimination and injustice, but trade unions must also understand that they are not there to cover the lazy, the incompetent and the inefficient.

Efficiency is a wide concept – you will agree. One of the obvious elements of efficiency which most people like to emphasise is punctuality. This meeting was called for ten. You should be here at ten. Efficiency for a rice farmer demands the learning of new methods to produce more rice per acre – an understanding that a man cannot work somewhat over 30 days in a year and expect to draw an income to keep him and his family alive for 365 days. Efficiency in the case of the sales girl should take the form, not only of knowing what products are there to be sold, but what alternative products there may be to those which the customer may ask for and the store or shop may not have. It should take the form of despatching the customer quickly and leaving an impression on the customer that he is important and wanted. Efficiency in the case of an administrative officer may take the form of being able to arrive at decisions promptly, being able to take into account the relevant facts and factors and acting with despatch, whether it be by the telephone or a minute in a file. Efficiency takes so many different forms for so many different people. It is all so dependent on the particular job which the person is doing. Therefore, it has been thought necessary to bring into participation in this campaign all sections of the community – private, public, commerce, industry, everybody.

It is hardly possible for us to have the entire population of Guyana here, but we sought to have representative organisations here; organisations we think can influence, by precept and example, their members and those who look up to them for guidance. It is proposed therefore to set up a National Efficiency Committee. This committee will be representing all sections, or as many sections as possible, of the community. Naturally, I would expect that from amongst you here there will be representatives. But, may I, as one Guyanese, to others say this, don't accept an appointment on the National Efficiency Committee unless you are convinced that you have the time and the will to carry out the duties which membership of the committee connotes.

One of the causes of inefficiency in this country is the anxiety with which people seek to have themselves placed on committees and the defaults and lethargy and irresponsibility which they disclose having achieved this Olympian height. How many secretaries know executive committee members who appear only at election time and then like the tale told by an idiot are heard no more? We find it in private organisations; we find it in public organisations; we find it and you will accept my word for it, in politics as well.

I expect that from amongst you there will be representatives on the Efficiency Committee. I am sure, therefore, that those of you who are put on that committee will carry out your task effectively and efficiently. But, even though, at the two meetings we have held, we have met the organisations broadly representative of the people in every walk of life in this country, we must not believe that the National Efficiency Committee will be the repository of all wisdom.

I would not like us to believe that we in the committee make all the decisions. You must work out some structure, find some means so that the public may have access to the committee – the public, who may not be directly represented, the individual who may not be directly represented will have some means of making proposals.

I think that it is the essence of efficiency to realise that you do not know all. There can come wise and sound suggestions from others whom you might have forgotten. A National Efficiency Committee may not find it possible to cover every aspect or every major sector or section of the nation's activities.

In urging efficiency or ensuring the re-education which is necessary for efficiency (and it has been proposed that there should be sub-committees responsible for particular subjects or sectors) I can see that there must be, servicing this committee and servicing all the sub-committees, a public relations committee or sub-committee. It will be necessary to explain things to the public; it will be necessary to involve the public; it will be necessary to make it clear to Guyanese what's in it for them – why they should be involved. May I suggest also the necessity to recognise by tangible means, certain awards for instance, efficiency when and wherever it is worthy of recognition.

I have spoken much longer than I had originally anticipated because I have got a conviction that here this morning we have a number of Guyanese who are as anxious as I to see greater efficiency and effectiveness of action, greater productivity, and greater economic and other forms of progress in the country.

18

'A New Era for our Amerindian Brothers.' Extracts
from speeches to Amerindian Leaders Conference,
Chamber of Parliament, Georgetown, 28 February–
8 March 1969

*In building a new nation, Forbes Burnham is determined to build it
for the benefit of all the people and at the exclusion of none. The
indigenous Amerindian population, amounting to about four and a half
per cent of the total population, had long been excluded from any
real part in or benefits from the investment in progress.*

*The policy of the past, under the British and successive P.P.P.
governments, was to treat the Amerindians as a primitive people and
isolate them on reservations. The Prime Minister immediately following the 1968 election took steps to change this policy.*

*The Amerindian population lives in isolated areas of the interior
easily accessible only by aircraft. Politically, since 1961, they have
aligned themselves with the United Force and as a consequence
Burnham assigned the responsibility for Amerindian Affairs in the
1964–68 coalition government to a U.F. minister.*

*The U.F. sought to make a cause célèbre of the Amerindian neglect,
but advocated a policy of continued isolation.*

*In complete contrast, Mr Burnham urged a policy of rapid develop-
ment of the Amerindians in order that they may take their place in
Guyanese society with equal status and with equal opportunity with
the rest of the Guyanese people.*

*With this in mind, the Prime Minister, for the first time in the
country's history, called a full conference of Amerindian chieftains to
meet with the ministers and senior officials responsible for interior
development. The Prime Minister addressed both the opening and*

closing sessions of the conference which lasted over a period of eight days.

Fellow ministers, ladies and gentlemen: The honourable Minister of Local Government has already welcomed you, the elected leaders of the Amerindian people, to this most important conference. But I personally, on my behalf, as head of the government of Guyana desire to give you a special welcome. I thank you for being present here today, especially since I know what long distances you have had to travel – from the Rupununi, the Mazaruni, the Corentyne, the North-West and some of the furthest reaches of our rivers. The fact that you have made such a sacrifice proves to me and to us your interest in the development of our country, your willingness to cooperate in making Guyana a great land and your burning desire to plan for the resolving of the many problems, with which you are faced and which have to be overcome, if the new life to which you and other Guyanese are entitled is to become a fact.

This conference has been called in fulfilment of a promise which the government made to itself and which was referred to on Sunday, 22 December 1968 at Independence Park – that we cannot and will not permit the original peoples, the indigenous peoples of this country to be bypassed in the same way as the native and indigenous peoples of other countries are bypassed, ignored and exploited.

May I emphasise that in a young country like Guyana problems and difficulties face all sections of the community and nation. But these problems and difficulties can be got over only by our working together as a people, giving and taking in the common interest of others for the benefit of our fatherland.

Sometime late in last year, I thought of inviting you to this meeting to discuss a number of matters of common interest to us all. It turned out, however, not to be possible because of the election campaign and the holding of elections in which so many of my ministers and colleagues and you yourselves were involved. Now that the elections are over and a new government has been elected, you and I can, in a calm atmosphere, as friends, get down to a sensible discussion out of which can truly come sensible decisions. You will notice that there are here present today, a number of ministers like the Minister of Finance – a very important person who holds the purse-strings.

The ministers are here so that they can fit into their programme for the coming year and for years to come those projects and services which are agreed with you. I want you to know that the projects and services will have to be agreed with you. We have not invited you to have discussions with us to tell you what we think is good and right for you. We have invited you so that you can discuss with us and come to conclusions on the basis of what you feel is best or good for you and the communities of which you are the elected leaders. The members of the Interior Development Committee are here so that they can, in cooperation with you, plan for the joint development of those areas of our country from which you come and which you know so well.

Ours is a vast country and the resources and the money which government has at its disposal will have to be distributed and divided among all the regions and all the people so that every citizen of Guyana gets his fair share of the national cake.

I would like you to understand, as leaders of your people, that you have a most important role to play and a great task to perform. You must not come here as if you are beggars seeking favours. You must come here with the conviction that you are full-fledged Guyanese citizens who, working together with other Guyanese citizens, can develop the resources of this country for the benefit of all of us.

There are some who, for their own personal and material motives, would like to separate you from the rest of the community, pretending to be your friends but, in fact, lining you up for greater exploitation on their own behalf. This must cease.

You must not feel inferior here at this conference. You must not feel that you have not got access to the government. A man and a people are as important as they feel and as important as the contributions which they make to the building of the nation to which they belong. But that contribution, gentlemen, can only be made if they are given the best opportunities of developing themselves, their experience and the abilities which God has given them. That is why my government has decided that all Guyanese, whoever they are and wherever they are, should have the best training and education which this country can offer; they should have the best medical services which Guyana can afford. The schools in the interior, for instance, must be as good as the schools on the coast and you will note that last year, amongst those who were sent to the United States of America for training to become good and competent ranchers were two

Amerindian citizens from the Rupununi. Another batch of Guyanese will be going on a similar course this year and, again, Amerindians will be included.

There are Amerindians today attending our best secondary schools; there are Amerindians today who are being trained to become good and successful farmers at the Guyana School of Agriculture; there are Amerindians today who are trained as teachers and technical men; and this process shall, and must, continue. In keeping with the promise which I made at Waramadong[1] on Sunday, 1 December 1968, I propose this year to select at least two qualified Amerindians to be trained at the government's expense in medicine and engineering abroad.

I know that many of you, as the spokesmen for the people whom you lead, would like to know what is the position with respect to your lands. As you know, an Amerindian Lands Commission has been sitting and visiting various parts of the country since September 1967. The honourable Minister of Local Government, has already made reference to this commission. Although the chairman of the commission, Mr Forte, has been away for some weeks now as a result of illness, the commission has written and submitted to government an interim report. Government awaits the final report and recommendations of the commission, but I can tell you today that I have already started to take steps to have transferred, with full title, to the Amerindian village communities settled in villages, those lands occupied by these villages and additional lands which the people can farm and develop for the benefit of themselves and those who come after them. Let me say that your government, through the Ministry of Agriculture and Natural Resources, will give every assistance, advice and training so that this farming and the development of these lands will bring you profitable returns.

In referring to the development of your lands, I include your right, with proper licences, to win from the bowels of our earth precious stones and metals; and government will see that the results of your toil are not stolen from you for little or nothing by those who, under one guise or another, in the interior of our country seek to rob you.

You, as captains, you, as leaders, of your communities I know carry important responsibilities; and it is to you that the government looks, not only for full cooperation, but also for responsible and

1. An Amerindian settlement in the Western Mazaruni visited by the Prime Minister during a 'Meet the People Tour'.

patriotic leadership. My colleague the Minister without Portfolio who sits on my left, will be working out what should be the proper allowances, for instance, to be paid to captains throughout Guyana and what other privileges and responsibilities should be given to you, the captains.

The responsibility for interior development which, naturally, includes Amerindian development and welfare, will come under the Prime Minister himself as from tomorrow, 1 March 1969. The department which will form part of the Economic Development Ministry will be called the Interior Development Department, and for a good reason.

In places like the Southern States of America you will find a large number of societies and organisations established for helping the Negroes but yet at the same time the Negroes there are discriminated against and have the most inhuman treatment perhaps in the world meted out to them. It is not your government's intention to permit a similar situation here and to make a mere plague of Amerindian development and Amerindian welfare separating them from the rest of the community and treating them like second-class citizens.

The Amerindians of Guyana must be brought into and become an important part of the whole community. For this reason there will be, not an Amerindian Development Committee but an Interior Development Committee. It must take care of the rights and interests of all the people who dwell and live in the interior and this automatically includes the Amerindians. Interior development is being transferred, as I said, to the Prime Minister as from tomorrow. This is being done so that things can move faster and decisions, with which we agree among ourselves, can be implemented at the very highest level.

If you and I are to build Guyana there must be not only cooperation but also loyalty to Guyana. In this world we cannot hope only to receive, we must also be prepared to give, and the least you are expected to give is your loyalty and devotion to the nation of Guyana.

Many will come to you – perhaps they have already come to you – and they will try to tell you that your future lies in working with persons and groups in other countries hostile to Guyana and who want to steal our land. But let me say this – and it cannot be disputed or disproved – what your government has done for you, no neighbouring government has done for your brothers. What your government plans for you, no neighbouring government plans to do for your brothers.

This country belongs to us all and to no one else outside. In this country we all are first-class citizens. In this country, every man has an opportunity to reach the top. In this country, so long as I am Prime Minister, no Amerindian or other citizen will be exploited and kept at the bottom. All of us can and will be men of spirit and dignity, making of Guyana a model country.

I wish you every success in your conference and look forward to joining you from time to time in your discussions and speaking to you again finally on the completion of the conference.

May God bless you all.

EXTRACTS FROM SPEECH CLOSING CONFERENCE

It has been said that this is a historic conference. It is the first time in the history of our country that the leaders, the captains of the Amerindian communities, have been invited to attend a conference to plan for the development of the country and more particularly the areas from which the Amerindians come. As my good friend and colleague Mr Duncan[2] said, this is but the first of similar conferences. As I said when I opened the conference in the House of Parliament on Friday last, we do not want the Amerindians to be separate and apart. When the British were here they wanted to keep the Amerindians as a group apart; they called them 'children of the forest' and they never gave them an opportunity to enjoy all the services which the rest of the community enjoyed.

After the British left, there were still some who wanted to keep the Amerindians separate and distinct from the community so as to be able to exploit them politically and economically. But that must cease now; and it has ceased as from the beginning of this conference. Anyone who attempts to interrupt this new way, this new approach, will be dealt with firmly and swiftly. We will not permit in our country the exploitation of our people – the Amerindians – just to suit the whims and fancies of a small group who pretend to love them but who have been exploiting them to the bone.

You will notice that on Saturday, 1 March, when there was a complaint that the Amerindian Lands Commission was not representative of the Amerindians, I gave you an opportunity to choose your representative on that commission; and I want to congratulate you upon choosing your representative democratically and also to congratulate

2. Amerindian, Parliamentary Secretary, Ministry of Local Government.

Mr Bennett, who has been chosen as your representative. I wish Mr Bennett every success in his new job; and I look forward to his serving his people and the country as he ought, with all the ability that I recognise that he has. Never before has any government in this country, or any group of people, given to the Amerindians their proper place in the society as this government has done.

In future, as Prime Minister, I am not going to permit other people to tell me what the Amerindians want; I am going to find out from the Amerindians what *they* want. It is all well and good for people to be pretending to speak for you, when sometimes they are speaking for themselves and are nothing but wolves in sheep's clothing. This is a new era, a new age in Guyana.

What gives me great pleasure, and what to me is very important, is the fact that from the Corentyne to the Waini, down to the south of the Rupununi, all of the people are asking for better education and training. That is important and that is significant, because we have learnt in this age that unless we are trained, unless we understand modern techniques, we cannot make a success of developing our country.

I remember some months ago, I stopped at Barima Bridge on my way from Matthews Ridge to Port Kaituma,[3] and I met an Amerindian captain and his people and I asked him what did they do, and he told me that they grew cassavas and a few other things for themselves to eat. And I said, 'What else do you do?' He said, 'Nothing else.' Well, one thing we have got to learn in this world today is that if we are to be able to get some of the things which we need, we have got to produce not only for ourselves, but must also produce a surplus, which we can then sell or exchange, for the things which we want and which we ourselves do not produce. That, basically, is the difference between subsistence agriculture and economic agriculture. Subsistence agriculture means that you grow enough for yourself to eat and therefore you are without the surplus to get things which you do not produce yourself. But economic agriculture means that you not only grow for yourself to eat, but you also grow enough to sell to others, so that you can get money to buy other things which you need, so that you can cease being beggars, you can cease asking favours. If you do not grow enough to sell to get the surplus to buy clothes, you'll have forever to be begging for cast-off clothes.

3. In the North-West District of Guyana about 15 miles from the Venezuelan border.

We've got to move, in the Amerindian areas as in all areas of Guyana, beyond the subsistence level; but if we are to move beyond the subsistence level, it means we've got to learn how to grow new crops and we've got to learn to produce from the same amount of land twice as much in crops as we produced before. And we cannot learn that, unless we get training, unless we get education.

I was attracted by what the Minister of Education said, that we want Amerindian teachers. We have got a number; I met one last night who is a teacher at St George's School in Georgetown. But we want more; and we want more Amerindian teachers not only to teach Amerindians, but to teach anywhere in the country, so that there can be the interchange and movement among all the peoples of this country.

We cannot develop the coast separately from the interior. We've got to develop the coast *and* the interior, and it is my own personal conviction that the development of the interior is likely to yield much more for the country as a whole than the development of the coast.

It is time that we develop the resources and riches of the interior for all of us. And I stress 'all of us', because again, some will come and tell you that the riches of the interior are for you alone – and those are the same people who buy your diamonds below the market price. It is not that they believe that the riches of the interior are for you alone, but that they believe that the riches of the interior are for you to give them an opportunity to rob you of those same riches. Let it not be felt that as Prime Minister I do not know what happens in some parts of this country – about those who come with the Bible and leave with the diamonds. There must be an end to this. Some of them, I understand, have been public servants who go in to serve the people and buy their diamonds cheaply, and encourage them to keep out other people so that they could better exploit the people that they call the 'children of the forest'. If you are 'children of the forest' all of us are 'children of the forest'. If we are not 'children of the forest' you are not 'children of the forest'. We are all the same whether we are 'children of the forest' or not 'children of the forest'.

Let us get it straight, Guyana belongs to all of us; Guyana is to be made richer and better for all of us. You cannot do without the other people in the country and the other people in the country cannot do without you. And when anyone comes along and attempts to separate you, think carefully what plan he has in mind for you; ask yourself if he doesn't look like those who have kept you where you have been for all these years. We want this country for all of us.

I want to speak to you for a few minutes on this question of the Lands Commission. I would like you to accept two things as evidence of my government's honesty of intention with respect to your lands. Those two things are the appointment of your representative on the Lands Commission and secondly my undertaking on Friday, that we are moving immediately to transfer to villages, as communities, the lands occupied by these villages as well as some extra lands, which they can farm for themselves and those whom they have to feed. Now that we've got the extra member, your representative, on the Lands Commission, I shall formally ask the Lands Commission to proceed as fast as it can towards the submission of the final report. And let us in fairness say this about the Lands Commission: they had to consult the wishes of the people in the Waini, Moruca, Pomeroon, Essequibo, Mazaruni, Demerara River, Mahaicony River, Mahaica River, Corentyne and the Rupununi, only to mention a few of the places. And they are not magicians or obeah-men;[4] they cannot finish their work overnight. When they make their final report, it must be a report that is fair and its main recommendations must be such as can be acted upon by the government.

I want at this stage to thank you on behalf of the government, for the resolution of loyalty[5] which was passed yesterday. From the point of view of the government, this is something that is very welcome. It is welcome in that the government can now learn officially, and beyond the shadow of a doubt, that the leaders of an important section of our community are supporting the government in the conflict which it now has with a foreign power. And it is good for you, too, to let the world know that you have nothing in common with those traitors, who started the uprising in the Rupununi and now, like the cowards they are, seeking and enjoying the safe asylum of Brazil and Venezuela. It is good that the rest of the community knows that you are loyal citizens of Guyana. And it is good that a warning be given to those who would want to make excuses for those traitors who have defiled our country and have lost every right to enjoy anything which Guyana produces.

I think that by and large we have had a good conference. We might

4. Black Magic practitioners.
5. A publicly-signed resolution by the Amerindian chieftains pledging their loyalty to the Guyanese government in face of the Venezuelan claims.

not have been able to discuss everything we wanted to discuss, but we've set a pattern now of discussion and interchange of ideas. We've set a pattern of everyone being involved, instead of some of us being treated as children and told what is good for them and what is bad for them. Indeed, it does seem to me that in the same way as independence came to the whole of Guyana, and Guyana as a whole is in a position to decide what it wants for itself, even so you are enjoying that independence by being consulted for the first time in history, to say what you want and to advise government how best what you want can be achieved by us all.

19

'Guyana Has Prospered.' Speech to nation at mass
open air meeting on occasion of third anniversary of
independence, Queen Elizabeth II National Park,
Georgetown, 26 May 1969

*Three years after the attainment of independence the Prime Minister
points to the achievements that have been made. Though the progress
has been considerable the Prime Minister is not satisfied to let the
nation rest on its laurels and once again he assumes the role of
lecturer in an effort to urge the people of his young nation on to meet
the still very considerable problems that lie ahead.*

Fellow Guyanese, comrades! Today is the third anniversary of that
Thursday morning when for the last time the Union Jack was lowered
and for the first time the Golden Arrow-head of Guyana hoisted. We
mark, today, the third year of independence; for it is now three years
since we set out to sea.

UNDOUBTED PROGRESS

Since then we can point to many achievements at the material level.
There are better roads and a new highway, more elaborate drainage
and irrigation works, a modern airport and an expanded communications system, more schools and an improved sea defence network,
more hospitals and more health clinics, greater production, not only
of bauxite and sugar, but also of animal stock. Not only has our gross
national product increased, but also our income *per capita*. Many a
village which lived in darkness now boasts electricity. Our studies and
plans for the erection of a hydro-electric complex proceed. The

Arakaka-Kaituma area is fast moving towards becoming a bread-basket. We now mill our own flour at a cheaper price to the consumer than that of imported flour. A wood pulp industry will soon come into being and there have been promising finds of radio-active minerals. All these indicate undoubted progress and give reason for confidence in the future if we were left alone to develop our resources along with those who help – progress which even the jaundiced eye cannot miss, for it is there to see.

Let us, however, not believe that we are anywhere near creating Utopia in Guyana; though in comparison with other developing countries our national income *per capita* is high, it is miserably low as compared with that of the developed countries. Though unemployment has been reduced it still remains to plague us and no government, no people in Guyana can be satisfied when thousands of fellow citizens remain without work. While we may claim that our distribution of wealth, income and resources is the best in the Caribbean, if not in the entire developing world, let us remember that we still need more, much more, to distribute amongst our people.

GROWING SELF-RELIANCE

At the spiritual and psychological level, we also can identify un-doubted achievements – achievements of the spirit, the mind, the attitude, which are reflected in physical, material and economic movement forward. To many of the prophets of doom, to the lineal descendants of Jeremiah, the growing self-reliance of our people has come as a shock and surprise. There is not a community of any size or significance which has not got its self-help group or groups. There is not a community of any size or significance which cannot point to projects erected or laid out by the community itself with the assistance of government.

The largest primary school has been built by self-help at Leonora, and a secondary school to accommodate 500 students has been constructed at Mahaicony, and these are only two of the many. The provision of a sufficient number of school places to meet the needs of our nation is within sight and all thanks to self-help. Taking into account our size and our population it is not an idle boast to say that Guyana leads the world in self-help.

One may ask: how has this happened in a country in which less than five years ago, self-destruction seemed the object of so many sections of the community? The answer is simple. The destructive energies of our people have been transformed into constructive energies and these have been utilised for the common good and national progress. The government and the people have found new goals and together they are achieving them.

Cooperative bank

The achievements of the spirit find expression also in the cooperative sector. In the last year alone, there have been over 80 cooperative societies established, including two of small loggers. This proves that many of our little people, instead of mewling and puking in their mothers' arms, are prepared, with government's assistance, guidance and help, to build their own economic empire. Since our last anniversary, 25,000 acres of land have been allocated to cooperative societies, and by our next anniversary there will be a cooperative bank.

These activities contribute to national economic growth: they represent a husbanding of domestic savings which are being turned to productive uses. The time has come also for a complete reorganisation and expansion of the cooperative Division of the Ministry of Economic Development, and this will take place next month.

We have noted some of the things that we have done together, we have pinpointed a few of the achievements which, with the help of friends, have been ours. We have alluded to the new spirit, to the self-confidence which has seized and inspired the majority of our population, but let us not imagine that there are no dark sides to the picture.

BUILDING GUYANA

Though they are a minority, a small minority, there are still too many Guyanese who do not yet appreciate that the building of a country, a nation, is primarily the task of its own people. The free man is he who frees himself. The slave looks to others to free him and still remains a slave. A country like Guyana cannot afford the parasite, the lazy, the inefficient, the colonial who hopes that someone will till, and feed him. We look with envy and admiration at the economic power of nations like the United States of America and Russia, but this did not come by wishing, or seat-warming. These countries may vary in political ideology. We may agree or disagree with their economic structures or motivations. We do not aspire, like them, to reach the moon or to control other nations, but they all teach us one lesson; that is, that hard work, sacrifice and the imagination of a people are a pre-requisite of economic development.

There are still too many amongst us who would like to see overnight in Guyana the structures, the institutions, and the standards of luxury, which are to be found in North America and Europe, without realising how much hardship and sacrifice went into providing these. There are still too many of us who want to pattern our life on foreign standards, forgetting that the Americans, the British, the Germans, the French, the Canadians, the Russians and others have in each case evolved their own cultures and set their own economic and social goals. To what end will we build skyscrapers when thousands are unhoused and underhoused? How in the name of God can we cultivate wants and glorify them into needs when they are based upon the economies of affluent countries and are excited and encouraged by deliberate propaganda and salesmanship? Independence must be twinned with realism. We must look at our condition, take into account our special circumstances and, free from slavish imitation, fashion for ourselves a society whose goals reflect the genius and the needs of our people and the uniqueness of our State.

We are a developing country but we cannot, we must not, seek to create a replica of any of the developed countries. We have our problems, but the developed countries have theirs too. There is no perfect country which we can and should hope to copy. We are all seeking a better life and in that search Guyana, guided by realism and goodwill, has as good a chance as any.

UNITED FRONT

During the last three years our nation has been moving towards that identity of purpose, that consolidation of enterprise, so necessary if we are to present to the threats to our existence, the united front which alone can save us from certain disaster.

We are learning that we are a people; that though in the distant past our forbears came from many lands, with varied and varying cultures, we, who are born here, share a common heritage, and that today the ties that bind us are faster and more numerous than the differences which would keep us apart. Today in Guyana, it is heartening to note a new awareness of the value of our diversity and respect for, and acceptance of, the customs and cultures of the peoples who comprise our country – customs and cultures out of which we can create richer ones uniquely Guyanese.

But this very diversity and the fact that we operate in a society of freedom has its dangers too. There is the danger of the promotion of selfish sectional interest above the interest of the nation. There is the danger that criticism, so necessary to a free society, can degenerate into spiteful invective. There is the danger that some, impatient of the limitations imposed by our poor condition, will succumb to the blandishments and the false promises of those who would seek to recolonise and destroy us. Earlier this year we put down an uprising in the Rupununi, which was aided, which was encouraged and which was connived at by Venezuela. Let us remember the words of John Jay writing to the people of New York on the 7 November 1787, when we consider our situation and the baseless claim to more than two-thirds of our land:

> If they see that our national government is efficient and well administered, our trade prudently regulated, our militia properly organised and disciplined, our resources and finances discreetly managed, our credit re-established, our people free, contented and united, they will be much more disposed to cultivate our friendship than provoke our resentment. If on the other hand they find us either destitute of an effectual government ... or split ... and perhaps played off against each other ... what a poor, pitiful figure will (Guyana) make in their eyes! How liable would we become not only to their contempt but to their outrage, and how soon would dear-bought experience proclaim that when a people or family so divide, it never fails to be against themselves ... weakness and divisions at home would invite dangers from abroad and ... nothing would tend more to secure us from them than union, strength, and good government within ourselves.

GO TO THE LAND

Increasingly we are turning our attention to the development of our interior. Our existence upon the coastland is the result of a pattern imposed upon us by colonialism. Our entry into the interior is an expression of our freedom. Already at Matthews' Ridge and Kaituma we have laid the foundations for a development which in time will spread to include the whole of the North-West. Our motto now and in years to come must be: Forward! Go West, Go South, Go to the Land!

We cannot allow our rich hinterland to remain almost uninhabited and uncultivated. The sight of these rich lands lying unexploited tends to excite the avarice of some covetous souls and to encourage the vaulting ambitions of others. We must possess these lands. To this end government is formulating plans for the orderly development of the interior. The Interior Development Committee is expected to hand in its report by July and thereafter speedy action will be taken to set up the necessary machinery for the settlement and development of our vast inland areas. In this development every Guyanese (without exception) will have a fair and just share.

But even though Guyanese respond with enthusiasm to the call into the interior we have to consider whether we alone with our small population can achieve those goals which we have set ourselves. Are we sufficient in numbers to exploit fully all our riches? Can a relatively small population like ours effectively hold so great a heritage as ours? The time has come to treat as a matter of urgency the question of the size of our population and its relation to the potential of our country. The time has come to examine the need for a rapid increase in population and the sources from which that increase should come. The swift but ordered development of our country, both as regards manpower on the one hand, and agriculture and industry on the other, is a vital necessity if our country is to survive.

GUYANA ADVANCES

This is the last anniversary of our independence that we shall celebrate as one of Her Majesty's dominions. Our next anniversary will find Guyana a republic. That will mark a further consolidation of our independence, another break with the murky past, a further development of Guyana as a nation.

There are those who are afraid of freedom. They prefer the security of a comfortable subservience to the challenges of national independence. They were afraid of self-government, they were afraid of independence, they were afraid of a government run by the People's National Congress. They are afraid of a republic. They see disaster in any change and tremble at the contemplation of the future. But Guyana has sustained the changes from colony to nation, and has survived and prospered. Guyana has prospered with this government. Under this government Guyana will advance as a republic. The fears of the timid will once more be confounded; the hope of the bold and free will be realised.

May God bless us all. Long live Guyana!

20

'The Cooperative Republic.' Extracts from speech
to People's National Congress Regional Conference,
Georgetown, 24 August 1969

*From the beginning of his political career Forbes Burnham rejected
the free-wheeling enterprise of an advanced capitalist society as a
means to develop Guyana for the benefit of the masses. Although a
student of Marxism from his early days at university, he found himself unwilling to accept the pat answers and ready-made ideology of
the communist world anymore than he could accept the capitalist
creed. Burnham believed instead that the solution for his country's
ills had to be found and evolved at home.*

*In 1961, still in opposition, Burnham enunciated his view that
cooperative enterprise and organisation would be the instrument
through which his party would establish a socialist society in Guyana.
In Washington in 1966 immediately after Guyana attained independence in his first major speech in the American capital he described
his ideological position in terms of cooperative socialism. Now in
1969, his People's National Congress for the first time in sole control
of the government, he sets about translating his vision of a cooperative
socialist republic into reality.*

Last year I said, 'Radical changes have to be made to our fiscal and
economic systems. To carry out these compulsory tasks, the nation
needs a strong progressive government that has the necessary mandate from the people – the electorate. That government must be a
P.N.C. government.'

Now there is such a government. There is no coalition partner to impede or inhibit. Though we cannot achieve the impossible, we must realise that any failure is ours, any disappointment of expectations we encourage, will be blamed on us. To win is good but that is not the end. We must now prove ourselves worthy of our victory. We must transform Guyana.

The eventual fiscal and economic reforms adopted must not be a hotch-potch but, regardless of the source from which the various ingredients may be drawn, must reflect the philosophy, goals and ideology of the government and party and be explicable in terms of such. Between 1964 and 1968 we carried out the operation of salvaging and preserving our national assets, of restoring peace and confidence. Not only were the attendant activities time-consuming, but there was also the further factor of our being in harness until November 1968 with another political party whose philosophical, ideological and social objectives were not really coincident with our own. It is true that we did agree in strengthening the cooperative sector of the economy and establishing the national institution of self-help. But a significant part of the four-year period was spent settling differences and executing compromises in most fields.

CONSOLIDATING THE NATION

I would put as the party's first goal the building and consolidating of the nation of Guyana. This means many things. First it means bringing together the various ethnic groups and inspiring them with a devotion to, and indentification with, Guyana. It is at the same time important and difficult, important because our country's rate of economic progress can be affected unless all groups feel that they have a place, and a contribution to make; difficult because our history is one of several divisive forces being at work on and in our society. When to this you add a tendency for Guyanese to vote along racial lines, the problem seems to become even greater.

Nation-building also means the fullest and swiftest possible development of Guyana's resources and their exploitation for Guyana. Our material resources are vast, at least in potential. We have forests, rich agricultural lands for crops and cattle, large rivers that can yield a fortune in fish and drive the turbines of hydro-electric plants. Precious stones and valuable metals, which we and the world need, are in the bowels of our earth. Guyanese have to accept the challenges. We have some of the skills already, others we shall have to acquire.

Certain categories of expertise and facilities we shall have to negotiate and pay for from outside. But one thing we cannot afford is sit and fold our arms. All this cannot be done in five years. It is important that we do not promise ourselves, or our audience, miracles or under-estimate the difficulties. But a significant beginning has to be made.

EXPLOITING OUR RESOURCES

I posited earlier that Guyana's resources must be exploited for Guyana. That means in the first place that we Guyanese must get the maximum or real benefit from such exploitation. In cases when for one reason or another, we do not have internally the means to be immediately responsible for the development of a particular resource we shall have to rely upon external assistance, public or private. In the latter case particularly we shall have to make the particular project attractive. There is no room for quibbling over this; philanthropy is dead if it ever lived.

What has to be ensured is that Guyana share substantially in the profits and advantages and is not raped, exploited and given the jackal's pickings. There will be occasions when rather than sell our birthright we shall have to refuse offers of assistance.

Government as the trustee of the nation will have to fix priorities and decide what type of investments are preferable. For instance, we do not want or need amusement parks and Coney Islands. We want what is good for Guyana and what will contribute to real economic growth. Guyana's vital interests must rank first.

Further, we must not imagine that the entrepreneur, local or foreign, will accept our priorities. That means that there will have to be heavy investments in the public sector. This sector gets its means from public contributions by way of tax and purchase of government securities. In the final analysis this means a higher level of domestic saving and a reduction of expenditure on conspicuous consumption or on non-essential items and commodities.

All this will call for considerable national discipline. It has to be conscious and deliberate. Many a parent in the past has gone without non-essentials or even essentials to provide an education for a child. Even so we shall have to make the sacrifice in the interest of develop-ing Guyana. There will be cynics and saboteurs in the wings to tell you how much you will be missing but what realistic alternative do they offer?

SHARING THE PIE

We come now to the sharing of the pie. When a colonial territory is struggling for independence, most of the sections of the community are involved in the movement but each for different reasons. The worker sees it as a stage, not merely where he is a citizen of an independent country with the attendant psychological uplift but also where his wages and conditions of work are better, where he gets a greater share of what the economy can distribute and his human dignity is recognised and accepted. The businessman or entrepreneur may see it as an opportunity for replacing the expatriate as the exploiter. The civil servant may identify the new status with his getting the administrative plums formerly reserved for the representatives of the colonial power. The politician divorced from the masses may equate independence with his occupying Government House and all the social kudos and authority that go with it. The middle and professional class may anticipate being the new élite replete with privileges but devoid of responsibilities to the society.

How does the P.N.C. see it? The worker, the proletariat, the little man must get that share of what is there for distribution, commensurate with his numbers, contribution and political significance. This economic strategy will automatically be reflected in the social organisation of the nation – a nation of equality, social justice and social democracy. In the Guyana which we must build there will be no place for privilege, discrimination or exploitation though there will be reward for service.

Because of the European influence on countries like ours, there is always the tendency to categorise our ideology and concepts of economic and political organisation in terms of European categories and tags like capitalism, socialism, Marxism, communism. For ease of reference and description, we ourselves use these terms. For us, however, they can only be broadly descriptive and more in relation to goals than means.

P.N.C.'s IDEOLOGY

Our ideology, our economic and political goal can be described as socialist because of what we seek to establish. Since, however, we have a different social and economic structure, qualitatively from that obtaining in European countries, we cannot and must not put ourselves into the strait jackets of their dogmas and tactics. We will, as a result, be suspect by both sides, who would like to continue a form of intellectual, if not also economic, colonialism, but that suspicion is the price we must pay if we are to fashion our own destinies and work out our own solutions. It is easy to shout, for international consumption, that we are capitalist, Marxist, socialist or communist and attract international notice. But of what concrete value are international plaudits to us?

In moving towards our goal of exploiting our resources and giving the masses economic power, we shall have to fashion new institutions, re-fashion old ones and put new content into others which already exist. The cooperative is one of the latter. It has to be expanded and adapted and given a new purpose. Investment by coops need not and must not be limited to agriculture and consumer goods but should extend into industry of all types. From the right and left there will be criticisms and caveats which are in fact rationalised prejudices. But we must know where we are going and see to it that we use our own vehicle to get there. Your government is committed irrevocably to widening and strengthening the cooperative sector.

You are already aware that republic day will be declared on the 207th anniversary of the Berbice Slave Revolt. This revolt, as you know, was led by Cuffy on the 23 of February 1763. In celebrating our becoming a republic we will at the same time be celebrating the revolt which Cuffy led and we shall be associating this final step to freedom with that first step taken by Cuffy who led the first significant slave revolt in this hemisphere. In becoming a republic, I consider it absolutely necessary that this change be identified with a Guyanese national hero and for the reasons I have outlined Cuffy shall be that hero.

In becoming a republic, we remove the psychological ties with the British Monarch, which in many cases have inhibited the thinking and coloured the attitudes of several Guyanese. Though in point of fact, the Governor-General is appointed by the Prime Minister, in theory he draws his appointment, position of dignity etc. from Her Gracious Majesty the Queen, Elizabeth II of Guyana. When the President of the Republic of Guyana is elected by secret ballot in the National Assembly, there can be no doubt, either in theory or in practice, that every power, every dignity, every right with which the President is clothed comes directly from the elected representatives of the people.

In becoming a republic there must also be a change in the content, a change in strategy and a change in the outlook of the State. This is one of the reasons, though by no means the only reason, which led to our decision, ratified at our last Annual Congress, to have the Republic of Guyana a 'Cooperative Republic'.

What do we mean by socialism in the context of Guyana? We mean, as we have said many times before, a re-arrangement of our economic and social relations: a re-arrangement, which will give the worker, the little man, that substantial and preponderant control of the economic structure which he now holds in the political structure.

At present, it is the common man who decides which party should govern politically, but if we look around Guyana today we are struck by the fact that, though we hold political power, we do not really hold the substance of economic power. It is true that wages and salaries have increased and conditions of work have improved. But when all that is said and done, the fact remains that the crux, the substance of economic power, is not in your hands, not in the hands of the small man.

The government has already begun to introduce 'workers participation' in the economic life of the nation, but this is at best only a step in the right direction. 'Workers participation' and 'profit sharing' serve to soften the rougher aspects of the system, but they do not change the system. It is similar to having a toothache and treating it with creosote or some other form of anaesthetic – which removes the pain for a time but does not alter the fact that you still have a rotten tooth in your mouth. What we want is to remove the rotten tooth and replace it with a good one. 'Worker participation' and 'profit sharing' are anaesthetics to ease temporarily the problem but the solution to the problem, the provision of the good tooth, will be achieved through the instrument of the cooperative.

You have been told by party leaders that the cooperative is the means through which the SMALL MAN CAN BECOME A REAL MAN, the means through which the small man can participate fully in the economic life of the nation and the means through which the small man can play a predominant part in the workings of the economy. This is not a new idea being put forward now by your party. Many of you will remember our campaign as far back as 1961 when we said that the cooperative was the instrument through which we would establish socialism in Guyana. But it was not until 1964 that we were able to participate in government.

From 1964 to 1968 our participation in government, with the mill-stone of the United Force around our necks, was very much a question of survival. That period, for us, was a holding period; we held to prevent things from getting worse while laying the foundations for improvement and movement forward later. The time has now come for us to make that move forward.

In passing, it is noteworthy that since 1961, when we first expressed our philosophy of cooperative socialism, the United Nations Economic and Social Council on 12 June 1969 passed a motion recommending the cooperative as an instrument for the achievement of a 'just society' in the developing countries of the world. The People's National Congress, as so often has been the case, was once again demonstrating greater foresight than others in this country.

Of course, the cooperative movement has made great strides in many parts of the world; in the United Kingdom, United States, in Canada, in Russia, and in other parts of Europe, both east and west. I want you therefore to understand the basic differences between the cooperative society we propose and the cooperative movements which you find in those countries – whether they be in the east or in the west.

In the west, under a capitalist economic system, cooperatives own chain stores, oil fields, housing projects and millions of dollars worth of property, and yet, and this is the important point, the cooperative movement in those countries is only an appendage to the economic system. The economy is still owned and controlled by small powerful groups and the decisions are still made by these groups; decisions which may at times benefit the nation generally, but which are primarily intended to benefit those few who own and control the nation's wealth.

In eastern Europe, cooperative movements are also to be found, but again their activities are only peripheral to the basic economic system. The basic system places economic power and control in the hands of those who run the communist party and they are the government. The decisions which those few leaders make are made by them because, according to them, they know best and not as the result of consultation with the people.

In Guyana, it is not necessary for us to waste our time criticising one system or another practised elsewhere in the world, whether it is in the east or the west. Rather we must spend our time doing what is best in the peculiar circumstances of Guyana. It is not our intention that, as in other countries, the cooperative movement should remain a mere appendage to the economic life of the nation. Nor is it our intention, as in the past in this country, to regard the cooperative movement as a social welfare exercise. Our basic proposition is this: the organisation of our human and material resources through the cooperative movement, with government providing financial assistance, management, training and administrative direction.

The small man will, through the cooperative, be able to own large and substantial business enterprises and make decisions which will materially effect the direction which the economy takes and where the country goes. In the Cooperative Republic we will be no longer 'drawers of water and hewers of wood'.

Comrades, even now, the cooperative movement in Guyana is not any longer a social welfare exercise. It has gone into building, into manufacture, into logging and we expect shortly into mining, but we still have a long way to go.

There is no doubt that even though cooperative capital holdings have increased by 150 per cent since we came into office in 1964, they are still those among us, even staunch party members, who are resistant to change and who will have to be educated and trained to understand the advantages to themselves, their groups and their country, of the cooperative society.

Comrades, I do not see any alternative. If there is to be economic upliftment of the small man in this country it can only come about through the cooperative.

I know that you still hear the story of the small man around the corner who started life as a messenger and ended up a millionaire, but let me remind you that for every individual success of this kind there are thousands of messengers who die messengers and thousands of others who retire in penury and poverty. There is only scope for the small man when our physical, our material, and our human resources, are brought together. The cooperative movement makes it possible for us to pool our resources.

The future is full of possibilities but the way ahead is not going to be easy and this we must understand. Up to now the cooperative movement has not been organised seriously to compete with private enterprise, but this is our aim for the future. We must be prepared to expect opposition and we must be prepared to overcome it in the interest of the small man and in the interest of Guyana.

For the cooperative movement to play successfully a major part in the economic life of the nation, cooperatives must be able to obtain adequate credit. Commercial banks are not a reliable source of credit for cooperatives and further they seldom prove to be a source of income for the country. Many of you, for instance, may believe that the foreign commercial banks are a source of foreign funds. Instead, these banks, rather than bring in money to the country, use local savings predominantly for local lendings. In order to provide an institution for saving and a source of credit for the cooperative movement in the future, we propose to establish a Cooperative Bank of Guyana. This institution will open its doors on the day that Guyana becomes a republic. In due course, the Cooperative Bank will become a national bank equipped to undertake commercial banking and then, as individuals, we will be able to bank there privately as well as through our cooperative groups.

The government is doing its part and you are expected in turn to do yours. For your part, it is necessary that you learn and understand the meaning and advantages of this change in our economic system. It is necessary that you get rid of the old attitudes of dependence on others and have faith in yourselves, in your government and in your country, and it is necessary that you grasp the value of coming together as a group, of pooling your physical, your material and human resources, so that *as small men we can become real men.*

Comrades, we cannot in Guyana hope to make heaven on earth but we can make sure that we get the dominant share of what Guyana has to offer us and of what we have to offer Guyana and we can do this through the instrument of the cooperative.

If, at this time in our history, we do not reap the benefits of what we have fought for so hard and so well in the past then I can only say with apologies to Shakespeare: 'The fault will be in ourselves and not in our stars that we are underlings.'

Part IV
A nation besieged

21

In 1962, the Venezuelan government, with Guyana moving towards independence, unilaterally declared an 1899 Boundary Award settling its boundaries with British Guiana null and void. She then raised a claim to all the territory of British Guiana west of the Essequibo River. The area claimed covers about two-thirds of Guyana's 83,000 square miles.

The British government refused to entertain the claim, and three months before Guyana's independence at a conference in Geneva, concluded an agreement enforcing Venezuela to pursue peaceful solutions to the controversy. On attaining independence, Guyana became an additional party to this agreement.

The agreement established a commission of Guyanese and Venezuelan representatives to meet regularly for the purpose of 'seeking satisfactory solutions for the practical settlement of the controversy ... which has arisen as a result of the Venezuelan contention that the Arbitral Award is null and void.'

In defiance of the agreement, however, and throughout the life of the commission, Venezuela had conducted a campaign of hostility and committed a series of aggressive acts towards Guyana causing the young nation to divert scarce resources from development to defence.

One of these acts was a decree issued in July, 1968, by President Leoni of Venezuela purporting to annex a nine-mile belt of sea running along the Guyana coast (of Essequibo) and extending to within three miles of it. The decree charged the Venezuelan armed forces with its execution. Prime Minister Burnham informs Parliament on the state of Guyana's relations with Venezuela.

The Prime Minister (Mr Burnham): Mr Speaker, hon. Members will have read press reports of a decree signed on Tuesday, 9 July 1968 by Dr Leoni, President of the Republic of Venezuela, purporting to annex as part of the territory of Venezuela, a nine-mile belt of sea extending to within three miles of the coast of the County of Essequibo. I have already elsewhere described this decree as a monstrosity in the sight of international law and indicated that in issuing it and the accompanying threats, the Venezuelan government was now openly embarking on a course of international piracy. I now desire at this the earliest opportunity to make a statement to the House on this most serious development in our relations with neighbouring Venezuela.

Hon. Members will recall the circumstances in which the Geneva Agreement of 17 February 1966 was signed. That agreement was duly laid before this House in Sessional Paper No. 1/1966 and was fully debated and approved by this House on 28 April 1966. Those circumstances, stated shortly, were as follows:

Our existing boundary with Venezuela was laid down pursuant to an award given on 3 October 1899, in Paris by an International Arbitral Tribunal whose judgment Venezuela had solemnly agreed by Treaty to regard as 'a full, perfect and final settlement' of the border issue.

Venezuela indeed accepted the boundary as so awarded and it was definitively laid down in the boundary maps agreed and signed by duly appointed representatives of the United Kingdom and Venezuela. However, as Guyana's independence approached, Venezuela began to contend that the Arbitral Award was a nullity because of alleged fraud and pressure.

The United Kingdom, which then had responsibility for British Guiana's external relations, firmly rejected the contention and asserted that the matter had been finally settled by the award. Nevertheless, in order to remove any Venezuelan doubts as to the circumstances in which the award was made, the British government, with the concurrence of the then government of British Guiana, offered to allow the relevant documentary material to be examined by experts from the United Kingdom, British Guiana and Venezuela. Mr C. T. Crowe, the United Kingdom representative who made this offer in the United Nations Special Political Committee on 12 November 1962, was, however, careful to say:

In making this offer, I must make it very clear that it is in no sense an offer to engage in substantive talks about revision of the frontier. That we cannot do; for we consider that there is no justification for it. . . .

Venezuela accepted this offer, and the documents were thereafter examined by experts from each of the three countries.

In the view of the governments of the United Kingdom and of British Guiana the work of the experts disclosed that there was not a scintilla of evidence to support the Venezuelan contention. The Venezuelan agitation nevertheless continued, and grew fiercer as Guyana's independence drew nearer.

The contention, however, remained the same – that the Arbitral Award of over 60 years' standing was invalid. Eventually, almost on the eve of Guyana's independence, the governments of the United Kingdom and Venezuela, with the concurrence of the government of British Guiana, concluded the Geneva Agreement.

Article 1 of the Agreement reads:

A Mixed Commission shall be established with the task of seeking satisfactory solutions for the practical settlement of the controversy between Venezuela and the United Kingdom which has arisen as the result of the Venezuela contention that the Arbitral Award of 1899 about the frontier between British Guiana and Venezuela is null and void.

The language of this provision does not admit of ambiguity. It must be clear to anyone reading it with detachment, and not bent on misrepresenting its meaning, that the issue which the mixed commission was established to settle was whether, as the Venezuelans contended, the Arbitral Award was a nullity.

Guyana has at all times been willing to examine this matter in depth with a view to securing a practical settlement of the controversy. Venezuela, however, has persistently refused to enter into a discussion of this fundamental question – perhaps not without good reason, from a Venezuelan point of view, having regard to the earlier work of the experts.

She contends instead, in defiance of Article 1 of the Geneva Agreement, and in the teeth of the history of the Agreement, that the task of the mixed commission was forthwith to re-arrange the frontier between the two countries on the assumption that the Venezuelan contention of nullity was well-founded.

Venezuela has therefore refused to come to grips with the real task of the mixed commission; but has instead chosen to accuse Guyana of obstructionism and intransigence simply because we have quite rightly refused to discard the arbitral judgment by which the boundary is now determined unless Venezuela first demonstrates to our satisfaction its supposed nullity.

These allegations of obstructionism and intransigence grew more strident when Guyana declined to agree to a Venezuelan proposal which would concede to Venezuela joint control over development projects in the Essequibo region of Guyana. This proposal was advanced in a sub-commission of the mixed commission set up with the simple directive 'to study possible areas of cooperation between Venezuela and Guyana'.

Guyana's proposals for such cooperation, which avoided any impairment of sovereignty and were conceived on terms of normal developmental assistance between countries, were rejected out of hand. Instead, in a display of bad temper, and in breach of their express agreement, the Venezuelans unilaterally withdrew from the sub-commission just over a week ago and announced that they regarded it as ceasing to exist.

This Venezuelan withdrawal from the sub-commission was yet another in a long list of violations of the Geneva Agreement by Venezuela prior to the recent decree. The most flagrant of these was the illegal occupation of the Guyana half of Ankoko Island by Venezuela military personnel in 1966 in clear defiance of the agreed and established boundary map and of the Geneva Agreement itself.

In addition, contrary to Article 5(2) of the Geneva Agreement, which prohibits both parties from making territorial claims outside of the mixed commission, Venezuela has on several occasions made territorial reservations in relation to Guyana's participation in various international meetings. One of the most serious instances of this was the major effort undertaken by Venezuela to prevent Guyana from becoming a signatory to the Latin America Denuclearisation Treaty.

More recently, but less successfully, Venezuela attempted at the Vienna Conference on Treaties in April of this year to dilute the provisions of the International Law Commission's draft Convention dealing with the sanctity of treaties. This attempt was obviously made in furtherance of her territorial ambitions. Nor have these violations always been overt. In 1966 Venezuelan diplomatic personnel in Guyana were engaged in a clandestine attempt to interfere in the internal affairs of Guyana through the subversion of members of Guyana's Amerindian community. As a result, it will be recalled, Guyana expelled a second secretary of the Venezuelan Embassy in Georgetown, Snr Talyhardat.

Within the last two months, in a concerted campaign of economic aggression against Guyana, Venezuela has sought to deter investment in Guyana by falsely asserting, first by statements of the Venezuelan Foreign Minister and later by a paid advertisement in the London *Times*, that the Geneva Agreement precludes Guyana from granting concessions of development in the Essequibo region of Guyana.

Indeed, the Venezuelan government has gone further and actually threatened sanctions against companies doing business in Venezuela and who have been granted concessions in Essequibo by the Guyana government.

Finally, only a week ago Venezuela violated the secrecy of the work of the mixed commission when, contrary to the rules of procedure of the mixed commission and to an oral undertaking given to the Guyana commissioners, the Venezuelan commissioners released a statement to the Press in Caracas relating to the Venezuelan withdrawal from the sub-commission.

Now there comes the preposterous decree signed on the ninth instant by the President of Venezuela. The decree is, we contend, a nullity and will be exposed for the unprecedented absurdity that it is. Whatever positions individual countries may take in relation to the breadth of territorial seas, it is palpably clear that only one State may possess sovereignty over the territorial sea relating to the same coast.

If this needed demonstration it is shown by Article 1 of the 1958 Geneva Convention on the Territorial Sea and the Contiguous Zone, which provides that 'The sovereignty of a State extends, beyond its land territory and its internal waters, to a belt of sea adjacent to its coast, described as the territorial sea.' Venezuela signed that convention on 30 October 1958 and ratified it on 15 August 1961, without any reservations relating to that article. The convention itself came into force on 10 September 1964.

Unless and until a decision in favour of Venezuela is forthcoming under the procedure of the Geneva Agreement, Guyana's sovereignty over the generally recognised continental shelf and territorial seas cannot be disturbed. Indeed, Venezuela has at all material times heretofore recognised Guyana's sovereignty over the territorial waters in relation to the coastline in question, and she cannot therefore claim sovereignty over territorial waters relating to the same coastline.

In fact, by the same convention all signatories to it specifically accept that where States are adjacent to each other the territorial sea of each cannot extend laterally beyond a line projecting seawards from the common land boundary. There are differences of opinion as to how the line should be defined but there is no dispute as to the general principle involved that two States may not both have sovereignty at the same time over the territorial sea (whatever the limit) relating to the same coast. The reason for this is apparent when it is recognised that the doctrine relating to the territorial sea finds its origin in the requirements of security of the coastal State, in the furthering of its commercial, fiscal and political interests and the right of its people to the exclusive exploitation and enjoyment of the products of the sea within its territorial waters.

There is yet another fundamental question which the Venezuelan decree entirely ignores or callously disregards. It is indisputable that Guyana's territory extends seawards to cover the entire continental shelf and Guyana has consistently exercised sovereignty over it. Since the ownership of the territorial sea includes ownership of the sea-bed, the Venezuelan decree purports to relate to part of the continental shelf which is within the dominion of Guyana. Insofar, therefore, as the Venezuelan decree was based, as it is expressed to be based, on the assumption that Guyana's sovereignty extends only three miles seawards, the decree was founded on a false premise.

If further evidence be needed of the degree to which the Venezuelan decree outrages the established tenets of international law and practice it is to be found in the terms of the Geneva Convention on the Territorial Sea and the Contiguous Zone which, as I have said, Venezuela has both signed and ratified. Under Article 24(1) of the Convention Guyana has specified rights relating to police, customs, sanitation and other matters in the contiguous zone, i.e. the belt of sea within 12 miles from the coast, and the existence of these rights excludes the competence of Venezuela or any other State to extend her sovereignty or jurisdiction over any part of that belt of waters.

The Venezuelan decree is an unmistakable attempt to assert a claim to the Essequibo region of Guyana outside of the mixed commission and is therefore yet another calculated breach of Article 5 (2) of the Geneva Agreement which expressly provides that no claim whatsoever shall 'be asserted otherwise than in the Mixed Commission while that Commission is in being'.

It is serious enough on this account as one of a number of similar breaches, but what gives cause for particular concern about Venezuela's maturity and sense of responsibility as a member of international society is her threat, for such it is, to use armed force in support of the purported decree, since it must be obvious that any interference with Guyana's shipping, fishing or other rights would be an act of aggression violating the Charter of the United Nations and disturbing the peace of the hemisphere.

The conclusion is inescapable that Venezuela is prepared to renounce or ignore any international agreement, whether bilateral or multilateral, and to defy the Charter of the United Nations at any time that it suits her whims or seems to promote some particular interest that she may for the moment be pursuing. In the present circumstances I have asked our ambassador in Caracas to return to Georgetown for immediate consultations.

Yesterday, at the request of our permanent representation in New York the United Nations Secretary-General circulated to all Member States of the United Nations a report of the Venezuelan decree together with the statement I issued on learning of it. In like manner I am arranging for this present statement to be communicated to Member States as well as to be specifically circulated to Commonwealth governments through the Commonwealth Secretary in London.

I have conveyed directly this morning to the British High Commissioner in Georgetown, whose government is a party to the controversy with Venezuela and a signatory of the Geneva Agreement, the serious view which my government takes of this recent development and the responsibilities which in our view devolve on the British government as a result.

I have also held discussions with the accredited representatives of other friendly governments in Georgetown who are members of the United Nations *viz*. Canada, the Republic of India, Trinidad and Tobago and the United States of America, informing them of the development and inviting their support for Guyana in the face of the Venezuelan acts of aggression.

We are taking every step available to us to protect our interests and secure our territorial integrity. I also held lengthy discussions this morning with the acting leader of the opposition in the latter's unavoidable absence from Georgetown. This is a matter which transcends domestic political differences.

I cannot tell with any certainty where this ill-advised course of action on which the government of Venezuela has embarked will lead us. We must be prepared, however, for further and even more aggressive demonstrations of international lawlessness from the government of Venezuela. We will need all our courage and strength to withstand these efforts to break our will and despoil our land.

Venezuela has now made clear her intention to seek relentlessly to re-impose the yoke of colonialism on a young and small nation that has only recently succeeded in freeing itself from the tutelage of another imperial power. We have no quarrel with the Venezuelan people but we shall not lack courage or resolve in resisting aggressive demands of a Venezuelan government that is prepared to defile the traditions of Bolivar and to flout the precepts of hemispheric and world order and security.

In our stand for survival we shall call upon the conscience of all peace-loving people to speak out in our cause and we shall need all our unity as a people so that our voice may be heard in all corners of the world and in all the councils of the world's institutions for peace.

By agreement with the acting leader of the opposition I propose, sir, with your consent during next week, to be precise, Wednesday morning, to offer this House an opportunity to discuss and debate fully the subject of Venezuela's latest moves of aggression against Guyana.

Note: Further information on the subject of Venezuela's claim to the territory of Guyana may be obtained by writing to the Ministry of External Affairs, Guyana House Annexe, Carmichael Street, Georgetown, Guyana.

22

Radio broadcast to the nation on disturbances in
the Rupununi savannahs, 4 January 1969

*Immediately following the December 1968 general election, when
Mr Burnham's People's National Congress was returned to power
with 55·81 per cent of the popular vote, Prime Minister Burnham
is faced with a secessionist insurrection of rancher barons in the remote
cattle-rearing Rupununi savannahs. The revolt proved to be organised,
armed and financed by the Venezuelan government. The insurrection
took place after the Venezuelan Presidential Election at which Leoni's
Accion Democratica was defeated, but before Copei's President
Caldera took office.*

The picture of the recent disorders in the northern Rupununi
savannahs has now become sufficiently clear for me to place before
the public the facts of these tragic and sinister events as they have
so far unfolded.

On Thursday, 2 January 1969, at about eleven o'clock in the
morning, the township of Lethem – which is the principal centre of
government administration in the Rupununi district – came under
heavy gun-fire attack. The main target of the attack was the police
station which was manned by twelve members of the Guyana Police
Force and a number of civilian employees and which had radio communication with police headquarters in Georgetown. The station went
off the air immediately after the attack began and before any messages
about it could get through to Georgetown.

It is now known that the attack was made by a band of heavily
armed ranchers of the Rupununi district drawn mainly, but not

exclusively, from the Hart and Melville families. The Hart ranch is at Pirara, 15 miles from Lethem, and was the control centre of the operation. It was from Pirara that the terrorists had set out earlier in the morning for Lethem. On arriving at Lethem they opened shell-fire on the police station with bazooka and with bursts from automatic weapons. Policemen rushing out of the building were fired at and at least one was killed in this way. The attackers then entered the station and in the struggle that ensued shot and killed three other policemen and one civilian employee, Victor Hernandez, an Amerindian, who was at the time a member of the board of governors of the School of Agriculture. The senior police officer at Lethem who was at the district commissioner's office at the time of the attack was shot and killed there.

Nor were the security forces the only object of attack. The government dispenser who came down to the police station when the firing began was shot at and wounded as he sought to take cover behind his car. The terrorists then rounded up the residents – including the district commissioner and his wife – and held them prisoners and hostages in the abattoir. Other persons were locked into their homes. At least $10,000 (Guyana) of government funds were taken.

One of the early acts of the terrorists immediately after their attack on the police station was to block the air strip at Lethem with seven-ton trucks and other forms of obstruction, thus completely isolating Lethem except by a ground approach from some other points in the area. To make this isolation more effective the terrorists simultaneously with the move on Lethem blocked other airstrips in the area at Good Hope, Karasabai, Karanambo and Annai. This left open only the grass strip at Manari, five miles from Lethem, and it seems that the intention of the terrorists was to use this strip themselves with light aircraft. In fact, certain missionary priests who were at Lethem when the attack occurred were allowed to leave by road for Manari later on Thursday.

Contrary, however, to the expectation of the terrorists, news of the attack at Lethem had reached Georgetown by lunch-time on Thursday and the same afternoon a number of policemen and Guyana Defence Force personnel were flown into Manari by two Guyana Airways aircraft. Both planes were fired at on the approach to the Manari strip, but neither was hit.

Within the next eighteen hours a fully equipped and supplied contingent of the security forces was assembled at Manari and yesterday morning (Friday) they began to move on to Lethem. With the security forces advancing, the terrorists fled Lethem, probably for Pirara. On arrival at Lethem, therefore, our armed forces were able to re-assert lawful authority without any resistance. Their arrival confirmed the casualties earlier reported, and the wounded persons were immediately flown to Georgetown. The district commissioner is now engaged on assessing the damage, both of a public and private nature, and the security forces have been assisting in the return to normalcy.

Meanwhile, the terrorist groups that had crossed the airstrips at Good Hope and Annai on the morning of Thursday 2 January had also overrun the small police contingents there and closed radio communications between these outposts and police headquarters, Georgetown. So far, as we know, there was no loss of life at either Good Hope or Annai, but at both places the policemen were tied up, placed in trucks and driven off towards Lethem. By then, of course, Lethem was under the control of the security forces, and on discovering this on their return journey the terrorists abandoned the bound policemen and fled.

Today, the security forces have continued their operations to restore all points in the area to normal governmental control and to pursue and capture the criminal elements that are already responsible for the loss of nine lives. The police posts at Annai and Good Hope have been relieved and the centres of terrorist activity at Pirara, Good Hope and Sunnyside have been razed to the ground by our forces.

A number of persons have been arrested in the area and this afternoon word was received from the police authorities at Boa Vista[1] that seven of the terrorists had been taken into custody there in their flight from Guyana. Steps are being taken to bring these fugitives to face trial under the criminal law of the land they have defiled and betrayed.

On the basis of what I have already said the acts of insurrection and murder that I have narrated are of the most serious nature; but they are, in fact, even more serious and sinister than would appear on the surface. One of the terrorists who surrendered to the security forces yesterday has given an account of the entire operation – an account which places it in a very different category from that of mere criminal terrorism. From this account, it is now known that there was a

1. A small town on Brazilian side of border.

gathering of Rupununi ranchers on 23 December at the home of Harry Hart at Moreru in the northern savannahs. At this meeting a plan was unfolded for capturing the main government outposts in the Rupununi with assistance from the Venezuelan authorities and declaring the establishment of a separatist State in cessation from the rest of Guyana.

On 24 December a group of ranchers and ranch-hands numbering approximately forty were flown from the Hart ranch at Pirara to Santa Theresa in Venezuela where the party spent the night. On Christmas day, 25 December the group were driven to an airstrip at Santa Helena and air-lifted in a Venezuelan army aircraft to a Venezuelan army training camp at a point approximately two hours flying time away. They spent seven days receiving intensive training in the use of weapons with which they were supplied, including automatic weapons and bazookas. On New Year's day, 1 January 1969, the group was flown back to Santa Helena, again by Venezuelan army aircraft. The following morning, at dawn, they were flown to the Hart ranch at Pirara in a DC-3 Venezuelan aircraft. Upon arrival at Pirara they set out immediately for Lethem and the acts of terrorism and murder I have already related.

The insurrection as we know was planned, organised and carried out by the ranchers of the Rupununi – the savannah aristocrats. Such Amerindian citizens as were involved were employed in a secondary capacity and appeared generally to have acted under duress and in response to the orders of their rancher employers. Nevertheless, within a few hours of the attack on Lethem, the Venezuelan press and radio were reporting an Amerindian uprising in the Rupununi and suggesting that it arose out of the wish of these Guyanese citizens to come under the sovereignty of Venezuela.

In addition, Valarie Hart, the wife of one of the Hart brothers, and a candidate of the United Force, at the recent election, was taken to Venezuela by the aircraft that brought the armed gang. In Venezuela, Valarie Hart has been provided with facilities for broadcasting appeals for assistance in support of what she describes as an uprising of the indigenous population. These appeals are beamed to the United States but call for assistance from all possible sources.

The pattern of this Venezuelan involvement is easy to discern. Going right back to the Talyhardat incident[2] the Venezuelan authori-

2. A junior diplomat of the Venezuelan Embassy expelled from Guyana in 1967 for subversive activities.

ties have sought to manipulate the Guyanese Amerindian community to promote their spurious claim to the Essequibo region of Guyana. This was followed more recently by the abortive attempt to establish and finance a Guyana Amerindian party and in a variety of ways to promote an Amerindian movement favourable to Venezuela's territorial and imperialist ambitions.

At the twenty-third session of the General Assembly in New York last October, Guyana warned of the massive effort being made by Venezuela 'to subvert the loyalty of Guyana's indigenous Amerindian people'. We pointed out that it was an effort that had no lack of financial resources and which functions through hand-picked and trained agents working under the direction of the Venezuelan authorities from bases situated on the Venezuelan side of the border.

Into the campaign of subversion the Venezuelan authorities have now recruited this group of Rupununi ranchers who have traditionally resented the authority of the central government, more especially since independence when that authority passed from British to Guyanese hands. The results of the recent general election, which have confirmed the process of decolonialisation, was apparently the signal for insurrection among these people who have induced in themselves a conviction that the grass lands of the Rupununi savannahs are theirs and theirs alone to the exclusion of all others, including the Amerindian people, and especially to the exclusion of the authority of the government of Guyana. Not surprisingly, they have found common cause with the government of Venezuela who have once more – and again with a traditional clumsiness and indifference to Guyanese opinion – embarked on overt interference in Guyana's internal affairs with the object of advancing their territorial claims.

It is perhaps not without significance that at the same moment that Venezuelan representatives were sitting down with their Guyanese counterparts at a meeting of the mixed commission in Caracas between Christmas and New Year, Venezuelan army personnel were training and equipping saboteurs and terrorists and launching them on a campaign of insurrection in Guyana. Nor is it perhaps without significance that they chose for the scene of this campaign a part of Guyana which has a frontier not with Venezuela but with the friendly State of Brazil.

I do not know where these events will lead us or what other excesses of armed interference Venezuela may be poised to embark upon. This may well be the beginning of a series of similar incursions launched by the Venezuelan government and we must, therefore, expect further acts of aggression and intimidation from the new imperialism on our western doorstep. We must be ready as a nation to meet all eventualities and we must prepare ourselves for further attacks upon our national integrity from the combined forces of Venezuelan military authorities and disloyal and subversive elements in Guyana.

As you know, I was due to leave Guyana for London today to attend the meeting of Commonwealth Prime Ministers in London. It has not been easy for me to decide whether I shall proceed to London and as you know I have already deferred my departure. With the situation in the northern savannahs returning to normalcy, however, I have come to the conclusion that I should now proceed to London to attend this specially important Conference of Prime Ministers of the Commonwealth. Dr Reid, who will be acting as Prime Minister during my absence, will keep you fully informed of all developments.

Note: The Interior Minister for Venezuela, Reinaldo Leandro Mora, while denying the Venezuelan government's participation in the uprising, admitted that Guyanese youth had received military training in Venezuela but claimed that this was at the wish of their parents.

Reuter report, Caracas 9 January 1969.

23

Extracts from speech to People's National Congress Regional Conference on Surinam relations, 24 August 1969

Threatened with territorial seizure by sabre-rattling Venezuela on its western boundary, the government of Prime Minister Burnham also finds itself faced with the necessity to repel armed infiltration by Surinam into Guyana's south-eastern territory.

Surinam is an integral part of the Kingdom of the Netherlands and the government of the kingdom, resident in The Hague, is responsible for its external affairs.

Since Guyana's independence, the Surinam government has twice attempted to occupy areas within Guyana and on the last occasion this led to a confrontation between the Guyana Defence Force and armed Surinam personnel. Prime Minister Burnham chooses the occasion of his party's Regional Conference to re-state his government's position.

It is necessary today that I indicate to you the seriousness of the situation which our country faces and I want therefore to allude to what took place on Tuesday last in the New River Triangle.

First, let me recall for you the Venezuelan take-over and occupation of the eastern half of the island of Ankoko in the Cuyuni River. This was in October 1966 five months after our achievement of independence. The Venezuelans have been there ever since. You are also fully aware of the claim which Venezuela is making to approximately two-thirds of our territory.

Surinam also has been making claims to a substantial part of our territory in an area called the New River Triangle. This is an area of land between the Kutari and the New River, which is shaped roughly like a triangle and embraces about six to seven thousand square miles of land.

In 1967, a number of Surinamers were discovered in a camp at Oronoque, which is at the junction of the New River and Oronoque River. We removed them from the camp. The Surinamers, intent on re-occupying our territory – the Oronoque region being now guarded first by the police force and later by our army – moved further north to build another camp. On Tuesday last we had to take over this new camp. What we discovered there was most significant and yet it is interesting to see how calmly our people have taken it.

However, on this the first occasion on which I have had the opportunity to meet party members as groups since the New River situation developed, I want to emphasise how serious it was and perhaps still is. We discovered that this camp was not a mere camp for surveyors, or construction workers on an airstrip in the jungle. It was, in fact, a well-constructed military camp built with underground dug-outs and overhead look-outs. We captured a well-armed and imaginatively constructed camp; and let us not now believe that this will be the last attempt by the Surinamers to occupy our territory by force.

A captured map brought back from the camp on Thursday revealed that the Surinamers proposed to set up other camps and settlements throughout our territory. Their intention was to be able to say that they had been in physical occupation of the New River Triangle, if and when talks are held to discuss their claims.

The seriousness of the Surinam claim and the earnestness with which they have been pursuing it is all the more reason for concern, when we take into account the bellicose and hostile attitude of the Venezuelans to the west. It is not without significance that the Venezuelan President and Foreign Minister have been, to use a Guyanese expression, 'taking up the fire rage of Surinam', by making all sorts of abusive and ill-founded statements against the government and people of Guyana.

Those of us who have lived in Guyana for many years find it difficult to contemplate the idea of incursions across our borders. For us, border wars and border clashes are things that occur in the Middle East, Asia and Africa, but never in Guyana. This is the time in our history when we must seriously understand the problems which face our young nation. In the case of these border incursions, the problem has arisen essentially because we are now independent. When a world power like Britain was responsible for our defence and security, the Venezuelans and the Dutch, through Surinam, were prepared to behave correctly and to refrain from the use of force. Now they assume that because we are on our own – a young nation, a small nation, a poor nation trying to make its way in the world – it is easier to seize our territory by force.

Guyana is small and is relatively poor, but comrades we must not assume that because of this we cannot put up a fight and even win that fight. Guns are of some importance, but what matters most is the man behind the gun; and the man behind the gun is as good as the ideal he is fighting for.

On Monday 26 May this year, when we celebrated the third anniversary of our independence, we issued a call to the people to move into the interior in large numbers and with government's assistance. This call was made for two reasons. First, to assist in the reduction of unemployment and to expand our production in agriculture and forestry, and secondly, to provide settlements where trained persons can inhabit our interior and protect our borders.

Personally, I have been heartened by the response to this call from the young people of Guyana. In fact, the enthusiasm of the people has been so great that our promise still runs ahead of our performance, and in some cases anxious groups of young men and women have had to wait for three or four weeks before we have been able to settle them in an appropriate part of the interior.

I should point out at this stage that these young pioneers are not being merely sent by the government into undeveloped areas, but are being carefully set up with help, advice and instructions in the establishment of properly organised agricultural settlements. The markets for the products grown on these settlements are guaranteed by government through the Guyana Marketing Corporation. I want to make it clear that we are not sending people into the interior to have a holiday; we are sending people to make a living and to provide an important line of defence against any attack on our borders.

Let us have no illusions, comrades. In this world, you get as much help as you prove you are entitled to. We must not believe that by sitting down and counting on the friendship of larger, rich, well-armed nations that we will save Guyana for ourselves and our children. Help and assistance comes only to those who qualify for it. In any case we are our best and most dependable allies.

Part V
In regard to foreign aid

24

Speech to Aid Donors Conference, Chamber of
Parliament, Georgetown, 15 September 1969

*Guyana is a recipient of foreign aid from a number of countries and
international institutions.*

*On becoming Prime Minister, Forbes Burnham soon discovered
that foreign aid programmes were often duplicated and even at cross
purposes. He offers a unique proposal – an aided donors' conference be
held each year in order to avoid this duplication and encourage a
mutual understanding of Guyana's problems amongst the aid donors.*

*The Prime Minister's speech to the third of these conferences
raises many of the important questions of concern to all developing
nations in regard to foreign aid programmes. In particular, the Prime
Minister refers to the problems of 'tied' aid, harsh interest repayment
terms amounting to sums in excess of the aid received and the tendency of some aid donors to favour publicisable projects.*

Fellow Ministers, Your Excellencies, ladies and gentlemen, good
morning. This is the Third Aid Donors' Conference that is being
held in Guyana since 1967, and may I, as usual, express the government of Guyana's welcome to those of you who represent various
governments and international agencies.

Too frequently, countries like Guyana suffer from the disadvantage
of being the recipients of compliments, sometimes sincere, sometimes insincere, and we do not really get an opportunity to recognise
where we might have fallen down and where we can do better.

If I may observe. . . . There seems to be, from our point of view,
three factors which affect the fact and quantum of aid, at least from

the nations or countries here represented. One such factor is, of course, the particular nation's resources and its global commitments. That we cannot question because each nation is deemed to be the best judge of what its resources are and how those resources should be committed, domestically or internationally.

Another factor which appears to us is the national interest and priorities of the given nation. That factor, again, is not for debate or discussion so far as we are concerned. We may have our own private ideas as to what should be your international interests or priorities, but since we do not believe in interference in the domestic affairs of our friends, we do not voice our different ideas.

But the third factor which is of great importance to us is reflected in a tendency amongst national aid donors to know what is good for the recipient country. On that we can break a lance or join an issue.

There *may* be rare cases where there is a lack of sophistication and a total absence of expertise, which factors *may* put the donor countries in a better position to know what the recipients want or should have, but I think that Guyana over the years, at least since 1965, has shown its competence to know what is good for Guyana, to adumbrate its own priorities, and to recognise what particular projects would be best in the fulfilment of our general goal.

One of the purposes of this conference, gentlemen, it is hoped, is the opportunity being given to the representatives of Guyana to say what we plan for our future. If you can help us, we should be most grateful. If you cannot help us, thank you very much. But we have no intention in the year of Our Lord 1970 of having priorities dictated to us by our friends, no matter how kind they may be and no matter of how long standing may be the relationship of friendship.

I should like to observe that Guyana has not been a mendicant nation in recent years. Our achievements in the field of community development and self-help are well known, and there is no need for repetition. Good wine, they say, needs no bush. Our attitude in seeking to finance our own development programme is reflected in Paper I, where it will be observed that between 1965 and 1969 we have attempted, in spite of certain strains and stresses, to finance 48 per cent of our capital development programme.

In 1968, which was an election year, the revenue as a result of taxation represented 26 per cent of the G.D.P., and in 1969, 28 per cent, which we have reason to believe is pretty high, especially in a developing country. To my mind, that establishes the fact that

Guyana is willing to help herself, but argues that indeed, if she has friends, those friends may justly and properly be asked to assist in financing our programme to a higher degree than has been the case in the past.

When we arrive at the more informal and business sessions, certain points will be raised of particular importance, especially the terms of aid. Some of these terms preclude us very often from drawing down fully the commitment given by a particular donor. The automatic tying of aid to goods and services of the donor country and the absence of the resources to provide the local costs are inhibitory factors.

Let me, however, note that over the past two years in the case of the United Kingdom there has been (a) certain liberalising of their terms in that 50 per cent of the loan can be used for local costs, and (b) they have taken a more flexible and realistic view of what amounts to a 'project'.

The United States government, also, late last year by the 006 loan, gave us an opportunity to use to a large extent for local costs foreign exchange made available by that government and we would hope to see this type of liberalisation more obvious so far as all of our donors are concerned.

It is difficult sometimes to escape the impression, cynical as it may appear, that many donors are attracted to the prestige project which can carry the flag of the donor country, rather than to less dramatic projects like draining backlands to make our agriculture more productive, erecting sluices and putting down village roads so that the farmers may carry their produce more easily to the market-place. I have reason to hope that this attitude will not be prevalent after we will have completed this conference.

Since last we met, a very serious situation has arisen in Guyana. There was an uprising in the Rupununi[1] clearly instigated by our western neighbours. Guyana is in a very unfortunate position which may be compared to that of Job. To the west there is Venezuela, to the east there is Surinam and to the north there is the sea. We have had assistance, in so far as keeping out the sea is concerned, but in so far as protecting our borders and maintaining our territorial integrity are concerned the weight has fallen primarily on Guyana and the Guyanese taxpayer.

1. Cattle rearing and sparsely populated savannah lands in the south of Guyana.

We introduced in the budget for this year a 3 per cent defence levy against which there was no particular howl which again is evidence of the fact that the government and the people of Guyana recognise that they must help themselves first and, in fact, they are their own best friends. But the incident in the Rupununi emphasised the need for us to put as top priority the thrust into the hinterland, and the development of those resources which still lie dormant there.

Some of our aid donors would prefer not to operate in an area like that; some of our aid donors would like to tell us we should put roads in the back of Black Bush Polder[2]: excellent. But roads at the back of Black Push Polder will be priority Z in the circumstances, because if we were to lose our territory west of Essequibo there is no point in having roads in the back of Black Bush Polder when Guyana will not be Guyana any longer.

You will, therefore, find in the discussion that, the greatest emphasis is going to be on agricultural diversification and increased production, especially in the hinterland, and a desire to make a bold attempt to explore and exploit the resources of our hinterland.

Since we last met we have also decided that Guyana will become a republic on the twenty-third of February. That decision was made not merely for psychological reasons, but to give us an occasion and opportunity to put a new content into the state of Guyana, so to speak, to give us an opportunity to involve the entire population in the development thrust and exercise.

That is why our republic will be called a Cooperative Republic, because we plan to use the cooperative not only as an institution for mobilising savings and reducing conspicuous consumption, but also as an instrument through the Cooperative Bank, for extending credit in proper cases.

It will be used, we hope, as a means whereby the lowliest man in Guyana, in combination and cooperation with others of his ilk, will have a major share in the economy of the country, thereby reflecting both his political and economic importance.

You may say that basically you are not politicians nor ideologists and you have no interest in this. Maybe if one looks at it narrowly, but so far as our economic planning is concerned it is necessary that we attract this to your attention so that you can understand the

---

2. A coastal rice development scheme.

milieu in which you may operate as donors and the circumstances in which you may give assistance.

Our emphasis on the cooperative is not mere ideology; it is also something that comes from our conviction that the rapid development of Guyana will be enhanced, will become a fact, if we are able to involve in planning and in the undertaking of projects the largest possible section of our population.

Some of the bottlenecks in the drawing down of aid are to be found in the government of Guyana, let me be the first to say it, and you will hear later some of the proposals we have for removing these bottlenecks, but I think you will concede that there are also bottlenecks where the aid donors are concerned.

Sometimes in case of debt repayments we have achieved the interesting, if not awkward and embarrassing, position as we did in 1968 of paying to one aid donor $5·4 million (Guyana) in honour of our debt to them and receiving in assistance $5·2 million (Guyana).

This year, however, thanks to the liberalisation by that particular donor, we hope to receive $8·8 million (Guyana) and pay $5·4 million (Guyana), a net, according to my elementary arithmetic, of $3·4 million (Guyana). That is why we shall make serious proposals with respect to the liberalisation of aid.

We do not object to repayments, we are prepared to repay, but our contention is that if terms are liberalised we will both be able to grow and to repay. Otherwise we shall have to reconsider accepting aid in some instances.

Let it be pellucidly clear that this government of Guyana does not want, does not desire, is not prepared to dishonour its debt obligations even when as is the case now, those debts were contracted and their proceeds mis-spent by our predecessors in office.

Part VI
The international responsibility

25

Extracts from speech to Diplomatic Training
Course, Department of External Affairs, 3 January
1966

*The contribution, if any, that a young developing nation, without
military resources to back diplomatic persuasion, can make on the
stage of world politics has frequently been questioned and often
scorned.*

*On the eve of independence for Guyana, Prime Minister Burnham
addresses a Diplomatic Training Course and with engaging frankness
puts the question of a small nation's international responsibility in its
proper perspective.*

*In defining the role that his young nation can usefully play on the
international scene, the Prime Minister makes the essential point that
the value of an independent voice, however small, in the struggle for
power between West and East, is that it is an independent voice.
Ever since independence, Guyana has consistently articulated a policy
of non-alignment.*

Your Excellency, Sir John Walker,[1] Your Excellencies, Ladies and
Gentlemen,

For some, the term diplomacy is synonymous with spineless pas-
sivity, bent on pleasing everyone while believing in, and standing for,
nothing, absolutely nothing. To others, the term expresses a high
competence in hypocrisy and cunning. In our context, however, and

1. At this date the British government was still responsible for external affairs
   but Burnham appointed a minister without portfolio to handle external
   affairs.

that of the world today, the role of the diplomat is to portray and project a favourable image of his nation and to seek, within the limitations imposed by the grouping of the world into power blocs, to gain the maximum advantage for the country which he represents.

The task of the diplomat representing a small young nation like Guyana is much more difficult than that of his counterpart who speaks on behalf of powerful (militarily and economically) countries like the United States of America and the U.S.S.R. He has no armies, navies, air forces or nuclear weapons to add persuasion to his words. He has no deep purses with the contents of which he can buy friendship, support or friendly neutrality. Furthermore he does not enjoy the support and assistance of an elaborate machine generously and brilliantly staffed. As a consequence not only has he got to carry out a larger number of routine duties himself but also much more personal skill, learning, knowledge and judgement are required of him.

A diplomat representing a new country just rid of colonial domination is faced with the problem of survival in the modern twentieth century jungle. He has got to learn to live in a world and society which places a great deal of emphasis on forms which are frequently at variance with the substance and intention. He has therefore got to be able to show a keen appreciation of the difference between what is said and what is intended to be conveyed; and to recognise that though principles and ideologies are the broad bases of behaviour and conduct, the world is run by individuals who have to be persuaded, who have to be influenced, and who sometimes have to be made into active allies or proponents of a particular cause.

Many are attracted by the apparent kudos and relatively generous salaries and allowances which are attached to diplomatic appointments abroad; impressed and attracted by the round of entertainment which is supposed to be part of the way of life of the diplomatic world and by all the other status symbols; but if the Guyanese diplomat is to serve his country effectively, all of these things will have to be bought at a very high personal price of devotion, energy and physical and mental strain. There are some would-be diplomats who associate independence and overseas representation with imposing embassies and expensive means of locomotion in the capital of every nation. The prototype for them is the foreign service of older and richer countries, like Britain, France, the U.S.S.R. and the United States of America. Than this there can be no greater error, for, in the first place, there are the obvious limitations of the purse. In the second place, the setting up of embassies must be based on the real interests of the principal nation and, in the third place, the size and order of the establishment in one capital or another are dictated by the particular or specific interest which is to be served thereby.

In the circumstances, therefore, a government like ours has to make a very careful choice of posts, in many cases having to accredit representatives to groups of nations rather than individual or single nations. It has got to consider whether its mission in New York – which in any case is a must – should not be the means of maintaining and improving relations with a larger number of countries, and benefiting therefrom as is the case amongst many of the newly independent nations.

Under our independence constitution practically all of the postings overseas of members of the foreign service are the ultimate responsibility of the Prime Minister. This has been done for a good reason and not to provide another field of patronage to the head of government; nor yet again to disrupt the traditional security of tenure of the public servant. The fact is that the overseas representative is an extension of the government of whose basic philosophy and approach he must be fully seized and which he must, sometimes in trying circumstances, sell and portray. Having made this point, I give my personal undertaking that the Prime Minister's power in this or in any other field will never be exercised whimsically or capriciously. Indeed, there is no place for whim or caprice in this country's international relations.

Approximately five years ago, in an address to the British Guiana Trades Union Council, I stated that Guyana under any administration headed by me, would be 'no pawn of East or West'. You may say that those words perhaps, represent the politician's picturesque imagery, but it will be the job, nay the duty, of our diplomats abroad to translate them into practical terms and attitudes.

In the world today, though I hope that here I am carrying coal to Newcastle, there are two larger power blocs seeking to extend their influence and, in some cases, actual physical control. The one is headed by the United States of America, the other, by the U.S.S.R. though in more recent times, it is very doubtful whether Red China accepts the latter's leadership of the second bloc.

Apart from considerations attendant on the fact of our being geographically situate in the western hemisphere, I have repeatedly stated that we, in Guyana, share with the West its oft-pronounced dedication and firm attachment to the democratic principle. Further, my government will never tolerate the establishment of any military base aimed at aggression against any of our neighbours or any nation in the hemisphere. We have been the recipients of substantial capital and technical assistance from the West, for all of which we are most deeply grateful. But all of this does not mean that we automatically support the Western bloc or any of its members in any action or stand they may take on the international scene. For instance, at this very moment, my government is highly critical of the kid-glove treatment being meted out by Britain and her allies to the renegade and illegal Smith regime in Rhodesia and is utterly disgusted by the hypocrisy and cant latent in all this talk about the undesirability of stronger and more positive action than has been taken so far, and equally disgusted by the cynical banality of 'kith and kin'. That, however, does not interfere with our relationships with the West.

On the other hand we are not that naïve because of our painful experiences with Western imperialism to be anti-Western *ex mereo motu* and to ignore the facts and risks of other imperialisms. Ours is, and must be, as President Modibo Keita of Mali has stated: 'The refusal of a nation to lose its personality in a world where assimilation is the objective of every great power', and even of some not-so-great powers.

Some of our Western friends may seek to advise us against having any type of relations with the Eastern bloc and its members while they themselves – our 'kind' advisers – maintain the most elaborate diplomatic and trade relations with those against whom they warn us. We have got to find out for ourselves. We have got to have such relations as we think will be in the interest of our country and the interest of the community of nations. Even if we have to be burnt – then let us be burnt – then we will have learnt the lesson more effectively. For instance, there is a 'hot line' between Moscow and Washington in spite of their public differences expressed in forums like the United Nations. In the field of international diplomacy our objective must be to safeguard our independence and further our national interests and the cause of world peace. With this as our policy, let me assure you, our opinions and decisions in the international field stand to be more greatly valued and respected than otherwise.

Those who commit themselves automatically as satellites of one bloc or another earn little or no respect. Those who will represent our country abroad must know that one of the clear objectives of this government is to re-integrate Guyana into the Caribbean region and to work with our brother West Indians for the economic and political advancement of the area and the projection of the Caribbean Personality on the international scene. We West Indians are geographically close to and have a great deal in common with Latin America but we have an identity and a national personality peculiar to ourselves which we must never confuse or permit to be confused with other peoples' identities and personalities.

On the wider scene this government recognises the common bonds which exists between Guyana and the Afro-Asian bloc. They are not merely the almost accidental ones of ethnic origin, but more important, are traceable to the fact that we all, in common international parlance, are ex-colonial, formerly exploited and euphemistically described as developing nations.

We are all considered potential game for satellite status by the larger nations and we are all at the same time anxious to maintain true independence. The influence and significance of the Afro-Asian bloc in the Commonwealth and at the United Nations must not be underestimated. It is tremendous. The members of this group might not have in the past been successful in achieving all their objectives. But even so which group has? Some of us may be critical, perhaps hypercritical, of the failure of members of that bloc to pass a positive judgment on the Sino-Indian hostilities but no one equates Christianity with Satanic wickedness because of its failure in some instances to give the proper leadership one would have expected of it.

Let us not be brain-washed or cynically and deliberately flattered by the big powers into believing that this third force in the world today is without philosophy, or cohesion and merely the object of manipulation by one or other of the two major power blocs. It represents something new, something dynamic, in international politics. I am convinced that the existence of this group is symbolic of international democracy in that it provides an opportunity for the opinion of the small nation to have equal weight to that of the international Leviathans.

I have spoken or been speaking for all this time on general principles, policies and attitudes, but I conceive it my duty, even at the risk of entering a field that is not my own, and in the presence of accepted experts, to condescend to detail and give you some idea of what I consider, of what my government considers, to be the qualities you must acquire and develop, and the things you must do, if you are to be worthy of your salt as members of the foreign service of an independent Guyana. At this point I can do no better than quote from the work of François de Callières, *The Art of Negotiating with Sovereign Princes*. 'A Diplomat's aim should be to arouse the minds of his hearers by a sympathetic touch. . . . He should therefore at the outset think rather of what is in their minds than of immediately expressing what is in his own.'

In this respect a diplomat differs considerably from a politician. The politician's task – and you will grant me some expertise in this field – is to let his audience know what he thinks at the earliest possible point of time and to seek to brow-beat, cajole, bludgeon or persuade his audience. But as I understand it, the diplomat of a country must seek first of all to find out what is in the mind of the person to whom he is speaking. He must possess 'an observant mind, a spirit of application so necessary to be stressed in our present context, which refuses to be distracted by pleasures or frivolous amusements, and sound judgment which takes the measure of things as they are, and goes straight to its goal by the shortest and most natural paths without wandering into useless refinements and subtleties which as a rule only succeed in repelling those with whom one is dealing.'

The diplomatist cannot hope to discharge his duties with success unless he has taken the pains to instruct himself. It is obvious therefore that the diplomatic corps is no place for the brash and conceited young man. When a diplomat, for instance, uses harsh or strong language he must be using it knowingly and with the objective of achieving a particular purpose. He must not be using it by accident or under the influence of spirituous liquors. He must understand to whom he is speaking; he must know the foibles, the weakness and most important in these days, the mythology of his listener. His mind must have sufficient depth for him to be able to report back accurately what has been communicated to him regardless of the forms.

He must when making all his statements have clearly in his mind what is the objective to be achieved – whether it is to get an official statement from a friendly nation intended to warn off would-be aggressors – in our case that would be very relevant after the twenty-sixth of May – or the obtaining of a loan or technical assistance.

He must be capable of keen observation, and develop the ability of anticipating events which may be of great significance to his government and on which the latter may have to act or take a decision. He must learn to deal with charm with his fellow diplomats and represen-tatives, and representatives of governments to which he is accredited and this even though relations between his country and other country or countries may not be very good, whether it be in the Caribbean or the United Nations. The ideology of these with whom he speaks is only relevant in so far as it enables him to judge of their objectives and their underlying motives but is completely irrelevant as a criterion for dictating personal relations.

A diplomat therefore cannot be an unlearned idiot who has crammed himself through some formal university course. He must be well read, not superficially; he must be familiar with the Marxist and capitalist philosophies. He must know and understand, or at least attempt to assess, the motivations behind the foreign policies of not only the nation which he represents but also of other nations whose spokesmen and representatives he has to meet.

26

Speech to Washington's Women's Press Club on occasion of first official visit to the U.S.A., Statler Hilton Hotel, Washington, 22 July 1966

Two months after the attainment of independence for his country, Prime Minister Burnham accepts an official invitation from President Johnson to visit the United States of America. His speech to the Women's Press Club is his first official public address in the U.S.A. as Prime Minister of Guyana.

Ladies and Gentlemen of the Press, friends of Guyana, I desire to express my deep gratitude to Washington's Women's Press Club for providing me with this opportunity of telling you something about my country, Guyana.

Your presence here indicates an interest in the story of this small nation, situate on the the north-eastern littoral of South America, once described as the only British possession on the mainland of South America.

Since the assumption of office by my government in December 1964, it has been my custom to meet the Press regularly and to discuss with them matters of importance and topical interest, but I must confess that facing a group of this size is not a usual experience for me. Since it may be difficult for me to cover every aspect which may interest you I propose, as is my wont, to provide a relatively long period for questions.

First let me pay tribute to your great country for the warmth of the welcome which was extended to me by your President and other members of the government since I arrived here yesterday, and also to the unique and outstanding achievement by Gemini 10's Astronauts.

For a period of more than a decade ending in December 1964, British Guiana, as it was then called, had achieved for itself the reputation of being a land where political upheaval, turmoil, confusion, and even violence, were the order of the day.

The scene was changed as the result of general elections held in 1964. Peace, stability and order were established and, amidst colourful but dignified celebrations, Guyana achieved her independence on the twenty-sixth of May, 1966.

That independence has been achieved during my term of office is naturally a source of personal pleasure but I take pride in the fact that even in my country's most difficult days my party and I remained unequivocally dedicated to the early attainment of independence.

I did not then think and I do not now think that independence was or is the panacea for all ills, bringing in its immediate train a magic solution to our diverse problems. But my contention has always been that the status of independence forces upon a people the responsibility of finding answers to the questions that bedevil them.

Only shortly before the elections to which I have earlier referred there were serious incidents of communal strife instigated by my political opponents, but these came to an end when it became clear that my government was prepared to be impartial but firm.

As a result of a constitutional conference held in October 1965, a new constitution was drafted for Guyana. This constitution includes in it those essential guarantees for a free people, so long ago incorporated in your own Bill of Rights. It provides protection for minority rights and the creation of the post of Ombudsman.

In the dark days of the immediate past many in Guyana had come to assume that differences of political persuasion were insurmountable and national cohesion impossible. But in the few months of its existence, my government which consists of a coalition of two parties (the People's National Congress and the United Force, left and right of centre, respectively) has been able to demonstrate that in building a nation and carrying through the challenging tasks of reconstruction the various peoples of Guyana are capable of working as a team.

Guyana has responded magnificently and showed its confidence in the new administration. Guyanese contributed in 1965 approximately $15 million (Guyana) to a government loan by way of savings certificates and debentures. This act of self-help encouraged friendly nations like your own to give or commit themselves to economic assistance and aid.

During 1965 there has been an increasing growth of economic activity. Hitherto neglected roads have been rehabilitated, government buildings which had fallen into desuetude, repaired and restored. A comprehensive seven-year development programme has been approved in our legislature and unemployment reduced from 20 per cent to 16 per cent.

Guyana is a small country in comparison with those nations of the world who conquer space and reach for the moon, but in terms of the Caribbean our 83,000 square miles, our huge forests, swift flowing rivers and mineral deposits hold out prospects of great promise, not only for ourselves but also for our West Indian brothers.

We have something to say and it is about time that voices like ours be heard before it is too late. Our forefathers carried on a struggle for human freedom and dignity: witness the slave revolts in the Guiana of the 1760s; the Maroon uprising in Jamaica; the flight of the Surinam Djukas or Bush Negroes away from slavery to live in the forests in freedom. These took place in the same century as the Americans' revolt against their erstwhile British masters. Our sons gave their lives for the defence of democracy in the war against Hitler. We contributed our bauxite to the Allied war effort at prices which still left our people poor.

Historians agree that the West Indian sugar industry, in which our ancestors sweated and bled, financed the British industrial revolution which in turn contributed to many another industrial revolution, including the American.

We come therefore into the modern world not as mendicants or innocents but as people demanding their just deserts. If these are not achieved, disappointment and frustration, the parents of frightening instability, will be the inevitable result. It is my conviction that you have a vested interest in stability.

We believe in democracy. We believe in free and regular elections. We believe in the dignity of the individual and his right to express himself freely, but democracy does not flourish where dire poverty exists in the midst of burgeoning wealth.

We note with interest and pleasure President Johnson's declaration in Mexico in April last to the effect that 'the United States is committed to help its neighbours improve their rich resources" and we acknowledge the aid in this direction which Guyana received from the United States during 1965-6.

We do not seek handouts but assistance from friends while we make every effort to help ourselves. Our people subscribed voluntarily to their country's development, as I have noted before, to the tune of $15 million in 1965. The maximum contribution to revenue is made by way of local taxation, and domestic savings are encouraged.

We reject the communist dogma and system as being irrelevant and unsuited to our aspiration and needs. On the other hand, we do not see our solutions in terms of unrestricted and uninhibited free enterprise, with the government holding the ring for the exploitation of the little man who has borne the sweat and toil of the day and for whom such will mean the very negation of independence.

We propose to make use of many institutional forms. There will be a place of usefulness for the foreign and local companies, the public corporation owned and controlled by the State, the joint undertaking between the State and private investors, and municipal enterprise. There will be the workers' cooperatives, producers' cooperatives, consumers' cooperatives, industrial cooperatives, and tradesmen's cooperatives. Participation in all these will be voluntary.

It is my philosophy that the people's cooperatives, democratically controlled by the people themselves, will eventually assume an important and significant position in our economy. You may describe this as cooperative socialism.

We are not imprisoned by rigid and unrealistic dogma. Our only dogma is that Guyanese must maintain independent control of their own destinies and be masters of their own country.

We give firm and unequivocal guarantees to local investors. We do not say 'come in for the time being' and infer 'soon we shall have no use for you and will treat you accordingly'. We accept that investment in the private sector is needed for our country's development and welcome it on mutually agreed terms. We expect that this will include fair wages, modern trade union and industrial practices, making a proper contribution to revenue by way of taxes and eschewing any meddling in domestic politics.

This I venture to say, especially after the Canada-West Indies talks at Ottawa, is the generally accepted approach of the English-speaking Caribbean. With the latter we share a common history, political and economic, common tradition and cultural patterns.

Situate as we are on the Latin-American continent, we naturally feel a great affinity with our continental neighbours and have recently introduced Spanish into our schools. We welcome and are seeking to develop further cultural exchange with various Latin-American countries. But we consider it our first task to come together with our Commonwealth Caribbean brothers at the economic and other levels.

Our purpose and aim is to build a West Indian nation that is economically viable and therefore stable. This is all the more necessary in the context of the new constitutional arrangements being worked out with respect to the Windward and Leeward Islands. Guyana's natural resources and vast under-populated expanses of land can be fully exploited for the benefit of the Guyanese themselves and their brother West Indians and ensure that the Caribbean ceases being a collection of poor small nations and islands and becomes instead a really prosperous and viable unit.

A number of former British colonies in the Caribbean have achieved independence in recent years but to *achieve* our true destiny and bring our people the real fruits of independence we must face our common problems and the world as a region rather than as an agglomeration of units. Together we have become world champions of cricket. Together we can beat poverty and project the Caribbean personality onto the international stage.

I said before that ours is a small nation. Even as part of a large West Indian nation we shall not be able to match weaponry with the large nations of the world. But I contend that the world's peace will be guaranteed in the final analysis not by the quantum of arms abroad but by the goodwill of one nation towards another.

Of this type of goodwill we in Guyana have recently had evidence when the United States government on our Independence Day voluntarily returned to us a portion of our territory which had formerly been leased for 99 years by the British to the United States during World War II. For me this is a demonstration of the United States willingness to respect the rights and sovereignty of a smaller nation. To me it is indicative at another level of an acceptance of a small nation's right to pursue an independent and sensible policy in international affairs.

It is my firm belief that the smaller nations can and must act as a catalyst in the all too often explosive confrontation of the world's big powers. I am convinced that because we are small, because we can never be a threat and because we have no ambitions beyond our own borders, our voice can add perhaps the greatest contribution to the unity and understanding among the nations of this world.

It is my government's determination that Guyana will never become the pawn of either East or West. I have repeatedly stated and I state again that we in Guyana share with the West its oft pronounced dedication and firm attachment to the democratic principle. It must be understood, however, that our support of the Western bloc or any of its members in any stand that they may take on the international scene is not automatic. On every international issue we shall exercise our own judgment on the basis of the facts at our disposal, having regard always to our national interests and the cause of world peace.

Our friends must understand that it is the right of friends to differ and still remain friends. Our attitude can, I think, be adequately described in the words of an African leader: 'The refusal of a nation to lose its personality in a world where assimilation is the objective of every great power, and even of some nations of not so great power.'

27

Speech to the General Assembly of the United
Nations on the occasion of Guyana's acceptance as
a Member Nation, New York, 20 September 1966

Mr President,

Permit me, please, to congratulate you upon your election to the high
office which you now hold and to wish that, bringing to bear all your
known qualities and experience, you will guide, with success, this
Assembly through the difficult year which lies ahead.

May I also express my young nation's deep gratitude to the members of the Commonwealth and our Latin-American neighbours who
have sponsored our admission to this organisation and to them and
others who have expressed such kind sentiments and warm wishes.

Mine is a small country with a land mass approximately equal to
that of Britain and a population of about six-and-a-half hundred thous-
and. There are the indigenous Amerindians; there are the descendants
of the African slaves and indentured Indians who together form the
bulk of the people among whom are also Chinese, Portuguese and
others. All except the first have come to our part of the world as
part of that economic and political process of imperialism. As such we
share the experience and aspirations of the newer nations and are
determined to restructure our whole life and institutions, economic,
social and political, to ensure for ourselves survival and a better life.

In an ideal world, a new nation might hope to go it alone, but this
is not an ideal world and in this age, as in others, there is always some
factor that bedevils the existence of small, weak nations. In the last
century, it was the imperialist dynamic, which has not yet entirely
disappeared, especially in Africa.

In our time, it is the self-interest, albeit sometimes enlightened, of
great powers, and their concomitant desire to control and patronise

the smaller and newer nations. This is one of the reasons why, in our relations with our sister Caribbean nations, we devote every effort to the strengthening of Caribbean unity, the development and maintenance of regional cooperation and integration at all levels and the building of a strong, viable Caribbean community. At the same time, geographically situate as we are on the Latin-American Continent, we cherish the warmest feelings of friendship for our neighbours, the Latin-American nations, with whom we look forward to more than a lifetime of meaningful cooperation.

Mr President, I hope that you will not find it presumptuous if on behalf of the newest of the new, one of the smaller of the small nations, I declare that my government's and people's passionate desire for peace among nations is second to none. In Guyana we have experienced the misery of communal strife, which I am happy to say is now past, but it is because we have lived with what on a larger scale seems to be one of the major problems of the world, that we claim the right to challenge the nations, great and small, to cease from making war and implements of war. In Vietnam, for instance, it is my hope, which I feel sure this Assembly shares, that an honourable and acceptable means will be found to substitute discussions around the conference table for the bullets of the battlefield. And this, though I know how badly reason oft limps beside the striding soldier.

Mr President, our nation has neither capacity for, nor the intention of, conquering or dominating others. We want to survive and help to build the brave new world. Our major contributions are moral persuasion and, we hope, dispassionate thinking.

Guyana shares with her friends an active and undying dedication to democracy, political and social, and to the democratic process and ideals and is not committed *ex mero motu* to any major power bloc. We want to preserve our newly achieved independence to develop our resources with our own energies, and the assistance of friends. We know that we have to live in a world of stark realities, not fanciful dreams, but we are sure that given an opportunity to be heard, we can contribute to the stability of our hemisphere and the peace of the world. But what hope of peace is there when four million Africans are oppressed by a small white minority of a quarter-million in Southern Rhodesia; when Angola and Mozambique remain running sores; when the inhuman policy of apartheid continues in South Africa, and those who utter pious sentiments grapple to their economic hearts former admirers if not supporters of Adolf Hitler; when the people of South West Africa are denied the right to self-determination?

What has become of the loud protestations – I am sometimes inclined to say cant – about the dignity of the human being, the fatherhood of God and the brotherhood of man? I pose these questions. We shall not rest until they are answered and answered satisfactorily. We share with Lincoln, that great liberator, the conviction that the world cannot survive half-free and half-slave. As we in Guyana see it and here we claim no originality, there is yet another threat to international stability and therefore peace. I refer to the imbalance between the rich and poor countries. It is accepted that in general the gap between the underdeveloped nations and the developed ones widens year by year even though many of the former produce valuable basic and strategic material on which others grow fat and rich. In this the developed decade, there has been a decline rather than increase in the level of economic aid and flow of resources to the developing from the developed countries. The situation is grave and the most urgent consideration by this organisation is indicated. This is not a question of charity, it is one of stability and global prosperity.

Mr President, my government subscribes to the Charter of the United Nations. It has faith in this organisation of which it hopes to be an active rather than a sleeping member. It also hopes for and will work towards the United Nations being as truly representative as possible of all the peoples of the world, regardless of ideological and mythological differences.

Again, Mr President, thank you and your colleagues for admitting and welcoming Guyana. May I hope that as we trudge along the difficult road and wander through the tortuous paths we can rely on the helping hands of our older colleagues and the advice of our more experienced friends, and in our turn contribute from our experience to the deliberations of this august Assembly.

28

Mr Speaker, sir, at midnight on 25 May 1966, the lowering of the Union Jack and the raising of the national flag of Guyana, which was of great symbolic importance, not only meant that certain powers which before were exercised by the metropolitan power, were going to be exercised by and have since then been exercised by the elected Government of Guyana, but it also meant that the nation of Guyana formally set sail on the rather difficult, sometimes tempestuous, seas of foreign relations.

Nearly a year has passed since independence and during that period, the government of Guyana has sought, within the limits of its financial and material resources, to adumbrate a philosophy, a strategy and an approach in its relations with foreign powers.

What is the purpose, one may ask, of a foreign policy or what is foreign policy, rather? I would say, with special reference to the nation of Guyana, foreign policy represents the philosophy and objectives motivating our relations and dealings with foreign nations. A foreign policy as stated by various governments, usually has a high philosophic content and a large degree of idealism. There is nothing intrinsically wrong in that, I would concede, but I should rather think that behind all the high ideals, protestations and postures for public consumption, there is always the underlying fact and factor of a national self-interest, or rather what is good for the particular country – not necessarily what the particular country can get out of the pursuit of a particular policy by way of goods, services or finance, but what, in the whole context of the country's existence, is good for the country and its citizens in the judgment of the government of that particular country.

At the idealistic or philosophical level, I would say, sir, that the foreign policy of this government is motivated by a desire to play an important and significant role in the achievement of permanent peace in the world and putting an end to the exploitation and enslavement of man by man. But even this has a material side. Developing countries like Guyana will have a greater opportunity for developing their resources, human and natural, for obtaining assistance in such development, if there were peace and if the large expenditure by the super powers in the arms race were to be considerably reduced.

The tag which is accepted amongst the developing countries in these days is the tag of neutralism, sometimes the synonym in these circumstances, non-alignment, is used. It is important, sir, to note a great deal of difference between the term neutralism and the term neutrality.

Neutrality, to my mind, connotes an unwillingness to come to a decision and remaining completely neutral on many, if not all, important international questions; giving no opinion; coming to no decision and voting neither way. Not only is such an attitude cowardly, but I would submit, it is unrealistic.

Neutralism, on the other hand, connotes that there is no commitment to come out or make a decision on either side in a dispute before the facts are ventilated and the mind applied to such facts. Neutralism, I would describe, as the pursuit of an independent foreign policy, the exercise of an independent judgment on any international question. A country which pursues a foreign policy of neutralism is one which neither of the super powers or great blocs can depend on automatically to support it on any issue.

Countries like Guyana, which have experienced the colonialism of a Western country and which are anxious to confirm, establish and advertise their independence, are frequently led into a position where the emphasising and confirmation of that independence takes the form of a constant anti-Western posture. On the other hand, there are some developing countries, newly independent, who pursue an equally disgusting, if not more disgusting, series of postures, believing that the West is richer, believing that the West is more generous, that commit themselves to a primitive adulation of everything Western and to an automatic support of the West, even in cases when the West does not have right on its side and in circumstances which sometimes draw the contempt and surprise of those they support.

The image of a country which commits itself automatically to one way or another is no image. That country earns the respect of neither side and that country can justly be described as a satellite. The government of Guyana has, since independence, shown a willingness, and expresses that willingness tangibly, to be friendly with all other nations who are prepared to be friendly. And in the realm of realism, the last clause is important because there is little or no point in a government like ours bending over backwards to be friendly towards a government which has shown open hostility. We may not be able to match arms with arms, we may not be prepared to descend into the gutter of vituperation, but we certainly shall not be bending over backwards to show friendship to those who have shown us hostility.

In the world today, sir, there is too great a tendency to consider matters in terms of black and white, as if those are the only colours. Between the position of one group or one bloc and the position of another group or bloc, there are intermediate positions and the contribution which young, small nations like ours can make, in several cases, is to give the blacks and whites an opportunity to recognise the grey. We can be intermediaries, and we can employ powers of persuasion where those powers are relevant.

This brings me to another thesis: that a nation of the size and with the resources of Guyana should not fool itself that it can on its own make a tremendous impact and change completely the scheme of things or alter radically the trend of events. There are certain issues on which we can exercise very little influence one way or another. We had an example of that in 1965–6 when there was the big argument in the United Nations over Article 19 and Russia and France paying for the peace-keeping exercise in the Congo. A number of smaller nations made noises and passed judgments, some of them thought that they were seized with the wisdom of gods; but the outcome of that confrontation between Russia and the U.S. was dictated by what the U.S. was prepared to do in the circumstances and what Russia was prepared to do in the circumstances.

I think that if we young nations after our appearance on the international scene run around pontificating, we give the impression similar to that given by the little new boy at school who does not even know his basic alphabet, purporting to instruct the teacher and the class on the vagaries of third-dimensional physics. The government of Guyana certainly does not propose to be an ignorant little new boy. There is a great deal that young countries like ours have to learn, about what may be vulgarly, but accurately, called manoeuvring on the international stage; and some of us with more enthusiasm than wisdom can easily mistake the protestations for conviction and the posture for belief.

In any case, sir, the government of Guyana accepts frankly and unapologetically the position that since our entry on to the international stage is less than twelve months old, there is a great deal which we have to learn, a great deal which we have to understand and a number of nuances which we have to know more about. Guyana does not propose to make itself the protagonist or advocate of one or other of the super powers or blocs. Both super powers and blocs are armed with enough material force and wealth to look after their interest in cold and hot wars and both of them are armed with sufficiently brilliant and skilled advocates to have their cases presented according to their interests.

In the world today, there are two major blocs called the Western bloc and the Eastern bloc, and there seems some doubt in these days as to whether the Eastern bloc unanimously subscribes to one leader or leadership. But, sir, there has been what has been called a third bloc, but I don't know that it is really a bloc. What has been called the third bloc, consists of the neutralist powers or nations.

Guyana belongs to this third group. Most, if not all the members of this group consist of underdeveloped countries or nations. These underdeveloped nations are disappointed that the 'decade of development' starting in 1960, has proved to be a flop so far. It is my belief that these underdeveloped nations can, in spite of their limited resources, develop not only formal political links but trade and economic links, and can come together for their mutual benefit and protection. This can be done especially in cases where they are the sole producers of certain important commodities, goods and or minerals.

Guyana has a certain common history and also a community of aspirations with what are described at the United Nations as the Afro-Asian countries. We have been, since the attainment of independence, developing our relations with these countries or nations. A part of this relationship was our invitation to President Kaunda of Zambia, which he accepted. He came here.[1] Part of this also was a close working with this group in the United Nations, not only on questions like Rhodesia and South West Africa, but also on questions of trade and development arising out of the United Nations Conference on Trade and Development which was held in Geneva.

1. Prime Minister Indira Ghandi of India also visited Guyana later, in 1968.

Perhaps I should pause for a moment to comment on our member-ship of the Commonwealth. I recall that when the formal motion of our accession to the Commonwealth, after the achievement of independence was debated in this House, the cowards in the opposition abstained after putting up a number of facetious arguments against our continuance in the Commonwealth. Guyana's being in the Common-wealth marks a subscription by Guyana to the ideals of the Common-wealth – democracy, human dignity, equality of man. That is the idealistic side, but on the materialistic side Guyana benefits economically from being a member of the Commonwealth.

Our membership of the Commonwealth is a combination of idealism and materialism and so it is with a lot of other members of the Commonwealth; so it is with Britain, because since the war, Britain's trade with the Commonwealth has increased and the value of her trade has increased even more than the volume of her trade and it is of more than passing significance that the Commonwealth is no longer described as the British Commonwealth, but as the Commonwealth.

There are some members of the Commonwealth which are richer than others, there are some members of the Commonwealth that are more powerful militarily than others, but that does not mean that the Commonwealth is not a free association of all its members – a free association whose survival is dictated by a combination of idealism and materialism. At the moment, the government of Guyana is happy to be a member of the Commonwealth.

Let me refer also to the Organisation of American States. There has been a great deal of discussion in this country as to whether Guyana should accede to the O.A.S., but those who beat the drums and make noises are either unaware of the legal position or they are intellectually dishonest when they seek to give the impression that this government is on the way to becoming a member of the O.A.S. Under Article 3 of the Act of Washington, no country will have its application for joining the O.A.S. considered by the Council of the O.A.S. if there is in existence a dispute with respect to boundary with a standing member of the O.A.S., if that dispute arose prior to 1960 and was between one of the members of the O.A.S. and an extra-hemispheric power and if that dispute has not been resolved by peaceful means. In those circumstances, the application by such a nation cannot be and will not be considered.

So far as Guyana is concerned, within the meaning of Article 3 of the Act of Washington, there is no point in Guyana's applying for membership of the O.A.S.

We have, as I mentioned before, been working very closely with the Afro-Asian group in the United Nations and as everyone in Guyana ought to know, not only did we take a strong and unequivocal stand with respect to South West Africa but our government was one of the co-sponsors of the resolution which was passed by the General Assembly calling upon Britain to take strong action with respect to Mr Smith, including the use of force.

I do not consider it necessary to enter into a long dissertation on what is happening in places like South West Africa, which was originally a League of Nations mandated territory to South Africa, or on what is happening in Rhodesia and the obvious failure by the United Kingdom government to deal as firmly with Smith as its predecessors dealt with Jagan and Burnham in 1953. What is happening in those parts of the world is known, and I needn't sing a long song about what is happening in Mozambique and Angola. The attitude and stand of the Guyana government on these matters and such matters is well known and cannot be questioned.

Part VII
On the subject of youth

29

Statement to the nation on the occasion of National
Youth Week, 19 May 1968

*Across the world young people, no longer adolescents but not quite
adults, are today in revolt against a world with values they cannot
accept and a world in which they feel alienated.*

*In Guyana, almost 60 per cent of the population is under the age
of 20.*

*Prime Minister Burnham, in his own words, recognises the 'depen-
dence of the nation upon the contribution of its youth'.*

*The Prime Minister in recognition of this contribution introduced
National Youth Week to be celebrated each year and makes as the
central theme 'Productivity through Youth'.*

My fellow citizens of Guyana, today marks the beginning of National
Youth Week. The theme is 'Productivity through Youth'. The week's
activities are of great importance to the entire nation. But they are of
special significance for our youths who will during the period focus
the attention of the community upon what they have embarked upon
and what they must and will accomplish to make Guyana strong.
Theirs is a world to build for their parents, themselves, their children
and their children's children so that this and succeeding generations
may enjoy full and happy lives in this magnificent land of ours.

National Youth Week will be celebrated each year during the week
immediately preceding our independence anniversay.

About 60 per cent of our population is under 20 years of age. This
is a revealing, striking and significant fact. It emphasises the great
dependence of the nation upon the contribution of its youths for its

immediate and future growth, progress and prosperity. The government, therefore, through the Youth Division, which is a direct responsibility of the Prime Minister, in collaboration with voluntary youth organisations throughout the country, is taking positive steps to stimulate and encourage our youths into challenging and meaningful action.

During this week in particular, the youth of our nation will be called upon to examine themselves and their activities in the light of the national objective of greater efficiency and increased productivity. They will have to examine their past achievements and failures. They will have to plan for the future, long-term and immediate. They will have to arrive at an understanding of how they can individually and cooperatively increase the sum total of their contributions to Guyana – in agriculture, industry, commerce, academic and technical pursuits aimed at promoting the national good. It is hoped in this way that our youth will be aroused to a new consciousness, a fuller awareness of their worth to the society and be given an opportunity to exercise responsibility and mature judgment.

No country that sets growth and prosperity as its goals can chart its course successfully without the conscious and deliberate participation and contribution of its young people. The social, economic, political and other problems of youths are not peculiarly youth problems but problems of the society in which the youths find themselves. Nor are they limited to Guyana but are world-wide in their symptoms and expression.

Everywhere youths are rebelling and rejecting the cultures of their parents and are seeking to create for themselves sub-cultures to replace the existing ones. Often we hear of vandalism and riots, hippies and their addiction to drugs; all of these seem attempts to escape the contradictions of the adult-dominated world, a world of hunger amidst plenty, a world where pious protestations and hypocritical postures do not square with the facts of the selfish rat race at community and national levels, a world where the declared and actual objectives are poles apart.

Fortunately for us in Guyana the youths of our country do not manifest the more rabid signs of disaffection. But this nation cannot sit supinely by and piously wish that the good Lord will protect us from the problems that bedevil other countries. The power, energy and revolutionary zeal to be found among the ranks of our youth must be properly channelled and turned into a valuable contribution to national growth.

Youths are not children and even if they were, born as they have been in the space and jet ages, we cannot expect them to be mere appendages to society, mere marionettes whom adults can whimsically operate. They can and want to help to build a new nation of Guyana – shorn of its colonial attitudes, its snobberies and prejudices, its discriminatory practices, its poverty. We gave them the vision of an independent Guyana. Let us give them the chance to make it a better place than, a different land from, British Guiana.

My government, after very thorough and careful consideration of the situation of our youths (their predominance within the society, their value to the community, their power to make or break the country), has established the National Youth Corps, the nucleus of which is drawn from among our unemployed youth of all ethnic groups between the ages of 15 and 20 years. Very shortly we shall also be recruiting young women. The main objectives of the Youth Corps are to develop fully in our youths a sense of discipline, social unity, civic pride and national responsibility. Through the programme of varied activities planned, its members will be geared to make an effective contribution in service to the country.

The Youth Corps was launched in January this year and already the first 74 recruits have completed their basic toughening-up training under the excellent guidance of the Guyana Defence Force at Atkinson. By June they will be occupying their own camp at Tumatumari where they will be trained by a director and full-time staff over a period of 21 months in various skills, including agriculture, motor mechanics, carpentry and joinery, radio repairs and servicing and others. They will be inducted into the cooperative life – socially and economically. The basic training will be in agriculture, because the future economy of Guyana for some years will be based on agriculture. Certain academic subjects will be taught members in order to give them a background to Guyanese history, culture and traditions upon which they can build, upon which they can refashion. They will be encouraged to identify their role in the development of the nation and our relationship to our West Indian brothers and cousins in the other developing countries and the rest of the world.

You will no doubt appreciate that the ambitious investment in our youths is a very costly undertaking. Your government has undertaken the initial operation of the Youth Corps by allocating in this year's Budget the sum of $130,000 (Guyana), meagre indeed, to youth training and welfare. But because every living person in this country is involved in the destiny of our youth, I take this opportunity to call upon every citizen, all of you, in every walk of life, the artisan, the farmer, the salary earner, the businessman, large and small, to identify yourselves with this great exercise of nation-building through our youths. You are offered the opportunity of contributing generously, money and equipment to the Youth Corps.

These are *our* youths; the most valuable resources any country can have. If *we* do not invest in them who will? It is our duty to ensure their meaningful preparation for their roles as the pioneers, the builders, the leaders of the nation. Your support of the Youth Corps is imperative. It is a national duty. Neglect it, neglect our youth, and Guyana will reap the chaos we see elsewhere.

To the youths of the nation, I say: this first National Youth Week is an opportunity for you to demonstrate palpably your real worth to the nation. It is an opportunity for you to examine your lives and your environment to see what is wrong. It is an opportunity to set new goals, to plan for the future of Guyana and yourselves. It is an opportunity for you to re-dedicate yourselves to the achievement of high ideals. It is well that I should remind you at this time that true greatness is not measured in terms of jingling coins and crispy notes, but in terms of service to one's country, to one's fellow men, to humanity. May I be so immodest as to lend you my own motto – 'Service is its own reward'.

You have a nation to make, a world to conquer and your government is at your side.

God bless you.

Part VIII
The struggle of other colonial peoples

30

Speech in the Legislative Council in debate on
disturbances in Nyasaland and the detention of Dr
Hastings Banda, 13 March 1959

Motion:

Be it resolved that this Council expresses concern over the disturbances in Nyasaland, the detention of Dr Banda and other Nyasa
leaders, the banning of the African National Congress, and the kill-
ing of several Africans.

And directs that Her Majesty's government, through Her
Majesty's Secretary of State for the Colonies, be requested to intervene to secure the release of the detainees, the lifting of the ban on the
African National Congress, and the taking of immediate steps to
ensure the just national aspirations of the people of Nyasaland.

Mr Burnham: Mr Speaker, the Colony, or to be legalistically accurate,
the Protectorate of Nyasaland, has been very much in the news, and
there are certain facts which do not appear to be in dispute. One is,
that Dr Banda, who recently returned to his country after many years'
absence, has been detained without trial, along with others of the
Nyasa people.

The African National Congress, an organisation which seeks to give
form and expression to the national sentiments and aspirations of the
Africans of Central Africa, has been banned, and a number of people
have been killed.

It is very interesting to note that an official statement purporting
to come from the government of the Central African Federation and
the government of Nyasaland gives the excuse that there was some
conspiracy between the natives of this territory, along with natives
of Northern and Southern Rhodesia, to slaughter and murder all

Europeans and Asians in the territories, and the government 'anxious' as ever that law and order should be preserved, has decided to institute the emergency and take the drastic steps that have been taken. But the most unusual thing about what I consider to be a fabrication, is that, although the 54 Africans have been killed, not one single European or soldier of the Central African Federation has even been injured.

I believe that most Members of this Council are aware of the fact that the native African of the Central African Federation is treated like a member of a sub-human species in spite of the fact that the Africans number over two million – this against five seats held by the Africans in the Legislative Council. Their rights as human beings are not respected and we hear from time to time such hypocritical prating from those who lord it over the natives as 'the natives are not ready to be adapted to modern society'.

You even hear such a disgustingly spurious bit of logic coming from a member of the House of Commons to the effect that the European had hundreds of years of civilisation and education and is well ahead of the native, who has only been introduced to these things about 60 years ago. Of course, according to the mythology of colonialism, those who say these things are entitled to their points of view even in a country that is not theirs; in a country that belongs to the Africans in the same way as Britain belongs to the Britons!

We who have had the experience of detentions without trial, we who have had the experience of arbitrary restrictions, feel an affinity with the people of Nyasaland and a deep sympathy for them at this moment; for all these people are aspiring to is the right to rule their own country. And it is particularly unfortunate that in this, the second half of the twentieth century, the British government has connived at and initiated such actions as we have noted in Nyasaland recently.

It has been said that the British government is not directly responsible, but unless my knowledge of British constitutional law, practice and history is faulty, until such time as dominion status is achieved by a colony or an ex-colony, there is in it the ever active interest of Her Majesty's government – an interest which can be translated into action. Still we see a European, a Labour member of Parliament, ejected from this country recently, because he was sympathetic to the Africans.

The people of Nyasaland object to being part of the Central African Federation, not because they object to being part of a larger unit, but because this federation consists of a number of countries where representation varies inversely with numbers, where the few thousands get practically all the seats, hold almost all the administrative posts and in fact behave as if the country is a feudal estate. It is understandable that the largest section of the people of Nyasaland do not want to be part of the Central African Federation.

This type of attitude of people coming from outside to tell us when we are ready and when we are ripe persists. It is true that that stage is well past in certain parts of Africa, and it is true it is practically passed in the Caribbean but we, as Guianese, are particularly sensitive about it, because we know it has not passed in British Guiana. I do not accept the excuse proffered in one of today's dailies that Her Majesty's government is not responsible directly, legally and morally for what is happening in Nyasaland.

That is why in this motion I am asking that a request be sent to Her Majesty's government, through Her Majesty's Secretary of the State for the Colonies, to intervene to secure the release of the detainees, to lift the ban on the African National Congress and to take immediate steps to ensure that the just national aspirations of all Africans are realised.

Her Majesty's government is competent to do it in the same way as Her Majesty's government is competent to suspend constitutions and send troops; Her Majesty's government is competent to intervene in the cause of democracy, in the cause of justice and the cause of right.

It is a heavy burden that Her Majesty's government has to carry, if in the twentieth century we are going to be subjected to such disillusionments as this one. What happens to all the talk about cooperation and all the talk about partnership? Is this talk of partnership meaningful only where they *have* to withdraw, or is it sincere?

We shall see whether all the talk about the glorious Commonwealth with its multiplicity of peoples springs from a sincere conviction or whether it is an empty phrase and an empty description to attract the attention of the world and beguile us natives.

If British Guiana does not do something about this and does not take a strong stand against the dictators of Central Africa, what right would British Guiana, or the British Commonwealth, have to point its finger at any other nation and talk about slaughter in Hungary?

In the Bible it is written: 'Take the beam out of thine own eye before thou takest the mote out of thy brother's eye.' It seems to me that this in an opportunity for Her Majesty's government to take the beam out of its own eye, to clear the way, to impress us with the sincerity of Her Majesty's government, to give us some conviction that it is worthwhile to remain members of this Commonwealth.

EXTRACTS FROM SPEECH CLOSING DEBATE

Since it seems as if every member who has spoken so far is in complete agreement with the motion, it may be thought that the exercising of my right to reply is an unnecessary imposition on this Council. I, however, do not think so, for while everyone has paid lip-service to this motion, there are certain misconceptions that have been introduced more especially by the hon. Nominated Member, Mr Tasker.[1] We have heard from the hon. gentleman about the hard work and determination of the whites in Central and South Africa without being told that it is the sweat and blood of those people to whom they refuse to give political rights that has given them (the white settlers) the prosperity which they now enjoy. We do not have to go to Nyasaland to know that those hard-working people are not the settlers but the natives who are supposed to be over-paid at 8 cents per hour!

The natives are huddled together like animals, and the settlers have stolen their lands. A certain amount of objectivity is necessary, but no pseudo-objectivity or criticism made by the settlers who are interested in the matter can fool people who can think.

Dr Banda is a gentleman who, according to the standards imposed on us, is most respectable especially as compared with the political leaders of British Guiana. Dr Banda is no revolutionary. He is a leader of the old school, well over 60 years of age, a polished gentleman who believes in evolution, and he is the man they have placed in jail. No wonder we are not persuaded by the nonsensical suggestion that communism is responsible for these disturbances.

I know Dr Banda personally, and he has made it quite clear that there need be no fear on the part of right-thinking European settlers; their properties will not be confiscated; their businesses will not be taken away. The position is *not* as Mr Tasker wants us to believe. Those white settlers are worried because they will no longer be looked upon as gods. Responsible leaders have told them: 'We do not want to send you home or confiscate your property, we just want

1. An Englishman representing big business and nominated by the colonial Governor into the Legislative Council.

to get our rights. If you behave yourselves like human beings some of you may remain.'

Another misconception that was introduced into this debate by the same hon. gentleman was that a number of people were in favour of federation. If it would not have been thought unparliamentary, I would have described that statement as sheer nonsense. I happen to know some of the leaders of the people in Northern Rhodesia and Southern Rhodesia personally. They were my contemporaries. I do not agree with what has been said in the U.K. on this issue, and I feel that what has been said by the few white settlers is absolutely inaccurate, to use a polite description.

I understand that the majority of the people has admitted that the majority of Africans are against federation because they feel it is an attempt to bring together the leading groups in the three territories, and that conditions would be worse for them in the end. The Asians are also against federation. If the majority of Africans are against it, how can the hon. Nominated Member argue that the people are in favour of it? I think the hon. Member used the words 'large proportion', and I apologise for misquoting him. In a majority of millions I cannot see how a few hundred thousand can be considered large.

All this talk about the economic benefits that will accrue to the people in Nyasaland is good theory. The question is, who gets the economic benefits? Is it the people who strike because they are being paid 8 cents per hour, or the people who are making the money out of the sweat and blood of the natives?

The same specious arguments being used here about vested interest and hard work were used in England by the people who sought to keep the American colonies under their thumbs. In this twentieth century we are still hearing the same old arguments – in days gone by it was the pianola, but today we have the tape recorder. It is high time that persons like the hon. Member desist from insulting our intelligence. This is the epitome of impudence.

As I see it there is nothing wrong with people wanting to be free. What is wrong is that other people do not want to see them free. I am not looking at this matter in terms of the shade or colour of the people involved. If the people in British Guiana want to rule themselves what is wrong with that? We are always grateful for the solicitude of our rulers, but it is our democratic right to insist by all means, yes, all means at our disposal that we be given an opportunity to rule ourselves. We object to this cynical and hypocritical solicitude on the part of the imperialists and their representatives.

If we want to make fools of ourselves, give us an opportunity to make our own mistakes. This interest in the people, this protection of the natives is sheer hypocrisy and is used to veil the economic interests of the white settlers. The colonials all over the world want to rule themselves and not by the minority who, in the past, have been so barbaric towards us. Times are changing rapidly, and this is but the last assault of the dying lion. History is on our side.

Events have shown that we have got to win. As individuals here we may not live to see the end. But time is on our side. When the whole colonial world wins, as win it must, we shall treat properly and humanely that minority who now are such barbarians. Those are the sentiments which I wish to express.

It is obvious that I feel very deeply because I have had my own experience, perhaps at another level and on another scale, and I am happy to see that this particular motion has met with approval of both sides of the Council. To my mind it is significant that, whatever may be the differences between us – and God knows, the gap is unbridgeable on many occasions – when it comes to the question of the freedom and the right of people to rule themselves, our enemies cannot hope that there are differences between us. We may differ as to who should take over the government, or whose ideology will bring prosperity to our country, but there are no differences when it comes to the question as to whether Guianese should rule.

Further, I say this: we would wish that something be done expeditiously; we want the immediate lifting of the ban. In another place and at another time I propose to move that we should observe a day of mourning for those people who have died. We wish not only that Nyasaland be free, not only that Central Africa be really free, not only that Africa be free, but that all those who today do not enjoy freedom, which is a God-given right, should be free.

31

Speech in the Legislative Council in debate on the
boycott of trade with South Africa, 16 November
1960

Mr Burnham: Mr Speaker, I think it was during the month of March
this year, that the civilised world was shocked by the massacre of
24 Africans at Sharpeville and Pondoland; and it was during that
month that the motion expressing solidarity with the relatives of the
deceased and criticism of the government which was responsible for
that massacre was passed in this Council.

During that month also, Mr Speaker, there were demonstrations
and public meetings throughout the world, and British Guiana saw
some of those demonstrations and public meetings. There has also
been started a fund in British Guiana for the assistance of those who
are fighting apartheid in South Africa and the relatives of those who
had been slaughtered as a result of the shootings at Sharpeville and
Pondoland.

But, Mr Speaker, it seems to me that it is not sufficient merely to
join in those expressions of solidarity. It seems to me, too, not sufficient to express pious sentiments directed against the philosophy of
the South African government. Something much more definite and
active must be done, and that is the reason for my moving this
motion, which, incidentally, I tabled last year and which had to be
renewed this year, on the ninth of January.

I must express some concern and disappoinment at the fact that
this government[1] has taken so long before bringing this motion to this
House. I cannot understand the reason for their sleeping on it this
long, and I cannot see that there are any complications whatsoever.

1. The P.P.P. government led by by Dr Cheddi Jagan.

The whole South African government's policy is to be deprecated, and the shootings at Sharpeville and Pondoland were just the culmination of that most disgusting policy. Not only are the native Africans – the original inhabitants of the country – robbed of their political rights, but they are also destitute of human rights. They are not allowed to organise trade unions in the same way as the whites are, it is an offence for them to strike, and the trade union leaders are, from time to time, prosecuted.

Since the Sharpeville and Pondoland incidents, there have been mass arrests, particularly of Africans and a few well-meaning members of other racial groups. Since these incidents have taken place, countries like Ghana, Malaya and Jamaica have decided to apply a total boycott of South African goods. If we are not in a position to use force. I submit that the most potent instrument is that of economic sanctions. Unfortunately, the United Kingdom government does not see fit to do what Ghana, Malaya and Jamaica have done, but there is a movement in Britain which is gaining momentum; and I feel that we, in British Guiana, as a colonial territory soon to be independent, should take our cue from countries like Jamaica, Ghana and Malaya.

The boycott which has been instituted against South Africa has had severe effects, and the Minister of Transport in South Africa, speaking in August this year, has had to concede that if the boycott by the various parts of the world were to continue, an economic crisis would be reached sometime in South Africa. That is exactly what we want. We want an economic crisis to be reached as a result of pressure from outside, so that there may be some change in the government.

British Guiana's imports from South Africa last year were valued at $213,612 (Guyana). This year, between January and July, we imported from South Africa $57,347 (Guyana) worth of goods. On the other hand, during last year we exported only $400 (Guyana) worth of goods to South Africa, but between January and July this year we have exported $34,331 (Guyana) worth of goods to South Africa. It is true that our imports from South Africa do not represent a very substantial part of South Africa's trade. For instance, the whole of the British West Indies between January and July, 1959, were only responsible for 0·2 per cent of South Africa's total trade. It is not merely the amount that matters but the principle. Further if a number of countries, each of them not importing a great deal from South Africa, were to decide, all of them to boycott South African goods, there is no doubt that the cumulative effect would be to cut down considerably South Africa's exports.

During the first six months of this year, for instance, South Africa's unfavourable trade balance as a result of the boycott by several countries of South African goods amounted to £20 million more than the unfavourable balance for the same period in 1959, and I think that we in British Guiana can make our contribution by refusing to import any South Africa goods. South African canned fruits, South African wines, South African peanut butter and various other products of South Africa have no right to come into a country like British Guiana at all. They are cheaper than imports from other parts of the world because they are produced on the blood and sweat of the African who is treated like a dog.

We would be unfair to ourselves, our country and to humanity if we in any way contribute towards the economic prosperity of a government and a country, the philosophy of which is apartheid.

32

Mr Burnham: Mr Speaker, it was on Monday last that I heard over
the radio that Patrice Lumumba, the democratically elected Premier
of the Congo, had been murdered. Great was my disgust, but slight
my surprise, because many of us who have been following the events
over the past year realised that the day that Patrice Lumumba was
thrown off the Belgium plane as a piece of cargo, those who were
opposed to him and all that he stood for, would never rest until they
had made an end to his life.

There are some hypocrites who, in spite of the circumstance of
the atrocious murder of Lumumba, allude to the release from the so-
called Katanga government of Tshombe alleging that Lumumba was
murdered by African tribesmen. I shall assume, but not accept the
fact that he was murdered by African tribesmen, but to accept the
veracity of the allegation by Tshombe is to be as naïve as he who
would say that if A kills B with a knife, the murderer is not A but
the knife.

There is no doubt about the fact that from the time the Belgians
were forced to give up the richest jewel in their crown; from the
time the industrial barons of Belgium recognised that the Congo was
no longer there to be exploited, their machinations were innumerable.

When the Belgians withdrew, they did not withdraw because they
were filled with any sense of democratic duty towards the people of
the Congo. As Frank Barber, a correspondent of the *News Chronicle*
observed: 'When the Belgians withdrew, they withdrew too late, and
they withdrew with an absence of grace and generosity.' From the
time they were forced to withdraw, they planned to re-enter directly
or indirectly.

It is not for me to be repetitious and to note how much The Société Génèrale and Union Minière got out of the Congo. It is not for me to report what everyone in British Guiana now knows: that the Belgium regime was brutal in the extreme. It is for me to observe in supporting this motion – I have no qualms, I have no over-sensitive feelings of propriety – that if there is any criticism of this motion, it is that it is not forthright in its condemnation of the United Nations.

Of course, we were entertained by stories of the so-called atrocities perpetrated by Africans after the Congo's independence. We were told many civilised Belgians were raped and murdered, but we were not told about the millions of Africans who have been raped and murdered in cold blood over the last 80 years. And the most disgusting thing about it was that when Afro-Asian countries, which ought to know more about Africa and ought to be more deeply interested in the basic welfare of Africa, attempted a solution, those who pretend to know better what was good for the natives, rejected the solution offered by Ghana, Malaya, Libya and Egypt.

When North Korean forces invaded South Korea, what happened? An army was sent by the United Nations. When the Belgians re-invade the Congo, what happens? The Secretary-General of the United Nations goes to negotiate and those are the same people who talk about the atrocities in Hungary. But who can point a finger at the atrocities in Hungary when the West stood by and allowed the brutality in the Congo merely because Belgium is a member of the North Atlantic Treaty Organisation? There are some Guianese, obviously misled, to whom we must offer our profound sympathy, who talk a lot of nonsense about Lumumba committing himself. How did he commit himself? Lumumba was democratically elected.

On the fourteenth of July, the Resident-General, sent to the Congo by the Belgian government, called him in and asked him to form a government because his party held the largest number of seats. He was told that he had until 6.30 p.m. on the seventeenth July to form his government, but on the morning of the seventeenth the same Resident-General sent for Kasavubu and asked him to form a government. But Lumumba, perhaps more trusting than many of us who are more seasoned would have been, in spite of the suspicion which he felt when on the morning of Friday, the seventeenth, several hours before he was supposed to form a government, he was called in and told he was no longer required to form a government, did not say much, and accepted the formation of a government later the next week when it was obvious that Kasavubu could not form a government.

When the difficulties started in the Congo I heard one hon. Member talking about 'stooge of the Russians'. My comment is that they are 'six of one and a half-a-dozen of another'. They have one complex whether they are Left or Right, East or West. They believe they know better for everyone than the people concerned know for themselves.

But I am a little disgusted hearing an hon. Member talking here about Lumumba being a stooge of the Russians or committing himself. When the difficulties started in the Congo where did Lumumbo go? He did not go to Moscow, he went to New York. When he left New York what did he say? He said 'I have no use for the Russians.' That is the man whom some ill-informed people would describe as a stooge of the Russians.

It was after the West had rejected him that in desperation he sought aid from the East. And why did the West reject him? This is an indictment which the West will have to answer. It makes no sense to talk to us colonials about democracy and to honour it in the breach. It makes no sense to tell us how Krushchev murdered Imre Nagy, the Premier of Hungary, when you sit by and connive at the murder of Lumumba.

African bases are important. There is a base in the Congo, and as General George Revers said at the Seventh Congress of the European Centre of Documentation and Information, held significantly in Spain, 'Africa is the logical base for the defence of Europe in the context of missile war', and Belgium is a member of N.A.T.O. Therefore, anyone, like Dr Nkrumah of Ghana, who feels that his country, or the continent in which he lives, is not to be a base in a war between two sides, neither of which is particularly interested in the particular territory or continent, must be destroyed, and that is how Lumumba came to be destroyed.

After all some of the Western powers could not afford to let down their good friend, Belgium; they could not afford to let down a member of N.A.T.O. After all, who is Lumumba? According to them he was just an ex-criminal who wanted to get power after independence. He did not matter in the larger scheme of things.

As they saw it, the retention of Belgian control of the Congo was more important than the right of the Congolese people to be free. The rights of the Congolese people as expressed by Lumumba, the deep patriotism of African leaders – these things were unimportant. More important was that Belgium should be supported.

Would anyone have imagined that in the second half of the twentieth century, those who prate about democracy would actually connive at the re-invasion of the Congo by the Belgians, and advertise a few atrocities which are minuscule in comparison with the atrocities perpetrated by the Belgians up to last year?

It is important for us to accept the fact that a man like Tshombe allowed himself to be used – a despicable character if ever there was one. It is important for us to recognise that we, colonial peoples, as we move on to independence and as we achieve our independence, must rely upon our own devices and not become caught up in the propaganda of one side or another.

I sent a cablegram immediately as I heard the news of Lumumba's murder, and I was shocked when it was suggested by the local Press that Guianese did not necessarily share the revulsion which I felt and expressed at this dastardly act which was perpetrated by the Belgian government. Which Guianese of any humanity or any sincerity or any intelligence would not be revolted by what has happened in the Congo?

It is time for us to clear the air of all this cant and nonsense. It is time for us to understand that you cannot overlook the sins of one side and recognise only the sins of the other side. It is time for us to understand that we cannot be apologetic for the sins of one side.

What is all this claptrap about Lumumba being a stooge of the East? What is the fear in people's breasts to come out and say there has been a wrong? If my mother did a wrong I hope I shall be fearless enough to say she has done wrong. We are carrying our politics a little too far. I am not uncritical of those who permitted the murder of Imre Nagy, but I am equally critical of those who seek to gloss over the enormity of the crime which, according to some reports, was committed in the Congo since last week.

It does not matter what may have been Lumumba's personal idiosyncracies. He is not a man alone; he is a symbol. What he stood for was the recognition of human dignity, and there are lots of hyprocrites who speak in support of Lumumba but in other circumstances do not recognise the human dignity of people like Lumumba. He was a man who stood for the right of people to run their own affairs. He was a man who stood for a strong Congo, and those things for which he stood are sufficient to recommend him to people like me.

Lumumba is dead. Lumumba, however, will live because the things for which he stood are deeply engraved in the hearts and minds of many of us. People like Tshombe, even if they do not meet physical liquidation, will leave behind them names to adorn a special book that must be written concerning the traitors of the twentieth century.

33

Statement to the nation on Rhodesia following the
Commonwealth Prime Ministers Conference held
in London, September 1966.

I am prepared to forget – save for purposes of historical research –
Britain's imperialist traditions. I will be prepared to forget them if
Britain solves or cooperates actively and positively in bringing a
speedy, if not immediate and satisfactory, solution to the so-called
Rhodesian crisis.

The British government through its spokesmen, notably the Prime
Minister, has stated that Rhodesia is its responsibility. This I accept
... to a point. But the fact of the Lagos Conference points to Britain's
desire to consult and have the views and cooperation of other Commonwealth nations. The British Prime Minister himself at Lagos on
11 January 1966, admitted that the problem of Rhodesia which was
a Commonwealth and world problem presented a challenge ... to the
whole concept of a multi-racial commonwealth. 'This problem', he
said 'can be settled only one way if we are to maintain a world
civilisation based on equality.' *This* only way, as I see it, is removing
the Smith regime by force. This is not warfare.

Ours is a small country which numbers its population in terms of
hundreds of thousands rather than millions and is separated from
Rhodesia by thousands of miles. Guyanese, however, take more than
an academic interest in the present crisis, not merely because of the
ethnic similarity between the Rhodesian Africans and a large section of
our multi-racial society, but more because we sincerely and unequivocally subscribe to the concepts of freedom, equality and
majority rule and earnestly hope to see every vestige of colonialism,
in every form, wiped out. We who have passed through and successfully fought minority domination feel a natural affinity towards, and

desire to assist, those who still so suffer. This, in addition to the fact that we are convinced that the continuation of Smith and his kind in office poses an insult to the African personality, gives the lie to loud protestations about the dignity and equality of man and can constitute, in the final analysis, a threat not only to racial harmony but also to world peace.

Immediately on U.D.I. the government of Guyana (British Guiana as it then was) banned all trade direct or indirect with Rhodesia. That was the least we could do, even though it was our conviction, expressed at that time, that economic sanctions apart from being incapable of dislodging Smith would cause greater and earlier hardship to the African, as distinct from the white Rhodesians and that the use or threat of force was the one sanction certain to be effective.

Force ought to be used because economic sanctions have failed and are likely to continue to fail to achieve the objective, for which there is universal support of removing the illegal regime. Mr Smith's is still the *de facto* though not *de jure* government. So much is this a fact that the British Prime Minister has referred to 'the government's storage' and 'the government's own dictated price' when referring to the steps taken by Smith and his colleagues to protect the Rhodesian tobacco industry.

It is true that the board of the Reserve Bank of Rhodesia has been re-appointed and its personnel changed, it is true that Rhodesia has been legally excluded from the London capital market; it is true that practically all invisible payments to Rhodesia have been prohibited by law; it is true that an almost total ban has been placed on exports and imports between the United Kingdom and Rhodesia (in Guyana's case the ban is total and absolute). But it is equally true according to the statement of the British Prime Minister that the illegal regime has been pouring out money like water to get a succession of tankers into Beira, 'will be expending about £6 million per annum of scarce foreign exchange' and has found it necessary to make nearly 3,000 new appointments in the public service, so as to disguise unemployment.

The Commonwealth Sanctions Committee's Report disclosed that economic sanctions, including the attempted oil embargo, have failed to do anything except make life in Rhodesia marginally more uncomfortable for the whites. Even assuming the potential effectiveness of economic sanctions, does anyone here believe or even hope that South

Africa and Portugal will turn their backs on their ideological friends and natural allies, the members of the illegal Rhodesian regime?

References to statements, undertakings and prophecies made by the British Prime Minister especially at the Lagos Conference, establishes that the time for force has arrived. There, for instance, he conceded that the ultimate objective of bringing Rhodesia back to constitutional rule might justify the use of force though it was his view at that time, that the problem could be settled by other means. Those means have been tried and have failed.

He opined that successful oil sanctions could prove to be a new weapon to replace the need to resort to force which he obviously posited as the ultimate; and further undertook that if in the long run sanctions failed, Britain would have to consider all other possibilities including armed intervention. No other possibilities introducing a new dimension are forthcoming. Therefore, the answer? Force. A policy of sanctions is a policy of sanctioning treason and illegality.

In the circumstances, in view of the British Prime Minister's prognosis at Lagos, that the economic sanctions might well bring the rebellion to an end within a matter of weeks rather than months, no further time could be asked for by those whose responsibility it is to quell the rebellion.

In the final communique issued at the end of the same conference it was stated that 'the Prime Ministers discussed the question of the use of military force in Rhodesia and it was accepted that its use could not be precluded if this proved necessary to restore law and order'. There is only one interpretation of that language. It could not be that what was intended was the use of force on there being an uprising of the Zimbabwe people and a general internal challenge to the Smith regime – force which was not used in the first place to suppress the rebels.

Such an interpretation is so palpably absurd that I reject it out of hand and assume that the Commonwealth Prime Ministers, including the Prime Minister of Britain, were saying in select specific terms that military force should be used as a last resort against the usurpers after other methods had failed. Otherwise it calls for a great deal of intellectual ingenuity to discover the distinction between a rebellion and a threat to law and order in the instant circumstances. It is difficult to conceive of British military might being insufficient to cope with the rebel forces of Rhodesia, especially when the former has been guaranteed a base by Zambia, and I refuse to accept the uninformed suggestion that in these circumstances the loyalty of British troops would be in question. Such a thing is contrary to all the known and advertised traditions of the British Army.

At Lagos it was suggested, I assume not seriously, that it might have been necessary – but difficult – to withdraw from Malaysia 25,000 British troops if battle was to be joined with the 23,000 fully equipped Rhodesian troops – presumably all loyal to Mr Smith. I say 'not seriously' because I could not be persuaded that the British troops in Malaysia represented the total military resources of Britain. Even if that were so then, now that the confrontation of Malaysia by Indonesia is at an end, are we to understand that the British troops in Malaysia, or some of them, cannot be released for urgent and possibly active service elsewhere?

What then inhibits the use of force in the tradition of British colonial history? In Guyana, then British Guiana, in 1953 when U.D.I. was not declared, when the elected government had won the majority of seats on an overall majority of popular votes on the basis of universal adult suffrage, the constitution was not only suspended and the ministers removed from office, but the British Army as represented by the Welsh Fusiliers was brought in to maintain law and order. I do not want to believe, though in some quarters this point of view has been urged with conviction, that the difference between Guyana and the Rhodesian Europeans is that the latter are kith and kin of the British people, government and army. Can it be urged that if Britain took punitive action in her colony Rhodesia that either of the great power blocs would intervene in support of Mr Smith? No one has suggested or can suggest that either the United States of America, the Soviet Union or China would rush to the support of the rebel regime.

How can the use of force be justified to put down what we are told is communist subversion in Vietnam, and be morally objectionable if directed against fascist treason in Africa. It is time that the big powers of this world desist from asking us small nations for moral and other support in the pursuit of their interests and things that they hold dear when they become pacifists *par excellence* where our ideals are involved. 'O judgment thou art fled to brutish beasts, and men have lost their reason.'

It is difficult to escape the conclusion that the treatment being meted out to the rebel regime is, for some inexplicable reason, unusually kind, if not weak. The British Prime Minister admits that rebellion amounts to treason which is still punishable by death, yet far from having any action taken to bring the criminals to justice the British government indulges in 'talks about talks' with them. This is not only an insult to many of us members of the Commonwealth but represents a retreat from the position taken by the British Prime Minister in January at Lagos. For there he said that Mr Smith could only approach the Governor under conditions of surrender. Following that the Governor would convey peace terms to him.

A gentleman like Mr Smith, that survival from another age, cannot be handled with words and protestations of good intentions. But, alas, even at the level of words there is weakness on Britain's part. There are the beautifully but basically ambiguous five, now six, principles. In the light of the 1910 South African constitution and subsequent events, what do these principles mean unless there is a categorical statement and undertaking that independence will, in no circumstances be granted to Rhodesia until after there is majority rule? Why should there be one criterion for non-whites and another for whites?

In the circumstances while admiring the felicity and facility of phrase evidenced in the now famous five, or call them six, principles, I supported the two simple declarations sought by the Foreign Minister of Zambia:

(a) A period of direct rule by Her Majesty's government to precede the granting of independence to Rhodesia.
(b) Rhodesia not be granted independence unless and until it is governed by a government elected by the majority of the people on the basis of one man one vote.

These were straightforward and unequivocal.

With respect to the first, Britain's chief spokesmen took up an unrealistic position in the present circumstances. Said they, 'there will be a period of direct rule after the rebellion is crushed'. But since the rebellion, at the rate at which things are going and with the present technique being employed, will not be crushed in our lifetime, this step as a first step towards legal government seems rather remote, to put it mildly. But do we have to wait that long?

The 1961 Constitution of Rhodesia has been suspended and executive authority vested in the Commonwealth Secretary. But what else has been done? For once in her history as a colonial power Britain is helpless and her statutes and bodies are tinkling cymbals and sounding brass; full of sound and fury . . . signifying nothing. In the meantime we were regaled with regrets that there was an unfortunate cleavage between Nkomo and Sithole, both of whom incidentally had been imprisoned by the Smith Regime, and a bemoaning of the fact that the Rhodesian Africans were without administrative and political experience.

It is my view that there should be set up an interim government broadly based, representative of the entire Rhodesian population and including Nkomo and Sithole. That would make the dismissal of Smith a reality and the will of the British government, in the first place, effective in Rhodesia. I further contend that all the necessary armed equipment of the State should be used thereafter to keep that government in office and to secure it from subversion by treasonable rebels of the Smith persuasion.

During the second world war, the camp of the allies rang with praise of resistance fighters in Europe, who were dying to secure their human rights. The same camp looks with distaste on Zimbabwe guerrillas who are fighting an equally righteous cause!

In the two world wars, in the War of American Independence, the black man gave his life in the cause of freedom. But today the giants stand still, shackled by technicalities and 'impotent' in Rhodesia as they have been in South Africa, Mozambique and Angola.

This day, however, cannot last for eternity. For one day the blacks, the disinherited blacks of Rhodesia and elsewhere will rise up and let there then be no cant about brutality.

Part IX
Caribbean unity

34

*Guyana, though situated on the South American continent, is – his-
torically, traditionally, culturally and economically – a Caribbean
nation. Its people speak the same language, are of the same ethnic
origins, play the same sports and have inherited similar political and
legal structures as the people of the Commonwealth Caribbean islands,
all formerly British colonies.*

*Forbes Burnham, from the beginning of his political career, cham-
pioned the cause of Caribbean unity and eschewed the idea of a
'Continental Destiny' for his country.*

*When, in the late 1950s, the Caribbean islands formed a political
federation and the British Guiana government under Dr Cheddi
Jagan stayed aloof, Burnham tabled a motion in the Legislative Council urging that British Guiana join the federation. The motion was
lost and in 1962, the West Indies federation collapsed with the withdrawal of Jamaica.*

*Mr Burnham remained in the forefront of the movement to revive
Caribbean unity and, after winning the 1964 election, he entered into
discussions with Prime Minister of Barbados, Mr Errol Barrow, towards this end. One year later, in December 1965, these discussions
led to the formation of the Caribbean Free Trade Association between
Barbados, Antigua and British Guiana.*

*The C.A.R.I.F.T.A. Agreement left the door wide open for Jamaica,
Trinidad and Tobago and the smaller Commonwealth Caribbean
islands to join. Mr Burnham's efforts, combined with those of his
colleagues in the Caribbean, have borne fruit. The Commonwealth
Caribbean countries – both the independent nations and the associated
States – are now all members of C.A.R.I.F.T.A. and C.A.R.I.F.T.A.*

embraces today all the Independent Commonwealth Caribbean nations and all the associated States. But to Forbes Burnham this is only a beginning, and he restlessly champions the cause and advances the programme of Caribbean integration, through all the ways open to him.

In March of 1965, it will be recalled that the regular Caribbean heads of government meeting for that year took place in Guyana and that marked a re-entry for Guyana onto the Caribbean scene and the re-integration of Guyana to the Caribbean family. That has been followed by what can be accurately described as a vast improvement in the relationship between Guyana and the rest of the Caribbean.

Undoubtedly, from time to time, there have been slight differences and pin-pricks from one side or another, but those things are part of the facts of international life and should not unduly concern or disturb us. There is no doubt that our re-entry onto the Caribbean scene was welcomed sincerely and seriously by our Caribbean colleagues and we went further in December 1965, when there was signed the Caribbean Free Trade Agreement at Dickenson Bay between Antigua, Barbados and Guyana.

We do not say that the signing of the agreement was on the sole initiative of Guyana; but what we do say is that the Guyana government took a very active and important part in achieving C.A.R.I.F.T.A.

The government of Guyana appreciates very fully that though C.A.R.I.F.T.A., as it now is, does mean or represent a step forward, does have the possibility, nay, the probability, for an increase of trade as between the three signatory territories and the rationalising of their respective and joint economies, to stop at an association limited to three Caribbean territories is to do injustice to the concept of Caribbean regionalism and the Caribbean personality.

This is why Guyana welcomes the positive interest shown by Trinidad and all of the other Commonwealth countries in C.A.R.I.F.T.A.; that is why Guyana, along with the two other signatory governments of Antigua and Barbados, will shortly be jointly sponsoring two conferences to discuss positively and meaningfully the expansion of C.A.R.I.F.T.A. In those circumstances, the Guyana government welcomes the recent statement by the Trinidad Minister of Trade that Trinidad's accession to the O.A.S. is not considered by his government to be in conflict with Trinidad's interest in acceding to a free trade agreement encompassing the Caribbean Commonwealth countries.

I have recently come from the Caribbean and I have had the opportunity of assessing at first-hand the response not only of Caribbean governments but of Caribbean people (a) to Guyana's participation with the rest of the Caribbean in exercises like this and (b) to the concept of a Caribbean nation. In these days when already independent, large and, in some cases, powerful nations are seeking to come together, it seems elementary that such an exercise is desirable in the Caribbean.

It is true that the federation came to grief but it is also true that the West Indian peoples in fields other than cricket or in addition to the field of cricket, are most anxious that there be a coming together. We do not underestimate the difficulties. We do not for one moment attempt to ignore the individual problems which may arise, but of this we are sure, that the fact of a Caribbean nation will be in our time. And, secondly, that Guyana is in a peculiar position to make a tremendous and significant contribution to the achievement of that fact.

This government does so, sir, not out of a desire to rule anyone or run anyone's affairs. In fact, the Guyanese delegations at these Caribbean meetings are noted for their understanding, for their attitude of equality and for their unwillingness to talk down to anyone. It seems to us that if we are to have a West Indian nation we will have to get rid of the 'big island' and 'big territory' complex and attitude and to realise that survival for *all* is dependent upon the efforts of *all*.

We have dedicated ourselves to making an important contribution to the building of a Caribbean nation, starting from the level of trade, followed by economic cooperation and later, time and experience will show what form even closer cooperation will take for the survival of the Caribbean peoples.

35

'We Must Integrate or Perish.' Speech to Conference of Officials of the Commonwealth Caribbean
Territories, Georgetown, Guyana, August 1967

A gathering of such academic distinction and administrative experience needs no polemics from me on the vital importance, nay, the
inevitability of regional groupings, but perhaps I may be pardoned
for adverting to the global picture of successful regional schemes and
associations aimed at, and achieving integration of their members
and participants. We find them in Europe, Asia, Africa and next-door
in Central and Latin America. Perhaps I will be forgiven for reminding
even this gathering that the Caribbean can no longer, like the pro-
verbial ostrich, hide its head in our beautiful sandy beaches and
ignore the trends and impelling forces of change in the world economic order. Either we weld ourselves into a regional grouping serving
primarily Caribbean needs, or lacking a common positive policy, have
our various territories and nations drawn hither and thither into, and
by, other large groupings where the peculiar problems of the Caribbean are lost and where we become the objects of neo-colonialist
exploitation, and achieve the pitiable status of international mendicants.

The history of efforts at Caribbean collaboration fills the pages of
many distinguished, and not too distinguished works, and need hardly
detain us here. Suffice is to say that discussion, argument, rhetoric and
semantics without follow-up action, have served only to disguise the
failure to act. We may delude ourselves, but the judgment of posterity
and history will be cold, harsh and accurate. It is my hope, therefore,
that this conference while giving its attention to the ultimate, will
focus discussions on those areas and subjects from which we can have
tangible results in the form of immediate practical action. Hunger and

poverty are not relieved by philosophical pratings, or academic out-pourings.

No one can deny the need for action. It is that need which is itself the *rationale* and *raison d'être* of this conference. Today, we are where we were yesterday; precisely through our inability to concert and our incapacity to yield the form for the substance; precisely because we have failed to match words with action.

Our problems differ only in degree, not in kind. All of our economies exhibit an unhealthy ratio of foreign trade to national economic activity. Less than 3 per cent of our total trade represents intra-Caribbean trade. The other 97 per cent of that total trade is dangerously concentrated on commodities and products controlled from outside the region, like sugar, bauxite, bananas, to take three of the biggest earners.

We all have the persistent menace of unemployment ranging from 10 per cent to 20 per cent. Emigration outlets outside of the Caribbean in spite of high moral posturings, are closed to us. Ours is one of the highest birth rates in the world. The pressure is building up and unless we plan and act, the lid will soon be blown off Caribbean society with dangerous and world-shaking results.

Ours is a common problem of capital deficiency, of shortages in the professional and technological fields and of the ineligibility of nationally important social projects for international finance. In some cases, over the past decade, in spite of a few flashes of hope and achievement, our economy in this region has been stagnating and in some quarters there have even been signs of slippage. Let us to our own selves be true. These are the facts. This is the naked truth. Either *we integrate, or we perish*, unwept, unhonoured.

A perfect solution to, or institution for, integration cannot be hoped for. As a former Minister of Foreign Affairs in the Nether-lands said in reference to the European Common Market: 'International institutions may be more or less well conceived, they usually are far from perfect. They are always born from a compromise.' Had European leaders waited for perfection, they would still have been indulging in histrionics and idle debate. Instead, they launched an admittedly imperfect association upon which they have been able to improve with the benefit of the experience of operations over the past decade.

We cannot expect to start off with some ideal or perfect arrange-ment. Neither can we hope to be so prescient of the future as to be able to determine all the consequences and difficulties of integration. We can and must, of course, try to analyse and anticipate as best we can from available data, what the effects of integration may be and can be made to be, but it would be folly *par excellence* to wait for perfect foresight.

Complete integration will take some time and will involve a number of complex decisions at the highest levels but it cannot arise full-blown merely because decisive political agreements have been achieved. In practice, arrangements will have to proceed step by step and their success will be dependent upon the research and analyses of experts and officials like those present here this morning. And that is why it has been decided that this conference should be the precursor of the one of heads of governments in October in Bridgetown.

Doctors Brewster and Thomas in their study have posited the need for a regional integration policy body to give continuous direction to the integration process; I would add in the same way as the Central American Free Trade Area established the Central American Committee in 1952 only that we shall have to move with even greater despatch and speed. In our context Brewster and Thomas have designated the body as a regional commission. The name may or may not be acceptable to you and your governments but the name is unimportant. What is of vital importance is the institution, its terms of reference and scope of activity. There can be no doubt that it cannot function without a secretariat, that it must have access to or be responsible for an institute of applied research which can mobilise a wide range of professional skills – a *sine qua non* which has been referred to as 'the fourth and final factor in the process of integration'.[1]

Heavy demands will be made on skills and expertise especially in the fields of development administration where at the individual territorial levels there is a shortage. Obviously, provision will have to be made for advanced training and applied development technology.

Finally, a key institution, perhaps around which all other supporting institutions should revolve, is a regional development bank. An important part of this conference's duty, therefore, will be to give consideration to the recommendations for the creation of a regional bank made by the U.N.D.P. team. In view of the unanimously strong support reported within the Commonwealth Caribbean, it is to be

1. The Commonwealth Caribbean Secretariat was subsequently established in Georgetown, Guyana, in 1968.

hoped that your deliberations will hasten the rapid implementation of the proposals for this institution.

One of the positive advantages of integration is that it enhances the international stature of the region: it increases its bargaining power *vis-à-vis* the world. There are those who prescribe O.A.S. status as a short-term solution to our problems – and I emphasise short-term; there are others who propose an involvement in the Latin American Common Market which is to be established in 1985 (I hope that these proponents are not suggesting that we wait that long to take action as between ourselves), but whatever arrangements may be come to, our ability to get proper and favourable terms will be dependent upon our acting as one group rather than as a number of little specks in the Caribbean sea. It is for you the technicians to analyse, evaluate and advise on the various propositions. It is for you to propose new formulae.

The present government of Guyana stands willing to support and endorse any proposition or solution which the region as a whole holds valid. We will, unlike some who preceded us, not opt out of a regional solution and indulge in dishonest rationalisations and vacuous shibboleths and clichés with which it is sought to cloak narrow political ambitions. We will not stay out and criticise, we will join and work towards the ideal. So important is the concept and goal of integration that even necessary limitations on our sovereignty are a price we are prepared to pay, the Jeremiahs notwithstanding. *We aim not at more cooperation but integration.*

We in Guyana have acted in the belief that a Caribbean free trade area is a relatively simple first stage towards the ultimate of an integrated economic community. That explains why C.A.R.I.F.T.A. was formed. It may well be that this meeting will share these perspectives and we can begin serious discussion and bargaining aimed at an expansion of C.A.R.I.F.T.A. to embrace the entire Caribbean region here represented. We have always shared this hope and the legal instrument establishing C.A.R.I.F.T.A. has made provisions for accession of other territories. In some quarters, C.A.R.I.F.T.A. has been dismissed as not being an illustrative solution to Caribbean economic problems. It is true that it is limited to three countries at the moment, but so too was the Central American Free Trade Area at the beginning.

C.A.R.I.F.T.A. contemplates much more than a free trade area. For a free trade area cannot stand still. It must either move unto a higher level of economic unity or disintegrate. C.A.R.I.F.T.A. itself contemplates and formulates administrative machinery for dealing with the more involved problems of a greater degree of integration. These include the harmonising of industrial incentives, the adumbration of a common commercial policy and the streamlining of external tariffs in relation to the rest of the world. The agreement at the request of its signatories has been laid as a conference document and I would urge a serious examination and scrutiny. Let me say that in any case Guyana does not consider its membership of C.A.R.I.F.T.A., as constituted at the moment, an impediment to economic integration on a wider scale.

Guyanese in common with other West Indians expect from this conference action and tangible results. We take this question of integration seriously and do not look upon this conference as the occasion for an exercise in debating skills of which we have a surfeit in the Caribbean. As I have said before and in other places, Guyana is willing to place its not inconsiderable natural and other resources at the disposal of the region as a whole. Our hinterland is not a mere showcase for the passing admiration of curious anthropologists, archaeologists and tourists but a vast place to be peopled and developed. With whom better can we share our resources than with our neighbours, our brothers, our sisters? With whom do we already share a common historical experience?

May I wish this conference every success. May I hope that pragmatism and action will be your watch words. May I urge that we make this conference a landmark in our history when we as a people moved from the theoretical to the practical.

Part X

The power and responsibility of labour

36

*Forbes Burnham has been twenty years a trade unionist and seventeen
years President of Guyana's oldest trade union. Even as Prime
Minister he remains President on leave from his union, and therefore
wears the dual caps of employer and unionist.*

*At the time of his speech to the combined representatives of labour
in the Caribbean area, Mr Burnham confronts a crisis of conflict in his
own country between the need for economic stability and the rising
expectation of trade unions striving for better conditions.*

*Though the majority of the Labour Movement is politically behind
Mr Burnham, the Prime Minister faces the economic consequences to
the nation of an inordinate amount of industrial unrest.*

*In his speech, he talks to his audience as a fellow trade unionist but
yet manages to make it clear that he considers labour legislation
inevitable if the economic situation is to be stabilised. He makes the
point that the trade union movement in a democratic society carries
upon its shoulders a great burden or responsibility and carries within
it the power to make or break the nation.*

Mr President, Brother Minister, Your Excellencies, Comrades:

I am happy to think that I have been invited to participate in this
opening ceremony not because I am the Prime Minister of Guyana but
because rather I am the President of the oldest union in the Commonwealth – the Guyana Labour Union – to the memory of whose
founder, this building was raised.

May I congratulate the Caribbean Congress of Labour upon having reached its ninth birthday and may I also congratulate them upon the honour they have conferred upon themselves by holding this, their fourth triennial congress in the Critchlow Labour College of Guyana. The organisation also ought to be congratulated for being at one time in the history of the Caribbean the only regional organisation pursuing the concepts of a Caribbean nation – an integration of the peoples of the Caribbean – at least at one level.

The politicians made an attempt in 1958 and by 1962, the federation was in a shambles, but the trade union movement continued. I do not think that the federation failed because there were trade unionists amongst the government of the federation, rather, I should prefer to think that the federation failed in spite of the participation of trade unionists in the government of the federation.

There is another significance to my mind about the stand of this organisation. I am told that within the Caribbean Congress of Labour there is to be found a Surinam affiliate; so in one respect again, this organisation is leading the way, crossing human-made barriers of language and colonial history and seeking to bring together the workers of the area into one strong group.

Today, we are now seeing another attempt by the politicians to integrate the Caribbean and its peoples. The President of the Caribbean Congress of Labour happens to come from the country whose Prime Minister[1] first was inspired by the idea and the concept of a free trade association in this part of the world. This Prime Minister has been really one of the pillars of C.A.R.I.F.T.A. and I have no doubt that Barbados will contribute infinitely and definitely to a regionalism which goes beyond a free trade association, beyond, I hope a mere economic community, which will go into the field once more of political integration.

When I first entered the trade union movement twenty years ago, we had as the head of the Labour Department a distinguished gentleman (as a matter of protocol everyone is distinguished) who used to lecture at the trade union movement from time to time on the necessity of keeping far away from politics, though he came from a country where the principal support of the labour party was the trade union movement of Great Britain. I hope that there are few of us left here today affected by this nonsense and poppycock which was carted some years ago throughout the Caribbean. It is impossible for

1. Mr Errol Barrow, Prime Minister of Barbados.

a trade union movement to have any vitality and play its proper role in the scheme of things in the context of developing nations unless it takes an intelligent interest in politics.

I am not necessarily referring to partisan politics. As a political animal myself, I should prefer to see most of the trade unions in Guyana coming out fully in support of the party which I lead, but as a realist I know that such unanimity may be difficult to achieve.

A trade unionist must take part in politics in its widest sense; trade unions must assist in planning; must understand the objectives which any given government has; must also realise that in the final analysis, because of the structure of our system, most of the remedies are going to be political.

I am happy to hear this morning from the President of the C.C.L.[2] that the C.C.L. and its affiliates do not limit their vistas merely to getting better wages and better conditions of work. I am to assume that the C.C.L. and its affiliates share with my government the conviction that one of the prerequisites for rapid and harmonious development should be the participation of workers in policy decisions – decisions in the industry in which they are employed. The peripheral involvement of workers, that sop to Cerberus, which was so frequently thrown to the workers in terms of x percentage increase of wages, x decrease in the number of hours work is not, as far as I can see, going to answer the problem of underdevelopment and ensure total involvement of the society and community.

The time has come when employers, whether be they government or the managers of private industries, have got to accept the participation of workers in the making of vital decisions. What distinguishes a human being from a robot or a mere animal is that he wants to know that he is a human being and he wants to know that he knows and understands why he is doing something and he wants to know that he is making a contribution to the adumbration of goals and objectives within the particular operation in which he is functioning or of which he is a part.

When I say this, I should also like to emphasise as a brother trade unionist that there is a tendency for us to produce a labour aristocracy in the Caribbean. As a socialist, I do not believe in an aristocracy or élitism, but assuming that there is justification for aristocracy or

2. Caribbean Congress of Labour.

élitism, those of us who aspire to become a member of the aristocracy should at least recognise that membership of that group or class carries certain responsibilities. It should be appreciated that leadership has got to be selfless and not selfish; it should be appreciated that leadership means sacrifice, it also should be appreciated that leadership demands an intelligent approach to the problems of the day.

I have reason to believe, copying the picturisation of my good friend, the President, that the good ones, the good leaders in the C.C.L. are in majority and the bad ones in a minority. Unfortunately, however, most organisations and institutions are judged in terms of the bad ones and consequently, it would appear to me that it is the duty of the good ones to ensure a certain amount of re-education and reorientation of attitudes.

The trade union movement is one of the most important institutions in the Caribbean; it represents at a certain level the organisation of the workers; the organisation of the common man; the organisation of the proletariat. These are in a majority and these are the people who, more than any other group have a right to ask for a better society – a better standard of living. The trade union has its duties therefore, not only at a level of industrial organisation but at a level of national planning and national economics.

We, in Guyana, hope very shortly to have the trade union movement involved in the economic exercise of insurance and banking. But it seems to me that there is little point in emphasising the importance of the movement without attempting also to take care of the economic side of the existence of the members of the movement. And I hope not with any amount of conceit but in a sort of brotherly fashion that the example which we in the trade union movement hope to set in Guyana will become a matter of common practice throughout the Caribbean, spearheaded by the Caribbean Congress of Labour.

I have noted, looking quickly through the history of the trade union movement in the Caribbean, that the Caribbean Labour Congress floundered on the rocks some years ago because of ideological differences and the championing of one cause or another irrelevant to the Caribbean by one group or another within that organisation.

The Caribbean Labour Congress got itself involved in the cold war and you had opponents or satellites of both sides in the cold war. And so the C.L.C. passed away – R.I.P. Then the C.C.L. came into being some years after in 1960. I know that assistance has been given to the C.C.L. by C.A.D.O.R.I.T.[3]: I know that the I.C.F.T.U.[4] has given assistance to the C.C.L.; I know that the affiliates of the I.C.F.T.U. have been of assistance to the C.C.L. and most of its affiliates. But in the Caribbean today, we pride ourselves, even in the cases of the smaller territories, of moving away from colonial tutelage at least in so far as internal affairs are concerned.

I would like therefore to think that in the trade union field also, we have reached the stage where we must be independent and the C.C.L. must be a Caribbean organisation. Otherwise we are going to find ourselves caught up in other people's quarrels; we are going to find ourselves having to take positions on issues which are unimportant to us if not completely irrelevant to our situation; we are going to find ourselves being used as tools. If, indeed, we want to be a vital trade union movement, we must recognise the need for independence and a Caribbean motif and orientation.

If this is to be a Caribbean trade union movement, I am hopeful that out of the deliberations of this congress will come decisions which emphasise the Caribbeanness of your organisation and indicate at the same time your awareness of the problems of the territory and the area and the region and *pari passu* with that your willingness to put forward solutions.

You naturally will be most critical of certain matters which are at the moment the subject of controversy. You will of course criticise various governments, and comrades, that happens in the best of regulated families and societies. My seventeen-month old daughter criticised me up to this morning. I love her still and I have reason to believe that she loves me still. And I should like to think that the criticism which you make will be criticism based on your own conviction and not external inspiration.

There are many ways of colonising – you can colonise with gunboats and armies; you can colonise by insinuating ideas; you can colonise by subtle brainwashing; you can be told all manner of evil things; you can be told about the freedom and independence of the trade union movement – freedom from your own, but not freedom from the outside.

My comrades, you are intelligent men. You have gone through the battle, you understand what I am talking about. There is a relation-

3. Caribbean Area Division of the Inter-American Regional Organisation of Workers.
4. The International Confederation of Free Trade Unions.

ship of friendship which we must maintain but we must not allow our *soi-disant* friends to put us on the wrong track. We must understand the circumstances in which we have to operate and I have made this plea over and over again to the trade union movement. You must take advantage of courses abroad but you must be mature and intelligent enough to differentiate between the circumstances of the country to which you go and the circumstances of the Caribbean.

So far as my government is concerned it recognises the importance – the vital importance of the trade union movement in our society and economy. The trade union movement was consulted when the development programme was first drafted in 1965; the trade union movement will again be consulted as we rewrite our development programme in the light of experience and new priorities. The trade union movement, through its elected representatives, serves on all important bodies in Guyana. The trade union movement supported the independence movement and the trade union movement has shown undoubted loyalty and devotion to Guyana when we were assailed from the West and from the East and I am happy to note the remarks of the President of the C.C.L. on this question of territorial integrity. And I have good reason to believe that in spite of little differences which may arise from time to time, the trade union movement in Guyana and the government of Guyana will continue cooperating as equals and will together create a society where the worker becomes a real man.

The government of Guyana proposes to put through the Parliament a certain bit of legislation. We politicians, are noted for our hypocrisy and our ability at ballet dancing and tightrope walking, but when speaking to friends, hypocrisy and diplomacy should not be called upon at all. The government of Guyana proposes to put through Parliament a certain bit of legislation, I say again. But the significance is that this legislation came after a discussion with the leaders of the trade union movement and at the request of the leaders of the trade union movement sometime ago, and the trade union movement and the government have been in constant consultation.

The trade union leaders like any other set of leaders are entitled to have second thoughts not on principles but on minutiae and those minutiae are now being studied. I want to assure the trade union movement of Guyana and the C.C.L. this morning that the legislation which we are putting through is not going to be legislation to give the employers a Roman holiday. It is legislation which will be aimed at providing proper means and machinery for the ready settlement of industrial disputes, because this government is convinced that one of the reasons for some of the industrial problems which arise is the absence of proper machinery for a swift and condign settlement. I am almost paraphrasing the words uttered to me by the then President and Secretary of the T.U.C. when they saw me two years ago in my office at Public Buildings.

As a trade unionist, I would not superintend the government which outlaws the workers' right to strike. But as a trade unionist who is a nationalist and Prime Minister, I cannot allow industrial relations to deteriorate to a point where our very existence is threatened, let alone our progress. We will continue to discuss, but the legislation will have to be passed and I am sure that when the legislation will have been passed, you will recognise that it is not what some of your newfound friends are telling you, an oppressive piece of legislation.

We politicians, have a peculiar way sometimes of simulating friendship and there are some who are telling you today that the government of Guyana wants to take away your rights. But reflect on their history of just five years ago. May I finally, now that I have made my position as Prime Minister pellucidly clear, call upon my brother trade unionists to cooperate in the interest of getting the best type of legislation and the best out of the legislation which will be passed.

Thank you for asking me to be here this morning. May I wish you in your deliberations every success. May I hope that only the best will come out of your congress, and may I say to those of you who are not yet citizens or natives of Guyana that we want to be as hospitable to you as we possibly can even to the point of conferring citizenship upon you and giving you somewhere in Guyana to settle. It gives me great pleasure to declare open this, the fourth triennial Congress of the Caribbean Congress of Labour.

Part XI
Tributes

37

'To a President.' Speech in the Legislative
Assembly to pay tribute to President John F.
Kennedy, 12 December 1963

Mr Speaker, I received the news of the assassination of John F.
Kennedy, as it happened, while attending the funeral of a close friend.
I did not know him personally, yet the shock and grief I felt were
great.

John Kennedy was a young man, in the very prime of his life when
so tragically struck down. Those who would rationalise or sublimate
sorrow in circumstances like these, would offer the comfort that only
the good die young. But that is poor comfort indeed, for a world
deprived of a good man and great leader.

As I understand it, the late President Kennedy was no saint; he was
a man, but a man with ideals which claimed the admiration of all of
us who believe that there is still a great deal to be said for the preservation of the much vaunted but infrequently practised democracy.

No one who has followed his career and his statements over the
past two or three years, can let pass unnoticed the contribution which
he obviously made to peace in this world; in particular his successful
negotiation of the Test Ban Treaty with the Soviet Union and other
powers.

No one but the insensitive can forget the great risk of unpopularity
which he ran in furthering the rights of Negroes in the United States
and seeking to make them full-fledged first-class citizens.

No one I think, in this world with a place in his heart for humanity
can but regret the death of the late John Fitzgerald Kennedy.

At moments like this, most of us would wish that the dart, of which
a poet spoke, capable of slaying death, would be found. Most of us
would have hoped that he could have lived to see the fulfilment of the

things for which he stood, to realise the achievement of the ideals for which he fought.

The loss which the American people have suffered as a result of the act of a lunatic, is a loss which is shared by us in this country, and I am sure, shared by the entire world. I am convinced that his name will live on for a long time if not as far as human memory will run.

I believe that, even in his untimely death, those things for which he stood will be strengthened. In the circumstances, I am inclined to think that it is time for us to dry our eyes; it is time for us to pay attention to the things for which he stood and for which he worked and, I suspect, for which he died. It is time for us to reassure ourselves that he lives, and it is death that is dead, not he.

38

'To a Statesman.' Speech in the Legislative Assembly to pay tribute to Sir Winston Churchill, 27 January 1965

Mr Speaker, it has been the custom in this House, by whatever name it is known, for the members to express their condolences to the relatives of distinguished persons who have died. Very rarely, but not infrequently, we have had cause to move motions like this with respect to the passing of persons or citizens who have not lived in our country. This morning, one of the primary purposes of the meeting of this House, is to move a motion of condolence expressing our deep sympathy and regret at the passing of that great man – Sir Winston Churchill. The honour and privilege of moving such motions have usually devolved on the Premier, but on this occasion, I am doubtful whether this is an honour which I happily enjoy, or a privilege which I would have anxiously sought after.

Though it is true that some versed in the field of philosophy put forward the proposition that : 'To live is to die, and to die is to live', we lesser mortals feel very keenly what we consider the capricious cruelty of death.

Sir Winston Churchill died on Sunday last. He was not a citizen of our nation or of our country, but so great is the debt which the entire world owes him that we really might have considered him, with more justification than in other cases, a citizen of the world.

We, who are the inhabitants of the British Empire, and who have felt very keenly our God-given right to rule ourselves and to be independent; we who have thought for many years that we should be masters in our own land, and architects of our own destinies, have been wont in years past to remember the late Sir Winston Churchill as the Prime Minister who announced that he had not been appointed 'His

Majesty's first Minister to preside over the liquidation of the Empire'. Perhaps a proper perspective has led us and will lead others to recognise that though we quite rightly object to what we consider the inhuman attachment to an empire of subjects, we, in spite of everything, owe him a great debt of gratitude.

Most people are agreed that had it not been for his indomitable spirit and his unusual ability and custom to excite enthusiasm when defeat faced his nation, were it not for him, were it not for his sterling qualities, even the independence which we seek would have been further removed from our grasp, for we would then have been under the shackles of the Nazi dictator.

It is only right that we recognise, in spite of our anxiety to cease being colonials, in spite of our conviction that we have a right – in fact a duty – to assist in the liquidation of the 'glorious Empire', it is only proper that we recognise that we could not have indulged in these thoughts or these ambitions and aspirations had it not been for Sir Winston's achievements. Our aspirations would have been further from fruition had it not been for what Sir Winston Churchill did during the second world war.

In those circumstances I am pleased on behalf of my government, on behalf of the members of this House, on behalf of the citizens of Guiana, to do honour where it is justly due.

Sir Winston was undoubtedly a great man. Than he, there can be no greater; as he, there may be a few as great. His was a full life. He was an artist, a soldier, an orator and a statesman. He seemed to use his oratory not for the sake of ornate speech but for the sake and for the purpose of whipping up enthusiasm when it was flagging, and giving inspiration where it was needed. Many of us, no doubt, remember his famous words at the time of the Battle of Britain. We remember his words 'Never in the field of human conflict was so much owed by so many to so few'. That compliment to those who defended Britain and the world at that time has become, and will continue to be, immortal.

But you will forgive me, Mr Speaker, if I prefer to recall the tones in which he issued the incantation of the poem by our brother West Indian, Claude McKay:

> If we must die, let it not be like hogs
> Hunted and penned in an inglorious spot,
> While round us bark the mad and hungry dogs,
> Making their mock at our accursed lot.

If we must die, O let us nobly die,
So that our precious blood may not be shed
In vain; then even the monsters we defy
Shall be constrained to honour us though dead!
O kinsmen! we must meet the common foe!
Though far outnumbered let us show us brave,
And for their thousand blows deal one deathblow!
What though before us lies the open grave?
Like men we'll face the murderous, cowardly pack,
Pressed to the wall, dying, but fighting back!

He was not the poet who wrote those lines, but he brought to the attention of the world the sentiments in that poem. He made it the poem of all those who fight for what is worth fighting for. Were it not for him that poem might still have rested in obscurity. A poem which has a particular meaning to us had a particular meaning to him at the time when he repeated it and will continue to have a particular meaning until the end of time, I prophesy.

Sir Winston Churchill was one of those men who precipitated the argument as to whether history makes the man or man makes history. There has always been a great argument about it. It is not for us to enter into this philosophical disputation. It is for us to recognise that he was outstanding. He was much greater than lesser mortals, and yet he had his human failings.

It is for us to pay tribute to a man to whom even we in Guiana owe a great deal. It is for us to recognise that even after the chill hand of death touched him he fought with the same indomitable spirit with which he fought between 1939 and 1945, keeping at bay the barbarians. He was a fighter to the end of his life. Whether we agree with his political sentiments or his ideologies we fain must accept his greatness, we fain must accept that we are his debtors. In the circumstance I beg to move:

That this House of Assembly records its condolence on the death of Sir Winston Churchill and that an expression of its condolence be conveyed to the relatives of the late Sir Winston and to the government and people of Great Britain.

'In war he showed resolution; in defeat, defiance; in victory, magnanimity; in peace, goodwill'. I pray God that we can follow in his footsteps in that respect.

39

'To a Martyr.' Speech to mass open air rally to pay
tribute to the Reverend Martin Luther King Jnr,
Independence Square, Georgetown, 8 April 1968

*When the Prime Minister learnt of the assassination of Dr King he
ordered an official day of mourning and led the nation in a candlelight
procession through the streets of Georgetown. An estimated ten thous-
and persons from all over Guyana participated in the procession and
representatives of all the political parties joined Mr Burnham in paying
tribute to a martyr.*

On Thursday the fourth of April, we were shocked, the world was
shocked at the assassination of the late Dr Martin Luther King Jnr in
the summer of his years. And all the world mourns. For whom do we
weep? A mere man? No! For whom do we shed these silent tears?
Another Negro slain? No! We mourn, we weep, we shed tears for a
martyr, one great by any measure, a freedom fighter, one whose stature
transcends that of us little men, one who, like Jesus, like Jose Marti,
our own Cuffy[1] and others, sought to share his faith with the poor
peoples of this earth.

Now lies he dead, executed by a bullet. What was the crime that
led to his execution? What sin did he commit? He had the courage to
believe in what Christianity teaches and the American constitution
recites – that 'all men are created equal'. He dared to raise his voice
against segregation of the Negro, against lynchings, against bombing of

1. Leader of slave revolution against the Dutch colonists in 1763 and the chosen
   hero of the Republic of Guyana.

Negro churches, against the harsh, wicked, unchristian deeds of a large and significant section of a Christian nation!

His was the misdemeanour of organising successfully sit-ins and protests against segregated eating-houses and buses. For this, his home was bombed! His was the felony of leading marches and demonstrations of Negroes in pursuit of their God-given rights, of leading prayer meetings in southern court houses. For this he was jailed. His was the high treason of planning a march of the poor in support of poor black garbage workers who picked up slop and waste. For this he suffered the supreme penalty – and this in a nation whose revolutionary history begins with the Boston Tea Party, one of the heroes of which was a Negro called Crispus Attucks! – in a nation which reveres Abraham Lincoln whose description of democracy 'Government of the people, by the people, for the people' still rings in our ears and adorns many a thesis; Lincoln who believed that a nation cannot prosper, cannot survive half-slave and half-free.

A man of courage, a member of a repressed race, he was a leader of men, indeed a leader among leaders. He had no fear of death if that was the price he had to pay in pursuit of his dream. As he once said (May 1964) 'If a man hasn't discovered something that is worth dying for he isn't fit to live.'

One recalls as if 'twas yesterday, King's march on Washington on 28 August, 1963. Then at the base of Lincoln's statue, he put his dream in an outpouring full of pathos:

> I have a dream that one day on the red hills of Georgia sons of former slaves and the sons of former slave-owners will be able to sit down together at the table of brotherhood . . . I have a dream today . . . I have a dream that one day every valley shall be exalted, every hill and mountain shall be made low. The rough places will be made plain, and the crooked places will be made straight. And the glory of the Lord shall be revealed, and all flesh shall see it together. This is our Hope.

Out of this march there came a volume of civil rights legislation some of which has been passed but much of which, notably that on fair housing, still remains unpassed in the American Congress. Some of those who claim shock at King's cruel and untimely death can build a monument to him by using their influence and their votes to have Congress enact laws ensuring fair and desegregated housing for Negroes in the United States.

269

But the life and work of Martin Luther King must not be viewed only in the context of the American Negro's struggle for parity. Not only was his international reputation recognised by the award of the Nobel Peace Prize in 1964, but to blacks throughout the world he was a symbol and a beacon. Indeed, terrible is the black man's lot in many parts of the world. Some of us are wont to exclaim with the Jamaican poet the late Claude McKay:

ENSLAVED

Oh when I think of my long-suffering race,
For weary centuries, despised, oppressed,
Enslaved and lynched, denied a human place
In the great life line of the Christian West;
And in the Black Land disinherited,
Robbed in the ancient country of its birth,
My heart grows sick with hate, becomes as lead,
For this my race that has no home on earth.

Then from the dark depth of my soul I cry
To the avenging angel to consume
The white man's world of wonders utterly;
Let it be swallowed up in earth's vast womb,
Or upward roll as sacrificial smoke
To liberate my people from its yoke!

King's and the American Negroes' struggles are causally and directly linked with those of the Africans in Rhodesia, in Portuguese Africa, in South Africa. You cannot pay tribute to Martin Luther King in his casket and turn the blind eye on the atrocities of his murderers' kith and kin in Africa. But alas, Jesus was betrayed for thirty pieces of silver and King and his people are being betrayed for South African gold and diamonds.

Will Martin Luther King die in vain? We gathered here tonight and millions more answer 'NO!' The cause of the twenty million Negroes in the United States of America is ours. We must give them every support in every form. We call upon the United States, that vast and powerful bastion of democracy, to suppress those elements in its society which make a mockery of that historic and revolutionary document – the constitution of the United States – 'all men are created equal'. The arms of government must be used to ferret out and destroy those barbarians whose prophet is Hitler! . . . Did our brothers not give their lives and we our money and support to defeat Nazism and Fascism? Have we not got a right to demand that the devotees of these inhuman philosophies be prevented from venting their spleen and practising genocide on our blood brothers?

In memory of Martin Luther King we call upon the nations of the world – East and West – to practise what they preach and bring to justice men like Smith, Vorster and Salazar. The black man is more interested in the black man's dignity than in the argument about 'isms which all ignore our human worth. We are tired of being pawns. Even pawns can become bishops, knights, rooks and queens. And, indeed, pawns can check-mate the king and win a game. Those who have ears to hear, let them hear.

There is a duty imposed upon men of colour to fight with might and main to bring freedom to American Negroes as well as the suppressed Africans in Central and South Africa. We can never be free to enjoy our freedom while our brothers are in chains. We must speak out like King without fear. We must pool our resources and we must have no illusions. As the late Martin Luther King himself remarked 'No privileged group ever in history gave up its privileged position without a struggle.'

We must steel ourselves for that struggle, we must remove racial discrimination from our land wherever it appears, however subtle it may be – in the institutions, public and private. We must join hands with our brothers o'er land, air and sea. Our struggle, our fight, must know no geographical boundaries. If our Christian friends have no soul or if theirs is buried in prejudice and money bags, we shall have to go it alone. If needs be, we shall have to go it alone but 'We Shall Overcome'.

Index